MW01405937

THE INGENIOUS LIFE OF
Melbourne Smith

THE INGENIOUS LIFE OF
Melbourne Smith

One Man's Revival of Historic Sailing Vessels

BY PAUL WOOD

Woods Maritime | KAMUELA, HAWAI'I

The Ingenious Life of Melbourne Smith
One Man's Revival of Historic Sailing Vessels

WOODS MARITIME © 2015

Text | PAUL WOOD

Photos & Illustrations | MELBOURNE SMITH unless otherwise noted
Title page illustration | *U.S.S. Hornet*, proposed Sailing Ambassador for the State of FlorIda, 2015

Design | CURT CARPENTER

Thanks to Mick Philp for his eyewitness accounts.

NOTICE OF RIGHTS
All rights reserved. No part of this book may be reproduced
or transmitted in any form or by any means, electronic or mechanical,
including photocopying, recording, or by any information storage and retrieval system,
without permission in writing from the publisher.

ISBN 978-0-9964454-0-5

PRINTED IN THE UNITED STATES

Woods Maritime
Post Office Box 7049 | Kamuela, Hawai'i 96743

Contents

PART 1 | SAILOR

1	CAP DE LA HAGUE	1959	1
2	MANHATTAN	1957	12
3	CADIZ	1960	22
4	HAMILTON	1930	32
5	ANTIGUA	1960	44
6	GUATEMALA	1961	56
7	PLACENCIA	1962	70

PART 2 | SHIPWRIGHT

8	MARYLAND	1963	78
9	BRITISH HONDURAS	1965	86
10	BALTIMORE	1975	98
11	INNER HARBOR, BALTIMORE	1976	108
12	THREE DAYS NORTH OF PUERTO RICO	1986	123
13	ANNAPOLIS	1974	131
14	NEW YORK CITY	1841	139

PART 3 | DESIGNER

15	SPANISH LANDING	1983	155
16	ERIE	1987	177
17	PENOBSCOT BAY	1998	197
18	WEST PALM BEACH	2012	215
19	SANDY HOOK	1849	225

BIBLIOGRAPHY	237
CREDITS	238

PART ONE

Sailor

Many of the best sailing trawlers were built in Upham's yard in Brixham.

Cap de la Hague | 1959

*"Don't wear your sea boots
if you're going to abandon ship."*

—MELBOURNE SMITH

THROUGHOUT his Greenwich Village period, even though the purchase of a worthy boat was fantastically beyond his means, Melbourne Smith kept looking at sailboats, visiting them, studying them, and painting them. He undertook a succession of watercolor portraits of classic sailing ships. Each portrait was a side-view depiction of a single ship under sail, every detail exact to the original vessel, including the fine lines of the rigging, the taut sails, the curves and minute features of the hull. Often he would add a lively detail—say, the fluttering of a colorful pennant at the top of a mast. These portraits were not oil-thick dramas in which boats battled typhoons or tacked in a cannon-blasting turmoil of old naval warfare. Each was done in lucid gouache watercolor, each a celebration of the design ingenuity and proportions that characterize specific nautical breeds. They were instructive, finely drafted replications.

"I had the goal of doing three hundred of them," he said later, "all different classes of sailing vessels, fifty each—fishing boats, yachts, cargo ships, historic ships...." He took his paintings to a publisher in New York. The publisher praised them and suggested that Melbourne could find a better arrangement for this project if he went to publishers in England.

In 1959 Melbourne left New York and crossed the North Atlantic on the SS *Salacia*. He disembarked in Swansea, Wales, with over a hundred of these paintings in his luggage. But the paintings would have to wait. All of a sudden he had money in his pocket, enough to purchase a very fine sailing ship and to outfit it for adventure.

The money came like this:

He had read an advertisement for a cheap old sailing craft at a Staten Island boatyard, and he went to see it. He did a lot of that in those days—visiting boats, learning boats, wanting one. There's a fine line between pretending and visualizing, and Melbourne managed to cross it.

When he saw the old boat, he quickly realized that the vessel was derelict, not worth a dime. He should have known. The entire yard was that way, flat, cold, deserted, and choked with more-or-less abandoned vessels begging to be scuttled. The dark seawater lapped foamy gobs of rubbish against the pilings, and the air carried a bothersome stink.

As Melbourne finished his inspection and climbed out of the rotten sloop, he found himself standing next to an older man who had apparently responded to the same ad. But this fellow was clearly not the nautical type—short, pudgy, with thick glasses, a slender tie, sweater, wingtip shoes, a city-style woolen overcoat, and a homburg hat.

"Don't bother looking down there," said Melbourne cheerily.

"Why is that?"

Melbourne explained in detail the terminal ailments of the sloop in question, and the formal stranger smiled, quite impressed by the lanky young man's enthusiasm and detailed understanding of hulls and rigging and the principles of buoyancy. The man's name was Aubrey Young. He was an engineer from New Jersey who worked in New York and felt that he would like to purchase a sailboat.

"Why?" Melbourne asked.

"Why what?"

"Why do you want a boat if you don't want to sail?"

"Well," said Mr. Young. "It might be a good investment."

Melbourne looked at him, thinking about that concept.

Aubrey Young looked left and right, then said, "Well, I have two sons. They're not quite grown. But they... have a lot of... energy. I thought that some extended adventures on the open sea would...."

"But where would you keep the ship? Who would be the skipper? Where would she sail?"

"I don't know yet. As I say, I'm just testing the idea." When Melbourne didn't react, he said, "You, for example. You wouldn't want to purchase this boat here. So what would you buy—if you had the money? And what would you do with it then?"

"I'd go to England and buy a Brixham trawler," said Melbourne.

Mr. Young's face registered surprise and a slight smile. He had no idea what the fellow was talking about.

"I've been reading a lot lately about Brixham trawlers," Melbourne said. In fact, he had given deep study to Edgar J. March's recent book *Sailing Trawlers: The Story of Deep Sea Fishing with Longline and Trawl*. "I think one of them would make a great charter boat. I'd get a small crew together and sail her to the West Indies. That's my dream."

"The West Indies?" said Young. "Maybe I can help you out with that."

He offered Melbourne a kind of partnership deal. He would front Melbourne five thousand dollars. Melbourne would go to England, buy the boat, and go into business. Once Melbourne paid back the loan, the two of them would become equal partners. "And I know a couple of boys who could learn to crew for you once you get established."

MELBOURNE AND HIS YOUNG WIFE Gisela left quickly. They first went to Hamilton, Ontario, and put their toddler son, Sean, in the care of Melbourne's mother. She was already providing childcare services for others, and she welcomed her little grandson into the household.

They brought with them a potential crew member—his wife's best friend, named Maxine Ofield. Maxine's husband had abandoned her and gone out to Hollywood to find work in the movies. So she was at loose ends and ripe for an adventure. Melbourne said later, "Maxine was eager to learn and never flinched at adversity." The three of them went directly to the classic fishing towns fronting the English Channel.

It was bitterly cold and damp that November when they found rooms over a waterfront pub at Poole, near Bournemouth. Melbourne got work in the pub, where he served beer and sold loose cigarettes for tuppence each. His customers were mostly poor. They would order a glass of beer, tenderly sip half of it, then come back asking for a bit more to freshen the mug. Melbourne always refilled their glasses to the brim. Soon enough, the half-beer returns began to dwindle until customers were coming back with only an inch in the glass. If their timing was right and the owner wasn't looking, Melbourne would still top them off.

By day Melbourne haunted the waterfronts. Soon he found what he wanted—*Sanspareil*, B.M. 326.

She had a white hull, which made her unique among traditional black-hulled Brixham trawlers. And she was beautiful, built in 1912 by Upham, a historic boatyard founded in 1817. During her fishing fleet years she had developed a reputation for speed. Later, in 1931, she was converted into a yacht with a thirty horsepower motor added to supplement her sails, and she was furbished with no expenses spared. Her price was three thousand pounds sterling—in U.S. currency approximately ten thousand dollars. This figure being twice what Mr. Young had advanced initially, Melbourne had to renegotiate the deal via long-distance communication. Young agreed, and wired the additional funds.

A YACHT IS A CRAFT reserved for pleasure, for the art and joy of windborne cruising. So to turn a trawler into a yacht was comparable to turning a railroad car into a restaurant.

After all, a trawler is a commercial vessel used only for the industrial purpose of trawling—which is to drag a huge net along the sea bottom and scoop up the particular species in season, especially sole, cod, haddock, halibut, fluke, and turbot, then hoist this harvest up through the cold resistance of water. When trawling was done by power of sail and muscle alone, the work was grueling and primitive enough to ensure that the oceans would not be overfished.

But even as a commercial vessel, *Sanspareil* had possessed the beauty inherent in sailing ships, a beauty that industrial machinery could never match. The powerful steam and motor ships that followed her retirement soon swept the waters clean of plentiful fish harvest. And they stunk of petroleum and rust.

Here is the difference between the old clean technology of sail and the present progressive technology of sludge: sailing trawlers depended only on the wind. They had to be capable of at least nine knots free speed in order to maintain one or one-and-a-half knots with the heavy trawl down. It took a smart sailing vessel to sustain that speed. Speed under sail always creates clean, quiet harmony, because non-motorized inventions necessarily have to adhere to the great dictum: "Form follows function."

DURING the nineteenth century the boat builders of Brixham on the south coast and Lowestoft on the east coast of England created a design that enabled their fishing fleets to harvest the sea with ultimate efficiency. Their sailing trawlers all had plumb stems and long overhanging transoms (rear ends) to prevent squatting when hauling a trawl. Most were ketch-rigged with a vertical mainmast and a smaller mizzenmast aft and strangely raked forward. Both masts carried gaff sails and set topsails aloft. A staysail was set forward and a bowsprit was run out to set a flying jib. A running (that is, moveable) bowsprit was necessary in those days so it could be run in on deck

Sanspareil's white hull made her unique among traditionally black-hulled Brixham trawlers. Here she is easy to spot, making her way out to sea along with two other smacks.

whenever the sailing trawlers entered crowded fishing ports to land their catch.

These sailing trawlers became icons, particularly due to their reddish sails. In the bygone Brixham trawler tradition, sails were dressed with a mixture of cutch (a resin from India) and red ochre. This process was called "barking," and it was done annually to preserve the cloth. Iron oxides in the ochre gave the sails a deep red-earth hue. The look was featured often in paintings of the old maritime masters, with Turner-esque skies all gold-glowing in veiled sun and resentful shadows. Local shipyards built hundreds of these ships between the 1880s and the 1920s. By the beginning of the twentieth century the number of sailing trawlers totaled three thousand.

Today precious few remain. The Second World War was particularly hard on the fleet. Nazi submarines amused themselves by capturing Brixham and Lowestoft trawlers, shooing away the fishermen, then shooting up the boats as a form of target practice. Today Brixham's heritage fleet consists of only six vessels.

THE AGENT selling *Sanspareil* was George Cork, who owned Admiralty Dockyard in Falmouth on the peninsula of Cornwall.

Cork had a large, vivid indentation in his forehead. Melbourne asked him about it. Cork said that he'd first gone to sea as a boy, and his responsibilities had been to cook and to come up on deck quickly whenever the trawler tacked. When that happened he had to hold the fore staysail clew to windward until the captain shouted to let go.

After several miserable days of incredibly hard work and little sleep, young Cork thought he had mastered backing the headsail. One day, though, he let the sail fly before the captain gave the order, causing the vessel to miss stays. The sail had a large heavy block at the clew, and the sail came back with a vengeance. The block walloped him on the forehead, laying him out cold.

When he regained consciousness in his bunk, little Cork expected sympathy. But the captain came below, looked at the split head and blood, then ordered the lad to stand up and turn around. The skipper gave him a wicked kick in the butt and yelled at him: "You'll remember now, I suppose, to follow orders!"

Life under sail answers the sea's demands, and the sea carries a swift razor. Melbourne never forgot seeing Cork's damaged forehead. But a sharper lesson for him lay just ahead.

MELBOURNE BOUGHT *SANSPAREIL* knowing she needed repair. Her bottom was foul with seaweed and barnacles. Her transom had some dry rot. And she was making a bit of water, which probably meant that her caulking was less than tight. He puzzled over the best place to have her hauled out. England, it turned out, was expensive for this. Word among the tongue-waggers in the pubs of Poole suggested that he should sail her across the Channel—across La Manche, as the French call it, "the sleeve"—to a boatyard in Cherbourg. There, a boat owner could get a better deal. Melbourne liked that idea. Having spent time in Montreal, he could speak some crude outlander French.

But he had no charts for the trip, and he'd never sailed La Manche before. He needed to hire a trustworthy pilot.

Enter Mr. Leo Toms, a middle-aged Limey who rose one evening from his perch at the bar and announced that he knew the waters between Poole and Cherbourg "like the back of my hand!" He had been both a yacht hand and a yacht captain, he said. Melbourne decided to trust Mr. Toms, pay him to pilot the crossing, then pay for his passage back to Poole.

After what happened later, though, and for the rest of his life, Melbourne would stiffen his shoulders and growl whenever he heard that expression: "know it like the back of my hand!"

They studied the weather for several days. Then when the prospect looked good, this peculiar and rather understaffed crew slipped their berth at the first lightening of dawn.

They intended to motor-sail across the channel heading south under power with staysail and mizzen—small sails fore and aft—raised to keep them steady. A favorable wind from behind kept pushing the stern up, so the pilot had to pay attention to prevent yawing.

Problem was, the bilge began filling with water.

This leaking wasn't bad at first. Melbourne spent about five minutes each hour hand-pumping seawater. But the need to pump kept increasing by about five minutes every hour. Soon he was pumping as much as he wasn't. Something was going very wrong.

Whenever he could break away from the pumping, Melbourne searched urgently for the source of this incoming water—the through-hull fittings, the bearing on the prop shaft. Nothing. He started tearing up floorboards and some of the beautiful mahogany paneling, but there was no perceivable leak to be addressed. By then every hand was turning-to without cessation at the bilge pump.

As the frigid December darkness closed in, the wind freshened. Soon they could see the loom of the light from Cherbourg on the eastern horizon. There was no port nearer than Cherbourg. He knew they had about two hours, under good conditions, to make port. But Toms's "back of my hand" course had not allowed for the Channel current, and now they were perilously far west and leeward of Cherbourg.

The wind soon built to force seven. It struck them from the east and took control of *Sanspareil*. By then, the water in the saloon was hip-deep. The engine, now submerged, quit altogether. Suddenly they were almost helpless in the talons of this storm, which was driving them at its own pace right into Cap de la Hague, a sawtooth headland of raw pre-Cambrian granite.

They had lowered the mizzen long before. But now the wind tore the entire staysail from its boltropes and swallowed it in the darkness. The ship was now ungoverned, wavering at the mercy of the elements.

Stumbling in the dark across the wave-swept deck, Melbourne tried desperately to raise the mainsail, working both the peak and throat halyards, hoping to grab some navigational control over the vessel. Maxine, who had long since given up her role as cook, took up his slack. If the ship could just get enough sail to turn against the wind, maybe it could catch the tidal race, the currents that naturally swept around Cap de la Hague out into the open sea. That way, at least, they wouldn't smash to pieces against sea cliffs. Gisela was massaging Toms, whose hands and legs were cramping badly.

Then the bilge pump clogged.

Melbourne sent Gisela below decks to get the life vests, also the passports. She came back soaking wet. She'd had to dive for them. In the saloon the air space that remained above the water line was less than two feet.

Another hour passed. They could hear the roar, the noise of the shore, the smashing of wave after wave colliding against implacable rock.

Suddenly a large buoy appeared, flashing in the darkness. "Steer for the buoy!" Melbourne shouted. He could see its occasional flare in the surging confusion. The buoy was ten feet tall, perhaps six feet around, crowned with the usual grid of angle iron. The presence of the buoy marked the boundary between survival and sure disaster. Melbourne had heard of desperate sailors climbing onto such floating structures and clinging all night while riding out other terrible storms. He grabbed a hawser, played it out, then bent it into an enormous byte or loop. Like a lunatic cowboy he hurled the rope, hoping to capture the buoy. He threw it high into the air as hard as he could on that treacherously rolling deck.

Toms shouted from the tiller: "You're not allowed to do that!"

"What?"

"No one is permitted to interfere with the buoy!"

We don't know exactly what Melbourne said at that moment, something derogatory, no doubt, about the punctilious nature of a certain British barfly. No matter. The storm took that hawser and whipped it away forever. *Sanspareil* brushed against the buoy. Melbourne knew they were going in. He dropped the anchor full length, but there was nothing below on which it could catch.

This was about three in the morning and very dark. Through the pelting rain that shone in the light from *Sanspareil's* masthead, they could see sheer cliffs ahead. Directly to leeward were monstrous rocks and a small stretch of steep and rocky beach.

Then it happened. With a terrible breaking sound *Sanspareil* smashed her port side amidships. She had been holed by an enormous rock. Surf was crashing across the deck. The only hope of survival was to leap onto that conquering rock, then somehow get to the next one a bit farther, and from there to the beach.

When the surf pulled back, they could see bottom. It was as if they could just walk up to shore, if only the sea would stop moving. But five seconds later the next surge came smashing in.

Melbourne shouted, "When you see the next wave, go for the rock. Go!"

Mr. Toms made the jump first. He landed securely on the rock, then he was gone.

Maxine tried to jump. She had already cleared the deck when she screamed. Her timing was bad. A great chasm had opened between the rock and the ship's hull. Melbourne grabbed her, but he was too exhausted to actually lift her back over the railing. He held on. They both scrambled for traction. Then he caught hold of her pants, ripping them, and he pulled back, both of them tumbling onto the deck.

With the next surge Maxine leaped and landed successfully on the rock. She got up and disappeared into the freezing December blackness.

"Then Gisela and I both went together," Melbourne recalled. "I had her at the back of the neck, gripping her coat collar. I never let go of her." They fell together into the sea. Saltwater soaked into their layers of pants and coats, feeling strangely warm in contrast to the icy wind. The sea pulled them rolling underneath the doomed ship. It sucked them back out to sea.

The following is Melbourne's own account of the scene:

"The seas were a turmoil as we turned over and over fighting for air. One moment we would surface, only to be smashed against the rocks and be swept out again. The kapok life jackets protected us somewhat from the sharp rocks, but the seaweed would slip through our fingers as we fought against being washed away again.

"It is difficult to remember how many times we were washed in and out, but it was some time before we were lifted higher than the next wave could reach. Inch by inch we made our way up the rocks, exhausted, spewing up the water we had swallowed. In movies you see people depicted crawling up the beach. No way in this case. Our soaked clothes weighed more than we could lift. All we could do was lie there and let the water drain out of our clothes."

When they were able, he and Gisela crawled up the beach. Suddenly the wind seemed to encase them in ice. His teeth chattered so hard he was afraid to talk for fear of biting his tongue.

Mr. Toms was doing all right, sitting well up on shore. "Well, this will be a good story to tell when we get back to the pub!"

Crawl crawl crawl.

They'd lost Maxine. For a panicked time, they scrambled along the shore shouting for her. They heard her cry in the distance. She had been washed into a gully about a hundred yards away. The seas were breaking over her, but she had a firm grip on a rock. Her torn trousers were hopelessly knotted about her ankles and pinned in place by her waterlogged sea boots. Melbourne cut her free.

The light at the masthead still shone even though *Sanspareil* was beginning her metamorphosis into driftwood, a transformation that would entail the loss of every personal and essential item on board—all of Melbourne's original artwork, his watercolor ship portraits, everything gone. The flashlight still shone a strong beam. Melbourne could hear the commercial jingle in his head. "Eveready battery does it again!"

Another fierce set of waves began storming the land. "We've got to get inland," he shouted. "Let's go! Let's move!"

Slogging and nearly frozen, they began searching for some way to climb from the battered shore to the flat farmland above. They tried scaling the cliff, then fell back. Finally the flashlight revealed a nearly vertical footpath and they took it up and up, scrambling, the wind pushing them left and right and dousing them with icy sprays of rain. They made gasps and cries of pain that really sounded like the yearning to weep, but it wasn't time for that. The four of them reached a kind of plateau, a seaside cliff-edge. They looked back to sea. If they had come upon this precipice while out strolling on a lovely summer day, they would have reveled in the panoramic beauty, then glanced down and said, "Walk on that trail? Hell no." Now as they turned, the storm wind smashing into their faces, they could see the masthead light still burning. They imagined they could hear that Brixham trawler getting torn to pieces.

"Let's go," said Melbourne.

"Could we just sit and rest for a minute?"

He remembered a story he once read about a little Dutch girl who stopped to rest in the snow and never woke up.

"No."

They were standing in flat farmland, fields usually given to carrots and onions but now fallow and slumbering under a crust of snow.

"You know what happens when people do that. Keep going till we find a village or something."

"I don't see anything anywhere. Which direction?"

"How do I know? Let's go."

They trudged silently in their icy wet socks. Heading inland they crossed a white-crusted field—lumpy ground, weeds cold-stiff and bent—then met a stone wall. They jumped, climbed, and crawled over the wall. About forty feet later, another stone wall, then again. They had to hurdle at least three dozen of these stone-stacks till they found a sort of footpath. The flashlight illuminated a frozen manure heap. The footpath turned onto a sort of lane, and a quarter mile later they came onto what seemed to be a kind of country road. Night-blackness and silence covered everything, and the only way to endure the terminal shivering, the threat of hypothermia, was to keep moving. Like some manic record-skip, the jingle kept resounding in Melbourne's head: "Eveready does it again! Eveready does it again!"

Finally, they reached some sort of habitation site, a place (they later learned) called Saint-Germain-des-Vaux. A light burned in a row-house building. This was a stone structure with a horseless cart and a forties-era pickup truck parked next to the front door. They shouted. A woman opened her shutters and came to the window. By now the time was five in the morning. "May Day!" was all Melbourne could think to say in his limited Canadian French: *M'aidez*, the international code for "help me!"

"Maidez, s'il vous plait! Mon bateau est tous fini sur les rochers!"

But Canadian French is not exactly French French. The woman quickly closed the shutters, and the light from her room flicked off. Darkness again closed on them.

They stamped and shivered outside. Then a door opened. The woman had banged on her wall to awaken a retired police chief who lived in the adjoining structure. The old man came out and gestured, offering them shelter. He produced a bottle of brandy and telephoned for an ambulance.

Next morning the shipwreck victims woke in a hospital in Cherbourg. Later that day they learned that seven vessels had been lost that night in the Channel.

Gisela said quietly, "Thank God you have insurance on that boat."

Melbourne didn't reply.

He had filled out the insurance form and included payment. But he hadn't put the packet into a postal kiosk until the very morning they had departed from Poole.

As far as he knew, it was still sitting in a mailbag somewhere. ✶

Manhattan | 1957

"Life has got a habit of not standing hitched.
You got to ride it like you find it. You got to change with it."

— WOODY GUTHRIE

H E BUILT HIS FIRST BOAT in 1948, he and his school pal Ziggy. Melbourne—or Bill, as he was called in those days—was eighteen. For hull, he used a single four-by-eight-foot sheet of aluminum. He employed the sheet metal fabrication techniques he had witnessed in the little factory of his foster parent, Mr. Collins. In fact, he constructed the boat in the Collins basement.

He cut and fashioned one four-foot end of the sheet into a hard chine—that is, the angle of welding between sides and bottom. He gave the rest of the sheet a gentle shape while bending the sides to form a rounded stern. He fastened the aft end to a solid oak transom. Melbourne turned the sides of the upturned aluminum into gunnels by using half-round oak on the outer side and three-eighths inch oak strips with spacers on the inside. He strengthened the bow with a simple planked foredeck, added oarlocks, then created a stem and keel by bolting on lengths of one-by-two-inch aluminum bar stock. He finished the little craft with wooden thwarts and floorboard, plus coats of paint, white on the outside. The result was an eight-foot dinghy—a rowboat. They named her *Daffy*. He and Ziggy rowed her across Burlington Bay, the harbor where Hamilton sits at the west end of Lake Ontario.

A polluted bay (in those days), an open lake beyond, and all the rivers and channels leading to the whole blue world—how many young people have chosen to find their way forward by passing through such a fateful portal? Countless. Most of them fodder for disaster. But Bill Smith was no heedless vagabond. He wanted to make his way, literally, and make it well. He set out to learn how others had made it.

Sometimes experienced sailors would give lectures in Hamilton, and he went to the lectures. He read a lot of sailing books. Sailing became his obsession. He got hold of a copy of the old *Dutton's Navigation and Piloting* and actually read it. Without the benefit of the usual exhausting, university-level course to explicate the text, Bill Smith just read it and re-read it until he got it—navigational charts, magnetic compasses, the use of a sextant, spherical trigonometry. This feat was comparable to reading Dante's *Inferno* in the original with the help of an Italian-English dictionary. But young Melbourne discovered that he had a knack for it, for the mathematics and curvatures and calculations. *Dutton's* was a leading authority, first compiled in 1926 by the mathematician Benjamin Dutton. Later in life Melbourne would actually design a new twelfth edition of *Dutton's* for the U.S. Naval Institute in Annapolis, seizing the opportunity to clarify and simplify the book's tough lessons via illuminating diagrams and illustrations. But in the late nineteen forties he was simply a driven young man with a mind moving like a Manhattan street corner, reading the damn thing over and over until he finally got it.

BESIDES PLAYING in orchestras at night, his first job on graduating high school was working for a silkscreen company doing design work. He earned twenty-five dollars a week drawing decals and ads. Later he worked as a designer in engraving houses, his pay rocketing to a hundred dollars a week. By age twenty-five he had saved enough money to purchase his own ship, something considerably more sophisticated than an aluminum rowboat.

He had done his research. He already knew about Dutch botters when, in 1955, he saw an ad in the newspaper for the *Wooden Shoe*, twelve hundred dollars. And he bought her. The botter is an original Dutch fishing boat of forty feet, a type that used to crowd the Zuiderzee and the canals of the Netherlands, flat-bottomed, broad-beamed with leeboards, well suited to the calm, shallow waters of Holland. The wide bow thrust upwards, giving the vessel a big-chinned almost tugboat look. Its single mast bore a gaff-rigged mainsail, staysail, and flying jib. She was a very pretty boat, old, but with the grist of history about her.

Our hero had to hitchhike down to Georgetown, which lies on the Sassafras River in Maryland, deep in the recesses of Chesapeake Bay, to buy her. He had the dream of sailing her around the globe. But first he wanted

Wooden Shoe had leeboards in place of a keel.
She began her life on the Zuider Zee in Holland.

to get the boat back to Canada for a winter of inspections and repairs and calculations.

Running on an adapted automobile engine with three gears ahead and one reverse, he worked his way north and then west through the Chesapeake & Delaware Canal and down the Delaware River until he reached Cape May, the sandy tip of New Jersey. There the engine failed. He replaced the engine, then continued up New Jersey's Atlantic coast to New York City, and proceeded inland on the Hudson River to Albany. From there he followed the old Erie Canal and the Oswego Canal across Lake Oneida. He had to lower the botter's mast in order to traverse many fixed bridges and locks. But when he finally flushed into Lake Ontario, he raised the mast again, using a case of beer to persuade a friendly crane operator to help him achieve the task. After sailing the length of Lake Ontario, he was in Hamilton and it was winter. He hauled the boat out and fitted new deck beams up forward. He painted a Dutch shoe on her mainsail and put symbols on her sides representing each Canadian province.

Next spring he took off—south again, this time to New York City, the 54th Street boat basin. He tried to make a go of life as captain of a Dutch botter. In his later years he claimed, "I never made a penny." But he survived somehow. He hustled a job with NBC, the National Broadcasting Company, recording the sound of ship horns as they entered the harbor. He would cut athwart, whichever big vessel arrived, and record the ship's warning blast, then deliver that hoot to NBC's audio library. This was no way to make a living. But when you're twenty-six, it's at least a damn good story.

As the next winter closed in, he had to make a strategic financial decision. By then he had two crewmembers and no prospect of income during the idle months. He berthed the botter at Staten Island, with crew aboard, and hitchhiked his way north to find employment.

He went to Montreal.

He went with samples of his artwork under his arm—newspaper ads, bottle labels, illustrations, and packaging designs.

IN MONTREAL he changed his name. That is, he began using his middle name, Melbourne. This name had come to him through his paternal grandmother, who in her youth had experienced friendship with a lad from Australia. Years later, she couldn't remember his name, only the name of the town from which he hailed—Melbourne. It became a family name. So when our hero went to Montreal, he simply became Melbourne. In time the only place in the world where he could possibly get called "Bill" was Hamilton, Ontario.

Melbourne had one dollar in his pocket when he arrived in Montreal. He slept in a train station that night. In the morning he grabbed a phone book and started calling all the art studios he could find. It was a Friday and the day of a very exciting football game. At every call he heard, "Boss isn't here. Went to the game. Won't be back till Monday." Eventually, though, he got a click, a company with the dismal but honest name "Advertising Producers." The owner, a Mr. MacGruder, said to come on in. MacGruder looked at Melbourne's artwork samples and said, "How much do you want?"

Young Melbourne, fingering the lint in his pockets, replied, "Let me work for a week. Then decide what I'm worth."

This bit of swagger impressed Magruder, but it didn't resolve the immediate problem—bed and bread. Fortunately, one of the company's two other hired designers asked him, "Where are you staying?"

"I don't know."

The fellow lived in a boarding house on Rue MacGregor near Chemin de la Côte-des-Neiges, and he lent Melbourne twenty dollars to get through the transition.

As it happened, Melbourne stayed in Montreal all that winter, working for MacGruder, making "Seagram's whiskey labels and other little piss-ass design jobs," he later recalled. The boss would go out every morning, just like Leopold Bloom, and come back every day with enough work for his staff of three artists to execute.

WHEN SPRING eventually melted the muddle of his winter huddle, Melbourne made his way back to Staten Island to see what could be made of his proud little botter. He took it out, powered by sail, to test the open sea. He and his crew sailed the *Wooden Shoe* to Norfolk, Virginia.

The trip was a bust.

Besides the fact that a Dutch botter is flat-bottomed, just as slippery as a plywood raft, it has no keel in the traditional sense. Instead it is outfitted with leeboards, which are vertical fins mounted on each side of the boat. A leeboard is lowered on the lee side to counteract the force of the wind and keep things steady and the boat moving forward. On the raw, open Atlantic, though, such a boat is about as in-control as a rubber duckie. To quote Melbourne: "You really can't sail anywhere except sideways." So he had to kick the motor into action.

"You can't really go around the world on the motor."

He finally took the botter back to the same broker on the Sassafras River and put it up for sale. Then he returned to Montreal and MacGruder's art studio for a second winter refuge.

The Advertising Producers studio was located in Victoria Square, the public space inside Montreal's downtown district. The scene was a quadrangle of shops surrounding a park-like green, a multi-lingual mingling of characters, all very European. MacGruder's studio occupied a second-floor spot located directly above a branch of the Royal Bank of Canada.

There was a teller working in that bank. As soon as Melbourne saw her, he opened an account.

HE STARTED going to the bank every day to make deposits that were too small to camouflage his true intentions. Her name was Gisela, he discovered, and she was beautiful to him—slender and dark-haired, quiet without being shy—and she seemed both amused and engaged by his across-the-counter enthusiasm, his inability to respect the church-like hush of the bank. He could see that she possessed the skill he lacked. She knew

Gisela minds the tiller of *Coaster*, a Chesapeake bug-eye, during a delivery run from Cape May to New York City.

how to settle into the formless silence of herself, serene, enlivened not by knowledge but by intuition.

Eventually he invited her on a date, and she accepted. He carved her a broach out of mahogany, gluing a safety pin on the back. He took her to a restaurant, the Café des Artistes, and they forgot to order any food. She loved music, and she read a lot, and so did he. They just talked through the evening until the waiters, dressed in classic Parisian white and black, were standing around ready to go home.

"That was the love of my life," Melbourne later recalled, "she and her family." Her full name was Gisela von Nida. Her nickname was Froschie (froggie)—she and her four sisters all had animal nicknames. Her mother was a brilliant Irishwoman, the widow of a German military officer whose fate had played out against his reluctance over the rise of Adolph Hitler. At the climax of the Second World War, he died in the massacre known as the Allied firebombing of Dresden. After that, Gisela's mother provided her linguistic skills as a translator at the Nuremburg Trials, for which service she was given passports for herself, her five daughters, and a housekeeper—but not to the U.S. To Canada.

By the mid-fifties Gisela's mother was supporting her household by working as assistant to the key physician at Montreal Neurological Institute,

CHAPTER 2 | 17

a leading hospital. Melbourne fondly recalls her third-floor apartment in Montreal. "It was a very happy house. I lived there many times."

But he and Gisela did not marry right away. First, he took her to sea.

In previous ship-scouting excursions to New York, Melbourne had made a nautical friendship with a family named Higgins. The couple were members of the Slocum Society, which offered support to lone, wayfaring sailors. Jack Higgins worked as recording engineer for Riverside Records. (Higgins's name is on classic recordings of Thelonious Monk, Louis Armstrong, among others.) They became lifelong friends. While Melbourne was living again in Montreal, designing display ads for Mr. Magruder and romancing the bank teller, he got a request from Jack Higgins to help him bring a boat up from Cape May, at the mouth of the Delaware Bay. "I asked [Gisela's] mother if she could come with me, and we took off."

During this adventure he and she began dreaming up a plan to own a worthy boat, escape to the West Indies somehow, and start running charter excursions in a faraway and far warmer clime. Melbourne's enthusiasm must have been very persuasive. After they'd sailed Jack Higgins's boat up to New York, Gisela the bank teller married Melbourne Smith the artistic sailor at the Seaman's Mission on 42nd Street. They laughed through the ceremony—the minister was so short that he had to stand on a Coca-Cola case to officiate. "It was all laughing from then on. We went back up to Montreal, planning to get a boat and live happily ever after."

APPARENTLY their first plan (perhaps not carefully considered) was to get out of Canada and follow the breezes of opportunity. They moved to Greenwich Village, in Lower Manhattan, the home of beatnik culture and the wellspring of the folk-music revival, with the presence of Dave Van Ronk hulking here and there, Ramblin' Jack Elliott making appearances, Woody Guthrie, and so on. They drove down from Montreal in a tattered convertible MG sports car with a collie in back. By now Melbourne knew how to play guitar. He only fell asleep once on the road, hit a signpost, but didn't do any damage.

"A hundred came in every day," he said, loads of actors and artists. "Out of every thousand, maybe one would get a job. They all got swindled. Everybody was a con. Wonderful concerts in the street!"

Melbourne had no work, nothing going. But he knew someone who made income as a "super."

"I guess he promised he could get me a job as a super if I came down from Montreal."

And he did. Melbourne became the superintendent of a five-story walk-up building, for which he received a rent-free pad (two rooms, toilet in the closet, bath in the kitchen sink) plus fifty dollars a month to keep heat going in the coal furnace. In exchange he was responsible for trash-collection, hallway mopping, and every crazy circumstance that might arise in the building. This was subsistence living, pasta all the time (some days stars, some days elbows). They used to borrow a television now and then from one of the tenants. Once when they were down to their last dollar, he put that dollar on the bed and the dog ate it.

"These were happy days, though. New York is a wonderful place to be when you're in love. It's a terrible place to be if you're alone."

The Village in those days was half hippie, but still very Italian. Melbourne had to learn how to work the system. There was an Italian men's club down the street, everyone in there playing cards, but he knew he wasn't welcome. Then a guy named Sal came to the apartment. He said, "If anything goes wrong, don't call the police. Call me." And Melbourne did. When something got stolen, he called Sal. Sal said, "Give me a little time and I'll be back." Then half an hour later the stolen item would return. Or else Sal would say, "Now you call the police."

One day he saw a young woman leave two big bags under the hallway stairs. Garbage was always a critical issue in the apartment. He ran after her but didn't catch her. He looked in the bags. They were full of envelopes and pages full of numbers. He realized that this was a numbers drop for Sal. So he went to Sal. Sal said, "Yeah, we were looking for them. Did you look at them?"

Of course not.

The next Saturday Sal came around and sold Melbourne a number. For one quarter. "Now I was accepted. I had now arrived in the neighborhood. I felt much better."

Melbourne branched out and started managing two more buildings. Of course, he was provided a no-charge apartment in each building. So he rented out the other apartments. That was illegal, but supers always had to connive to make an income. It's the way of the city.

"In New York you learn how to talk to people. Tenants were always asking for help in throwing things away. I learned that those situations were a huge source of income. 'What do you mean? You want me to carry your chair? Why am I going to do that? What do you mean, a dollar? That's not enough. It's got to be five.' That's how the super makes his money."

Melbourne and Gisela were in New York for a year before he could find work as a commercial artist. At every job interview he demonstrated that how he could do everything from sketches to finished drawings; he could spec type, airbrush, and create fashion illustrations—the whole spectrum of commercial art. And yet, despite all those skills, his applications kept getting rejected.

At last he learned that in New York, you must specialize in only one skill. So when the next employment opportunity appeared—a job designing textbooks—the interviewer asked if he could illustrate the books as well.

He said no, I only design them.

He got the job.

GARBAGE was a major issue. If tenants threw trash in the street, he would get the ticket from the cops. The first week as a super, he got a trash ticket for fifty bucks—the sum total of his monthly earnings. When Christmas came around, the trash guy knocked on their door. "The boys are going to be expecting something."

"How much?"

"Fifty bucks."

"Fifty bucks!"

"Yeah, fifty bucks for each of us. We got six of us."

"How are we going to get that money?"

"You get it from the tenants. Look, you're mopping the floor. You bang on their door with the mop handle. They go, 'Oh yeah. Here's something for you.' It's ten bucks. You say, 'Ten bucks! What am I going to do with ten bucks?'"

Melbourne recalled, "You always had to run a scam. I kind of enjoyed it."

Cheap apartments were rare in New York City, and you couldn't sell or take bribes to get one. But if one came available, the prospective tenant could buy the furniture in the apartment. So Melbourne learned to put a junky old table in any available rental and sell that table for, say, five hundred bucks.

"I think I was just trying to make some money and find something I could do."

The pressure on him started pushing even more intensely when, not so long after their move to the Village, his young wife went into labor. The baby, a boy, was born in a taxicab. They were living in lower Manhattan and the hospital was well north, on 125th Street. They made it only to 14th Street, where there was a small French hospital. A huge nurse came out carrying a tub, and she scooped both Gisela and the newborn into the tub and carried them off. Melbourne, who had only twenty-five dollars, asked the cabbie how much. The cabdriver said, "That's okay," and drove off.

Now the challenge was getting back to their old soft-top MG before eight o'clock. Parking on the street was always a problem. He couldn't lock the thing, so he often came out and found homeless people sleeping in the car. But this night the issue was to move the car before eight o'clock or else it would be towed to make room for street cleaning.

Because of the birth of the child, Melbourne didn't get back in time. The MG was gone.

Melbourne went directly to the night judge to plead guilty. He explained that he hadn't been able to get back to the car until eight-fifteen—the contractions, the delivery in the cab, the nurse with the tub, the whole story. The judge congratulated him on his fatherhood and, because the judge didn't yet have the paperwork, remanded the case for several days. And because Melbourne didn't have fifty bucks to pay the fine, the judge sent him to a cell in The Tombs.

He was there for several days—four to six people in the cell. All of them laughed out loud when Melbourne protested, "Hey, I'm not guilty!" He was allowed one phone call, but the policeman, not he, had to make the call. So he wrote a note to his friend Jack Higgins for the cop to say, "Jack, I'm a police officer calling for Melbourne, now don't hang up, Jack. To pay the bail I need seventy-five dollars just to get out till Friday. We just had a baby. You have to help me."

Higgins heard the first five words of that policeman's call, and then he shouted into the phone: "Get lost!" He hung up.

The mess unraveled itself in a few days, but the MG was gone and stayed gone. After a while, a year and a half, Melbourne and his small family were ready to go, too. ✶

Cadiz | 1960

*"The French rhetoricians have a maxim
that there is nothing beautiful that is not true—
an axiom that applies to ships as well as other things.
From time immemorial first impressions...
have followed their possessor to the threshold of the grave."*

—JOHN WILLIS GRIFFITHS
Treatise on Marine and Naval
Architecture | 1849

THEY WOKE the day after the shipwreck in a hospital—a French hospital of course, so it possessed a sunny *je ne sais quoi* that he remembered ever afterward. Husband and wife were together in the same room. The question was: would they prefer wine or beer with their meals.

Besides cuts and bruises they were all in fairly good shape. Melbourne's knee was inflamed from a collision with rock; likewise Gisela's shoulder. But all injuries were minor and temporary. A few days of rest, and they went on. *Sanspareil*, on the other hand, had been utterly reduced to its elements, a scrap-pile of old timbers.

The local authorities visited, of course. They needed to file a report on the accident. When they asked for the monetary value of the loss, Melbourne told them five thousand pounds, which was the worth of the boat itself. But the newspapers reported that *Sanspareil* had been carrying five thousand British pounds worth of cargo. That figure set off alarms. What could they have been carrying—across an international boundary, no less—of such value? Agents from Interpol came to question Melbourne in the hospital. After some back and forth he started to realize that they suspected him of

Golden Hind was built in 1931. After the Second World War, re-rigged as a three-masted yacht, she became Melbourne's fateful infatuation—*Annyah*.

stealing Lady Docker's jewels.

Lady Docker was great scandal-sheet entertainment at that time for the British, most of whom lived in poverty, or at best severe austerity, in the aftermath of the Second World War. She was a former burlesque dancer who had captured the heart of Lord Bernard Docker, chairman of the Daimler Company. Throughout the 1950s she had amused the nation with her opulent spending, her mink stoles and champagne receptions, and above all her procession of custom-made luxury autos, especially her Daimler Silver Flash with red crocodile leather seats. But in 1956 this spendthrift Lord was ousted from Daimler, and the unfortunate couple fell on hard times. At the end of the decade a mysterious theft occurred—fifteen-thousand pounds' worth of Lady Docker's jewelry vanished without evidence of a culprit. Her insurance company, justifiably alarmed, urged the investigation of any possible lead, including that of a shipwrecked Canadian lad in a Normandy hospital.

As Melbourne watched himself become tabloid fodder, he brooded over his own insurance problems. How could he (and his American investor) be compensated for the loss of the vessel when the insurance company hadn't yet received payment on the policy? The day after the shipwreck, Melbourne contacted the insurance company. They wired back that they had never received his money. Melbourne thought, "Oh hell, I'm in trouble now."

The next day he received another wire. Yes, they had received the cheque now, and so the insurance policy was in force.

Melbourne marveled at this radical demonstration of British honour and fair play. But mostly he rejoiced that his catastrophe had suddenly boosted the value of Aubrey Young's investment. Stated in U.S. currency, Young's ten thousand dollars had transformed rapidly into a fourteen-thousand-plus shipwreck.

Melbourne's next move was to restart his search for a sailing ship, this time for something bigger and better.

WHEN MELBOURNE returned to England to settle the insurance claim, Gisela went on to Germany to spend time with her mother's sister. The year was 1959 and it was shortly before Christmas. Melbourne joined her in Preetz, Schleswig-Holstein near the Keel Canal in Northern Germany, in time for a classic Old World yuletide. Melbourne arrived by train wearing a spanking new officer's uniform, a gift from the Merchant Marines Benevolent Society, which provided such to any members who had suffered a shipwreck. The holiday played out like a nostalgic fantasy. An uncle had bagged a deer in the snowy woods. The family's tannenbaum bore actual candles on its branches. And Gisela announced a surprise gift. Thanks to their mismanagement of contraceptives (wisely provided by her mother), she now found herself pregnant with their second child.

Meanwhile, Melbourne had continued to pester boat-brokers and study the ads in yachting publications, determined to find the set of sails that would carry him and his young family into a whole new life. He concluded that the likeliest marketplace for this was Gibraltar—the British outpost tucked between Spain and Morocco at the mouth of the Mediterranean.

Clearly this set of circumstances presented a geographical challenge for the family.

Reflecting in later years, Melbourne said, "We decided that Gisela would go back to Canada to live with my parents and have the baby there, and she would join me later. She would teach my father to read."

Not that his father had never learned to read. He had just never used that skill to any particular purpose, such as reading a book. Wouldn't it be terrible (thought the young couple, nobly) for Melbourne's father and mother to grow old without the experience of reading books? So Gisela decided to stay in Hamilton for the duration of her pregnancy and volunteer her time for the cause of late-life literacy.

"A hopeless, silly idea," Melbourne said later. "My father's attitude was always, how could somebody know more than I do?" Gisela's period in Hamilton went badly. She would wash the dishes, then her father-in-law would wash them again. Then he would retreat into silence, sitting like a stone. After several months of this kind of friction, she scooped up her son and went to stay with her mother in Montreal, where she had the second child, Genevieve Patricia.

On his own very different mission, Melbourne went south by train, chasing a boat as yet unknown. Using Gibraltar as his base, he made excursions into Tangier, on the Mediterranean coast of Morocco. He prowled the docks, talked with sailors and boat owners, and hung out in the bars listening to conversations and asking questions. He learned how the tides and winds affected sailing passage in and out of the Straits of Gibraltar. He learned how smuggling operations worked between Spain, Italy, and other ports of call. He wrote letters to his wife every day, using those flimsy blue fold-up aerogrammes that came pre-postaged. He was hoping to find a good Brixham trawler or a French tunnyman, something that would fit his budget. He found a couple boats he liked, and then he found the one he loved.

He found her in a British yacht-broker's office. Her photograph arrested his attention. He studied her specifications. She was too good for him. Beyond his means. And yet, like a bumpkin enthralled by a dazzling courtesan, he had no intention of letting her go.

SHE was *Annyah.* Her frames were all galvanized steel. The hull planking, decking, and deckwork were entirely Burma teak. Hundreds of heavy bronze bolts fastened her three-inch-thick hull planking. Her gear was heavy, too. Standing on deck, a man could scarcely reach around her mainmast. It seemed her mainsail and gaff weighed about a ton. Raising that sail, pulling four hundred feet of rope, could break the spirits of even three strong men. She had been built to a Milne design as a two-masted yacht, launched out of Glasgow, Scotland, in 1931, one hundred and four feet on deck, a twenty-foot beam, and a draft of twelve feet three inches. Her name then was *Golden Hind*, a King's Cup contestant. Her original owner, wealthy of course, built her for racing, which she did with a professional captain and crew of six.

During the war, British defense authorities moored her in Portsmouth Harbor. They removed her masts and tethered a large barrage balloon—meant to foul enemy aircraft in its long vertical cables—to a huge ring on her deck. Later she was re-rigged with three masts, cut down, better for cruising than for racing. And she was bought by a retired British Army officer, a Captain G.C. Morton, who then left his homeland to avoid its taxes. Morton renamed the ship in honor of his Greek mistress.

"His mistress was named *Annyah* Panis," Melbourne recalled. "When I got there, they were living in separate hotels. She got kicked out of his hotel because when she was drunk she squatted on the dance floor to take a piss. Some high society is not what you think it is."

In 1960 *Annyah* was tied up on the North Mole in Gibraltar as a houseboat. Morton kept a Spanish crew aboard, but he had become a sick old man unable to supervise her maintenance. He knew she was fading. He advertised her for sale hoping someone would refit her properly and use her appropriately. It wasn't as though he needed the money. But the price he asked was well past Melbourne's purchasing power.

According to Mick Philp—who later joined her crew in the West Indies—to build such a boat at that time, some thirty years after her construction, would have cost about a half million dollars.

On a windy winter day Melbourne stood on Gibraltar's stone pier and studied *Annyah*. He saw her peeling topside and the long sweep of her sheer (the hull lines). Then he walked her deck and looked up at her tall spars. He went aloft in a boatswain's chair to her hounds*, thinking and dreaming. He knew he couldn't meet Captain Morton's price. He doubted, even if he did get her to the West Indies, that she would be in any condition to run charters. But none of that mattered, really.

He visited Captain Morton on board the yacht repeatedly. Morton was no longer fit for sailing, but he dressed like a gentleman, ascot and tweeds. His wardrobe consisted of six blazers and a dozen slacks, all of these identical. His ties all bore the insignia of the Royal Gibraltar Yacht Club. Melbourne talked excitedly about *Annyah*, and he talked about his goal, the English Harbour in Antigua, its narrow entrance and the sheltered cove marked by the remains of Lord Nelson's Caribbean headquarters. Eventually Morton, a fading vessel himself and weary of the whole matter, agreed to this enthusiastic young Canadian's absurdly low offer. He released to Melbourne Smith's command the astonishing *Annyah*.

---

*Projections on each side of a masthead which support trestle-trees for a topmast or top-gallant mast; and for nesting or supporting the eyes of shrouds.

Melbourne stands before the mast with the crew of *Wooden Shoe*. To his right is the big Irishman Bob "Paddy" Adam, who joined *Annyah* in Gibraltar.

MELBOURNE SHOPPED AROUND the waterfront bars and youth hostels to gather a crew of amateurs. They bunked in *Annyah*'s forecastle and worked long-hour shifts stripping and finishing the hull, brightwork, and spars in exchange for their keep.

Paddy Adam, an Irishman from Dublin, was working as an engineer on a ship in the Mediterranean. When his ship passed Gibraltar, he got off and joined *Annyah*'s crew. Paddy was a friend from Hamilton days. He and Melbourne had sailed together for a couple years in the *Wooden Shoe*.

Two Spanish fishermen joined her crew in Cadiz. Paddy and the Spaniards were to become fixtures of the *Annyah*'s final incarnation.

Suddenly, now that he was captain of this big vessel—one hundred and four feet long with a twenty-foot beam and three towering masts—Melbourne had new responsibilities. The engine would have to be rebuilt or replaced, not just cleaned up, and he had no money for that. More immediately, he had crew who needed pay—not so much, but they did need to eat.

The only real option he could see was a bit of harmless smuggling. For example, there was the "nicotine navy." Melbourne claims that he didn't join that scam. "They would never let me in on it."

These smugglers moved cartons of cigarettes—a dollar a pack duty-

CHAPTER 3 | 27

free but worth much more after slipping into Italy. They employed vessels that had been dumped after service in the Second World War, stripped down, the diesel engines replaced with cheap gasoline engines, drums of gasoline on the deck. The captains were frauds, remittance men, drunks who hung out in bars claiming to know something about the sea. "It took me a while to figure this out," said Melbourne. The true captain and engineer posed as deckhands. They would communicate to each other on the radio using whistling as a code. If the ship got nabbed by the Italian Navy—nabbing had to happen, of course, for the sake of Italian pride—the smugglers would sacrifice the drunken "captain," who would wake the next morning facing ten years in an Italian prison.

Though he may not have moved cigarettes, Melbourne did smuggle cases of Long John whiskey from British Gibraltar into Cadiz, sometimes at the behest of the British Consulate. In such situations, he carried two manifests, one covering the bogus transaction in case he got caught.

This was a game that kept him alive on the water while he prepared to sail with a crew from Gibraltar to the Caribbean to meet the unclear future ahead. In his aerogrammes with his wife, he asked if she would prefer to meet him in Gibraltar, with the children, including the infant daughter, or wait till he reached Antigua. She wanted to come now so that they could cross the Atlantic together.

By then he had moved *Annyah* to Cadiz, the port city in southernmost Spain. Cadiz faces a long, narrow bay that points the direction Melbourne intended to go. As he waited for his family to come, he learned how to get around, leaving the port by walking through a gate into the city. Every morning he went for a shave and haircut. While he sat in the barber's chair, local tradesmen would offer him products he could use, anything from bread to brass screws. He felt like a king. The barber would shave him twice, then slap him with brothel-potent alcohol. He would walk into the city for supplies. Once he walked a great distance to purchase toilet paper. When he reached the store, he told the shopkeeper—using his bad Spanish—that he would like to buy some paper for the toilet: *papel para el baño*. The shopkeeper was baffled by the request. For a moment Melbourne considered using a simple hand gesture to convey his meaning. But there were other customers present. He chose to walk all the way back to his quarters at the harbor and look up the proper expression: *papel higiénico*.

He finally reunited with his wife, ending seven months of separation, and he met his two children for the first time, or in the boy's case, as if for the first time. Sean Wolfgang was three. The little girl Genevieve Patricia was three months. Gisela was exhausted from the twenty-four-hour ordeal. He met them at the airport in Gibraltar and they spent the night there. She collapsed quickly into unconscious sleep.

THE NEXT DAY, a friend of Melbourne drove them in his automobile from Gibraltar through the international checkpoint into Spain and to Cadiz. They stopped for lunch at a beautiful old hotel in Algeciras, the Hotel Reina Cristina. The choice to stop there had been purely accidental. Then Gisela realized where she was. Her parents had stayed there, in fact resided there for some time, two decades before. As a German military officer, her father had been assigned to this station, directly across the bay from English-held Gibraltar, in order to openly spy on enemy comings and goings. The high command had refused to allow officers to bring their wives. But they did allow the companionship of a mistress. So Gisela's mother had assumed the role of mistress. Her mother later said that one of the best days of her life was when she left that hotel, when she could finally show her passport to the concierge who had treated her throughout their stay with the contempt reserved for prostitutes.

Now two decades later Melbourne and his wife sat in perhaps the same fateful seats.

IN CADIZ, six seamen lived on the ship. The whole situation was happy. The two Spaniards particularly liked playing uncles to the little boy. The baby swung in a cradle overhead. Everyone was working hard to prepare for the departure in two weeks.

After a day of rest, husband and wife went out for a night on the town, to little bodegas, small wine bars and restaurants in basements with singing and music and dancing.

The next day she felt terrible. Her gasping and trembling and crying out convinced everyone that she needed to get to the hospital. Paddy Adam was six foot four. He scooped her up and carried her off to the ambulance. When she got to the doctor, she said, "I think I have polio."

"No, no, my dear," said the doctor. "We haven't had a case of polio in years."

Oddly enough, she had written and mentioned a couple of times that she felt they should get shots for polio—not for the kids but for themselves. Was

Hotel Reina Cristina in Algeciras played a poignant role in the drama of Melbourne's first marriage.

that a premonition, he wondered then, as his wife fell into a dire physical decline.

After a full night of vigil, Melbourne left to get breakfast, hurried back, and found that the door to his wife's sick room was locked.

When he was later let into the room, he saw the contour of her body utterly still under a sheet. But he rather looked out the window in search of her.

"Evidently polio lasts only three days," he said years afterwards. "You carry it for weeks or months. Then you don't know what's going to happen. Some only get a cough.

"Some die."

H E TELEGRAMMED Gisela's mother. "Our beautiful Froschie has died from polio." She immediately sent Gisela's nineteen-year-old younger sister Biene to assist in any way.

The English Embassy came quickly to Melbourne's aid. They put the infant in the care of some very reliable Spanish women, and Melbourne provided the baby's formula that Gisela had brought with her.

To Melbourne the funeral was an absurdity. Neither the deceased nor the bereaved were religious in any way. He wanted to donate the body to the university, but the university was not accepting such donations at that time of the year. Cremation was out of the question because Spain was a Catholic country. He had to pay for a funeral, and for practical reasons it had to be a second-rate funeral, and so Melbourne's entire childhood and youth vanished in a puff. At the ceremony he recited Robert Burns's "My Luve is like a Red Red Rose," recited it to himself without knowing exactly what he was doing. Then she was buried.

There was a big investigation of this death. The U.S. Naval Station at Rota sent a doctor over right away. The British Consulate felt concerned. The local police investigated a horse and buggy ride they had taken that night in Cadiz. That investigation was utterly futile. Polio cannot be contracted from a horse's rump the night before you die. The thing had infected Gisela in Montreal well before she set out for the future.

For the future invented by them to be theirs.

"I don't remember paying the bill," Melbourne admitted. "I never never never thought something like that would happen."

THE CHILDREN were taken by their aunt Biene across the Atlantic and America to live with Helga, Gisela's oldest sister, in Manhattan Beach, California. No way could they participate in the work ahead. He had to continue with *Annyah*.

"I got very busy after that. I sailed back to Gibraltar, then left for Las Palmas in the Canary Islands. *Annyah* was ready to sail without an engine.

"But when you sail, you have a lot of free time. That's when it hits you. You try to find a reason.

"I'd always pick a star out at night. You see shooting stars all the time. I'd pick out a star. I kept thinking—if that star shoots, I'll jump into the sea and drown, join her wherever she is. That would be a sure sign. 'Leave the boat and join me.'

"Fortunately it never happened." ✶

Hamilton | 1930

*"The ship, a fragment detached from the earth,
went on lonely and swift like a small planet."*

— JOSEPH CONRAD | 1898

IN LANDLESS DARKNESS, under sail, steady and quiet and focused on great distances, the mind easily turns to memories of early days and the mute mysteries. "None of my family ever left town except to visit relatives," Melbourne realized as he traveled by wind power under starlight across the Southern Atlantic. But that thought wasn't quite true. His father once enlisted in the Canadian Army and was sent to Montreal. That was in 1939, in the fervent stirrings of the Second World War. Melbourne was nine. He still remembered his father's serial number (B11164), the puttees wrapped around his legs, and his itchy woolen uniforms. But as the recruits marched through the streets of Montreal, the French citizens, in a burst of Anglophobia, pelted them with garbage. Then his father developed some sort of medical condition, was hospitalized for a time in St. Johns, New Brunswick, and missed the chance to be shipped overseas with his fellow volunteers. That's all that the old man ever seemed to want to experience of the world.

That, and itchy wool.

"It's a funny thing," recalled Melbourne, "a sore point all my childhood. My father always bought Turnbull underwear, made out of wool. I couldn't stand wool on my body. I used to put a hankie on my back and pull it over that, or wear my pajama bottoms under my pants. You can't sit still in school irritated like that."

He mused: "Winter underwear ruined my childhood."

Whenever his father caught him padding his bum, the old man would shout, "I spent good money on that, and you're bloody well going to wear it!" When he got old enough to rebel, Melbourne attacked his father on this woolen underwear obsession, and his father said, "What's the matter with that? You turned out all right, didn't you?"

He never enjoyed doing anything with his father. Every outing ended with Melbourne—Bill, as he was known then—being sent to bed when they got home. "Stand up straight! Stop wiggling! Stop talking! Don't touch my tools!"—it never seemed to end. "I'm sure he thought he was doing the best for me, but I preferred to spend my time away from him." He thought of his own small children. He wondered what underwear they had on. At this rate, they wouldn't have a chance to prefer spending time away. He had robbed them of that choice.

Just as irritating as wool, upon reflection, was the family's faithful attendance at Houston Street Baptist Church, a service on Sunday morning or evening but always Sunday School in the afternoon. The only consolation for this earthly torment was the nickel or dime his mother would give him for the collection bowl. There was a drug store on the corner that charged a penny for a stick of licorice root. So young Billy would sneak a piece of that and chew it till he had a wad of hay in his mouth.

"That made Sunday School tolerable," he said.

When Melbourne got older, he negotiated his release from the Baptist church. He stated, and his parents actually agreed to the concept, that when he turned sixteen he would make his own decision about whether or not to attend church services. But the day he turned sixteen was a Sunday. "Never mind," his father said. "Get ready for Sunday School! Shut up, or I'll give you something to really cry about."

His mother, on the other hand, was fun. When she got together with the girls, she would be dancing around and putting something on her head. When she packed his lunch for school, she made sandwiches of Wonder bread, butter, and Spanish onions. Later Melbourne asked her about these onion sandwiches. She replied that she made them "so the girls wouldn't bother you!"

After school there were always fights, always somebody wanting to beat somebody up. Being a scrawny kid, his philosophy was "Spit far and run fast." But an uncle had advised: "Hey, you get insults, just punch him right in the mouth. Get the first punch in. Go on the attack!" So he tried that once. The big kid folded like a cheap umbrella. Fists and blood. Later the kid's mother showed up at the family door. Look what your son did!

Industry-friendly Hamilton, situated at the west end of Lake Ontario, served as Melbourne's unlikely launch pad.

Melbourne's mother replied, "Your boy is much bigger than Billy. Go put some bandages on him!"

Dear old Mom.

But Dad was a more complex problem. "I still have bad dreams about him," Melbourne admitted. "Why am I fighting him now?"

Melbourne's father drove a horse-drawn milk-delivery wagon. He would start at two or three in the morning and get back around noon, often sleeping on the return. Once the milk was delivered, the horse knew the way home. This was terrible work in winter on the shore of Lake Ontario, but the milk wagons had doors on each side, and a Coleman lantern gave a little heat. In those days ice was delivered to the house in fifty-pound blocks, and automobiles were odd. People walked. Melbourne spent most of his childhood walking, walking. Where?

"Don't even try," seemed to be the father's philosophy in Melbourne's recollection. The father never read, and he discouraged conversation around the dinner table. "Just shut up and eat."

FEW of the family members owned their homes at that time. They all rented. When they went to visit other family—there were aunts and uncles all over town—no one ever called ahead (no one had phones). They just got off the streetcar and showed up at the door.

There were no school buses. And lots of snow. The schools never closed no matter how hard it snowed. "Kids walked a hell of a long distance to get to school. I never saw parents bring their kids to school. That just never happened."

From grade seven on, he always had an after-school job—bicycle-mounted delivery boy mostly, everything from drugstore packages to fur coats. He remembered delivering two five-gallon bottles of Helene Curtis shampoo, one on each handlebar, sliding his bike around snow patches and streetcar tracks. Had to have a job. "I was always paid the same thing, five dollars a week. I got to keep a dollar. Saving for my college fund. Ha ha!"

In fact, nobody ever talked of college.

During the 1930s Hamilton was a city of just over one hundred thousand souls, an industrial town dominated by two steel manufacturing plants, Stelco and Dofasco. They used to dump their slag into the bay and light up the sky at night. Also, two big U.S. companies, Procter & Gamble and Beech-Nut Packing Company, were running manufacturing plants in Hamilton.

The city wraps around the westernmost point of Lake Ontario, situated at a strategic harbor inside Burlington Bay and conveniently located about halfway between Toronto and Buffalo, New York. One of the city's distinguishing features is the Niagara Escarpment, which runs right through its middle more or less paralleling the lake's contour and dividing the city into lower and upper portions, the steep rise between them being about eight hundred feet. The time it took to drive from there to the U.S. border and Niagara Falls was about an hour, but not until fast cars and decent highways had been developed.

Hamilton had no history of any significance to Melbourne. It was founded by a fellow named Hamilton, a British loyalist, after the War of 1812. It was incorporated in 1846, the same year that the first fast-moving clipper ship was launched out of New York City. It had nowhere near the geographical splendor, the beauty, and the cultural dazzle of French-speaking Montreal, located almost four hundred miles away (eight hours of travel time in the 1930s) at the other end of Lake Ontario and far up the St. Lawrence River. For a kid such as Melbourne, Montreal was the moon.

AS HARD as Hamilton treated Melbourne, he was just as difficult in return. He recalled getting kicked out of the Boy Scouts. Everybody was sitting around, maybe twenty-five kids on the floor, and he was sitting on the piano stool. He couldn't remember what the scoutmaster was doing, talking about bears or something. Melbourne wiggled and made the bench go *ee-ah. ee-ah. ee-ah.* The scoutmaster said, "Billy please don't do that." *ee-ah.* "Billy, I've asked you, please don't do that again." *ee-ah.* "Billy, you do that one more time and...." *ee-ah.* "Okay, you can go home right now!" Melbourne went home crying. "Why are they picking on me?"

Under the honest starlight of the Southern Atlantic, Melbourne imagined what he would say to such an irritating brat if he were that scoutmaster: "I wouldn't have waited five times to say, 'You're a real asshole, that's what you are!'"

He never had a crumb of respect for team spirit nor for tradition nor for doing the right thing. He was a terrible student. But he always did the artwork. He'd miss classes to do artwork. "Maybe it was the only way I could redeem myself," he thought now.

In grades seven and eight at Lord Tweedsmuir Public School, he took shop classes. One was drafting, the other metalwork, and he took two classes in woodwork. He learned how to draft in grade seven. That skill later gave him a livelihood. He learned how to handle power tools such as the lathe. More important, he learned the hand tools, the plane, chisels, and such. He learned the right names for original implements. In fact, he realized, that's what he liked most about ships of sail—the antique mechanism, the names of things, the power of simplicity.

In the ninth grade he learned how to set type: big flat boxes, small squares, California Job Case*, precision, accuracy of detail. Mostly, though, he liked to draw. He could remember the first thing he ever drew, a guy wearing a cowboy hat. He was always making posters for school. How they pasteurize milk. Or how electricity can start a fire. He laughed at himself recalling one poster he'd made: "Don't play with fire around electrical wires." He got the message a little wrong. But the artwork was good, and he got a prize.

He felt regrets. He was bad to his art teacher, a dowdy, bewigged old lady named Miss Hortense Mattice Gorden, who was well-studied in the principles of modern art and who used very practical assignments to teach "value, direction, harmony, interval, and form." Melbourne realized now that her ideas were the few that had lasted for him past high school. "I was really learning how to put a design together," he thought. "It's what nature is."

---

* This is a wooden box with built-in dividers, used to store moveable type for letterpress printing. It was the most popular such "job case" in North America.

Every leaf on the tree is different, in different relation with each other. "That's all she taught." But by the time he thought to thank her, Miss Hortense Mattice Gorden had already met her demise.

For a moment he regretted everything in life that he had ever done. "I have loads of relatives in Canada," he thought, "and I've slighted them. You don't have to leave the house to become a great person. It was a grimy, dirty town in those days because of the steel mill. Now they've cleaned up the lake. The whole town has grown up since I left."

But Bill Smith had to go, go, go.

NIAGARA FALLS wasn't the only crowbar that pried Billy Smith out of his stuck life in drab, neo-colonial Hamilton. But it certainly did help.

In his case, though, "Niagara Falls" does not refer to the crashing cataracts that have been such an attraction for honeymooners and hydroelectric industrialists. No, we're talking about the city itself, on the U.S. side of the river, a city that has never profited much from the tourism nor from the technocrats. In the mid 1940s, as Melbourne remembers it, Niagara Falls, New York, was depressed. On Main Street half the storefronts were boarded up, some of them rented for oddball purposes just to show signs of life. However, the place had the advantage of being located in the United States—just across the border about sixty miles from Hamilton—and by the end of the Second World War the British Empire was bankrupt and America was coming into its ascendancy. Melbourne's father moved the family there, looking for work.

Instigator of the move was his mother's brother-in-law Tom, who had been born in the U.S. and was employed. Uncle Tom and Auntie Annie offered their basement as temporary lodgings for the transition. Suddenly they were all living like Anne Frank's family—the two parents, the early teenage Melbourne, two younger sisters, and a coal-fired furnace in a space the size of a small parlor. If someone wanted to sit, someone else had to stand.

"Let me tell you something about my Uncle Tom," said Melbourne many years later. "He was an American, so my father thought he must know everything."

The uncle had a clock on his mantle that was set in a wooden case designed like a sailing vessel, something of a Columbus-style galleon with the timepiece embedded in the hull. The sails were chrome metal topped by wavy flags. But it pained Melbourne to see the obvious—the sails were being blown one direction and the flags were flying the reverse. That made no sense. So when no one was looking, he spun the flags so that they seemed to wave in the naturally proper direction. Uncle Tom came home and growled, "Who's been fooling around with my clock?' An argument ensued. His father stepped in to defend Uncle Tom. "Shut up! Your uncle knows what he's talking about!"

Melbourne later drew diagrams to prove he was right, but he never showed them. "That was a crushing event in my childhood," he admitted some seven decades later.

H IS FATHER tried for several weeks to find work in Niagara Falls. Eventually he landed a job, but he didn't like it. He decided to move the family back to Hamilton.

Melbourne, however, bested his father by getting a job for himself. He went to work as an apprentice sign-painter for the Harry J. Allen Sign Company. And when the family returned to Ontario, Melbourne chose to remain in New York. When it came time to begin high school, he didn't. Childhood was over.

All his life Melbourne was amazingly skilled at drawing lines. Here was early proof. He was one of two employees for Harry J. Allen—"a real nice guy," Melbourne recalled. "A wonderful drunk."

Apparently sign-makers have a natural attraction to booze. What else can you do after painting humdrum messages on depressed storefronts and unfared taxis? You stop at the bar for a shot of whiskey. "Give the kid a sarsaparilla," Harry would say. They painted bulletin boards. They made neon signs out of scrap bedframes. Young Melbourne learned how to carry a twelve-foot ladder upright, shuffling along from one signboard to another. He once painted numbers on the wings of an airplane. But the plane took off before the paint had properly dried, and he had to re-do the job.

And he was making money. Ten dollars a week. At night he worked as usher at the local movie theater—ninety-nine cents after Social Security was deducted. "It was all cotton, man," he recalled. "I had money jingling in my pocket." It went like that for months.

Then the principal of the public school in Hamilton that he was supposed to attend came to fetch him. This principal was a member of the Hamilton Kiwanis Club, and through the club he had contacted certain members, a childless couple named Collins, who were willing to accept a stray boy.

So Melbourne went to the Collins home to spend his first two years of

Royal Canadian Sea Cadet Melbourne Smith

high school. This foster home was just a couple miles away from his family in another part of town, and he still saw his family once a week, still took his laundry home. But the Collinses changed his life.

"They showed me a whole different world I didn't know existed." Mr. and Mrs. Collins never raised their voices. They never said, "Shut up and eat your food! Don't talk at the table!" They set napkins on the table, and they engaged in pleasant conversations. Friends would visit them to play euchre and bridge. They tried to teach him a new word every day. They encouraged him not to use no more double negatives. "They taught me to stop interrupting everybody else, to stop being a horse's ass."

They did go to church occasionally, but the church was far more Episcopalian than Baptist, no clapping and shouting of amens. "Everything was civilized," he said.

Collins had a small factory, Collins Sheet Metal Products, which made everything from stovepipes to garbage cans to breadboxes. "Never say fail," was the slogan, with the tag line, "Say never fail!" The factory, as Melbourne remembers it, was a little sweatshop full of poorly paid Polish ladies.

IN FACT, most of his buddies in those days were second-generation Eastern Europeans, the children of immigrants and political fugitives. His schoolmates included Ukrainians, Hungarians, Croatians, also Italians. He learned to speak Polish, first the numbers, then a conversational kind of Polish that he discovered later was archaic and Jewish-sounding. His best friend was a Polish kid they called "Ziggy." The two of them picked up work after school painting flowers on teapots from a local pottery. He and Ziggy painted thousands of teapots till they grew tired of the economics, ten cents apiece. Melbourne later sang in a Polish choir. He also learned to play trumpet and percussion, skills he sometimes contributed to polka bands and klezmer parties, weddings, and other such events. At Polish parties old people would come tottering in, then jump up and dance ecstatically, then walk out slowly, weeping because they hadn't danced like that in such a long time.

Many of his pals were large, slab-dimensioned immigrant boys, and he was wiry and hyperactive, a little guy. He remembers a Test-Your-Strength game at a local fair—squeeze down on a lever and make a ball rise. He watched his beefy buddies go at the challenge, then realized that if he froze his best grip and then changed the angle of his forearm, he could create a lever and trounce them. Important lesson: brains over brawn.

A similar lesson was sharpened by a high school track-and-field event that Melbourne wasn't supposed to attend. He wasn't on the team. But there was a bus ready to take athletes to a regional competition, and he realized that if he got on the bus he could miss classes. So he did. But when he got to end of the ride, he had to confront the fact that he would need to compete in some event or other. He chose the high jump. But he had never jumped before. He had no skills with the traditional horizontal, leg-over-the-bar-and-spin form the other boys all knew. Instead, he invented a completely vertical, pogo-stick jump that always landed him right on his head. With that technique he set a couple of school records. And then he never competed again.

He wanted to enroll in the typing class, but they wouldn't let him because he was a boy and the school assumed that his only real motivation was to be around all the girls. (This is a charge that he could not honestly refute in later years.) But he was talented and naturally skilled in art—in drawing, making posters, knowing the beauty of the well-executed line, and creating the clear visual image. In fact, the only reason the school let him graduate was his exceptional skill with making art.

As previously mentioned, he was horrid to his own art teacher, the stout, elderly Miss Hortense Matisse Gorden, who was well-versed in the techniques of modern art. "But she got her revenge," Melbourne later admitted. "She failed me bad. I had to go back and take all the exams again." That, plus a special art project demonstrating Melbourne's proven design skills, eventually convinced the school to grant him a diploma.

"THEN I had sort of an itch to travel," he remembered. (As events showed, "sort of an itch" was a bona fide understatement.)

Old Mr. Collins touched off that itch, perhaps unwittingly, when he took young Melbourne on the train to a trade show in Montreal. The very sight of Montreal startled the boy with images of a life more beautiful, more diverse, more international, richer in culture, noisier with voices, and juicier in physical sensation than anything he had imagined. Situated at extreme opposite ends of Lake Ontario, Hamilton was a lump of coal and Montreal a diamond. Imagine going from Bakersfield to San Francisco, or from Dublin to Paris. Around the time Melbourne was finishing high school, Montreal had become the second-largest primarily French-speaking city in the world (after Paris), a city of outdoor cafes and classic continental architecture, a city fairly anti-Anglo in character—during the Second World War its mayor had ordered the citizens to refuse being conscripted into the national armed forces—along with a lively Chinatown and Latin Quarter. The city was widely known at that time as the Cultural Capital of Canada.

By contrast, Hamilton, with one-third of that population, has been called the Steel Capital of Canada.

DURING four years of his early adolescence, Melbourne committed his attention to the Royal Canadian Sea Cadets, a kind of maritime Boy Scouts. Through the Cadets he began to learn what it means to sail.

The group met twice a week at their military-style base. According to Melbourne, mostly they wore uniforms and marched. Melbourne took the role of the lead drummer in the bugle band, and they went to parades all the time. They even marched in the Niagara Falls (New York) Magna Carta Day Parade, tromping in front of the great waterfalls across the Rainbow Bridge. With his drumming and trumpet skills Melbourne also marched with the Army Cadets. "You did those things at school," he said, "because you got out of class. I also played in the school orchestra—that way you could get out, too." Every summer the Sea Cadets would go camping for two weeks in Thousand Islands at the far end of Lake Ontario, sleeping outdoors, digging latrines, carrying "honey buckets," all juvenile simulations of the soldiers' life. After all, such duties had helped win the day in the last great war.

The most enduring lessons came from Cadet classroom training in maritime skills. Best of all, the boys experienced day-sail excursions aboard the HMCS *Oriole*, a hundred-foot yawl that is still in service today—and

The Orion Quintet, circa 1950, records a track for a proposed television show. That's Melbourne Smith on the maracas.

famous, being close to a century old—as a training vessel with the Canadian Navy. *Oriole* is a two-masted vessel, rigged fore-and-aft, in which the mizzen or after mast is quite short and stepped back toward the stern. Every Cadet was given a chore to do while *Oriole* was underway. Melbourne's duty was to manage the starboard main backstay. When a duty came up for any of the Cadets, they would all rush to assist. In this way all the lads learned the rudiments of sail, a profoundly traditional science that for centuries had enabled many a young man to slip away from the ignominy of his land-locked life to chase his own glory or, more often, his doom.

The implications of this training for Billy Smith far surpassed the fun of skipping school to play drums in a marching band. But he couldn't know that at the time.

He spent his ninth and tenth grade school years with the Collinses then moved back with his family once his father was employed and the household returned to some stability. But Melbourne's own rising sensibilities clashed increasingly with the values of his father. For example, although his best friend was Polish, and very courteous in his visits, the father kept grumbling about "the damn Polacks." When a family of Hungarians moved next door, the old man was livid. "Goddamn Honkies moving in!" Then the neighbor, mowing his own lawn with a push mower, walked over and voluntarily cut the little patch of grass belonging to the Smiths' home. "What the hell!" his father shouted as he stormed out to confront the trespasser. Melbourne was mortified. After all, this was the parent of a school chum.

His father was gone an hour then came home drunk. The neighbor had suddenly become his best friend.

Such a reform of narrow-minded thinking might have salved the son-father relationship at some earlier time, but by then it was too late. Melbourne was out of school and playing music for money—for good money. He was making more than his father. He played drums mostly, some trumpet, lots of polkas, but he filled in with orchestras at Club Norman in Toronto and at the Burlington Beach Inn in "beautiful downtown Burlington Beach." Once he played with Nat "King" Cole when his trio came to Canada on tour. He studied music theory and took banjo lessons, and he taught music at Borcellino's Music Store near home. With Alfie Borcellino he launched the Orion Quintet (guitar, accordion, bass, piano, and drums—"a constellation of stars"). They cut some records, even aspired to a television contract. To get around, Melbourne purchased a Model A 1931 roadster with a rumble seat (excellent for hauling the drum kit) and cloth top, fifty dollars. Later he sold it for seventy-five.

One winter he had to do an engine overhaul and used his father's garage. He pulled the head off the engine block, but then the weather turned too cold for him to get the repairs finished. His father yelled at him: "If you get that head back on, I'll eat my hat!"

The next spring Melbourne took a terrible delight in backing his roadster out of the garage and racing past the old man shouting, "Eat your bloody hat!"

IN 1953 he and a buddy hit the road. They crossed the Atlantic on the *SS Salacia*. Melbourne made some cash by painting signs at the coronation of Queen Elizabeth. They read "Liz is a Wiz," and he sold a hundred of them. The newspaper next day described these signs as the work of a "disrespectful American student."

A cheap airplane ticket got him back to Hamilton via Iceland and Newfoundland. He pondered his next move. He began thinking intensely about boats and about navigation by sail. Such thoughts turn almost inevitably to reality. Time is the only variable.

THESE MUSINGS and others drifted past his mind as time's barriers evaporated in the silence of sail under starlight in the South Atlantic. ✶

Antigua | 1960

*"If you want to build a ship,
don't drum up the men to gather wood, divide the work and give orders.
Instead, teach them to yearn for the vast and endless sea."*

—ANTOINE DE SAINT-EXUPERY

HE HAD PASSED eight months in Cadiz and Gibraltar. Now as autumn approached he caused *Annyah* to slip through the Strait under full spread of sail and escape the grip of the Mediterranean. Her sails had been patched by the two Spaniards, who would remain the most steadfast of his crew. Others on board were a couple of Dutchmen, his late wife's cousin Klaus from Germany, and a contentious mate named John Horn from South Africa. A couple of paying passengers joined them in the Canaries. The big Irishman Paddy Adam was on board as crew, also as the ship's engineer. But he no longer had an engine to care for. A cracked block had finally ended the beautiful vessel's capacity to travel by any means other than the wind. Melbourne's adventures in smuggling had not raised enough revenue to cover the cost of a replacement engine.

Unable to motor through the Strait of Gibraltar, he sailed out under the restrictions he had learned in many tavern talks with experienced mariners—tacking his way out three days after the full moon when the tide was running quickest and the Levante wind was in force. From this point on, he was going to have to negotiate harbors and dockyard slips in the antique manner, by means of nautical prowess alone.

He knew that the lack of an engine was likely to hurt his ability to run charters once they reached the West Indies. But what could he do about that? He needed to move, to follow his sextant, his fate, and his luck.

They sailed southwest to the Canaries, a flotilla of volcanic peaks that lie

In Gibraltar, Captain Melbourne Smith prepares *Annyah* for her Atlantic crossing to Nelson's Dockyard, Antigua.

just off the southern boundary of Morocco. For centuries these islands had been the rallying point where sailing ships could catch the prevailing winds and ride them due west to the Caribbean.

This first leg of the voyage went smoothly, much of the crew's attention being applied to the adjustments required by life beyond shore. The Spaniards had laid in a supply of excellent dried venison. *Annyah*'s own stores included some oddities—for example, big cans of lentils. The cook knew how to prepare them, but "nobody liked them," Melbourne later recalled. And there were several cases of jars of pickled walnuts. "Every once in a while, we would open one and throw it overboard."

Though she lacked an engine, *Annyah* had come equipped with two antique generators, both manufactured by Stuart Turner in Henley-on-Thames. These chunky contraptions were fashioned of heavy dark-green components, including a solid steel tank for petrol, all twisted together with brass piping. Vigorous cranking in the manner of an old Model T got the generators to sputter into life, after which they banged away like unmuffled dirt bikes.

In short order the crew raised La Palma, the westernmost of the Canaries. Melbourne had no chart for the harbor. But he knew that every incoming ship was required to take on a local pilot who would assume control of the arrival. So they hung a blue light over the side, the signal for a pilot to come out, and then waited half a day. By this point one of the two generators had expired. Now the only motorized sound they heard was the knocking of one device that wanly lit a few bulbs in the ship's saloon.

When the pilot finally did come out, Melbourne explained to him that they had no engine. But the harbor was downwind, so they would have no trouble getting in. They just needed to know which berth.

It was a very narrow harbor, crowded with big ships. The pilot pointed, as if to say, "That's where you're going." As they entered the harbor and began to turn, the pilot cried, *"No, no! Sigue adelante"*—keep going all the way to the end and turn around.

"But we have no engine."

"No, no. Sigue adelante."

Hearing the bang-bang of the generator, the pilot had decided this noise was *Annyah*'s engine, and he trusted his ear over the young Canadian captain's wretched Spanish.

Melbourne's words: "So we went to the end and turned around, then tried to keep going but couldn't. He was gesturing us, 'Come on.' Finally I showed him the engine room. Empty. And we had another thousand yards to go. We pulled ourselves along with arms and rope, with others helping us, until finally we got into our slip.

"The next day the pilot came back with a bunch of pilots. 'Look what I did!' he was saying to them. 'I brought in a ship with no engine!' He was very proud of himself."

A*NNYAH'S* destiny still lay far ahead, almost three thousand miles across the Atlantic Ocean in the West Indies. The *British* West Indies. Any ship registered to a British citizen (Canadians included) could claim privileges in a British-held port. That's why Melbourne was determined to reach Antigua.

On this island's southern coast English Harbour and Falmouth Harbour lay side by side and intertwined, a pretty little shelter of clean sea and ridged headlands. The port, as mentioned earlier, included the remains of Captain Horatio Nelson's naval headquarters, which he had commanded in the 1780s—before he became a hero—while defending British interests against the American rebel trading vessels, not to mention the rebellious tendencies of the Antiguans themselves. In the early 1960s the English Harbour seemed like a smart place for Melbourne to catch onto the growing interest

Annyah's crew and passengers pose before setting sail for the Canary Islands.
BACK ROW: **seaman Klaus Barth from Germany, American passenger William Gillies, engineer "Paddy" Adam from Dublin, captain Melbourne Smith, American passenger Donn Perish, and mate John Horn from South Africa.** KNEELING: **the Dutch cook Hank van Asperen, Spanish seamen Manuel Aguila and Luis Garcia, and the cook's brother, seaman Kas van Asperen.**

in charter yacht cruising and to take advantage of his Canadian citizenship in the later days of the collapsing British Empire.

Shortly after they sailed out of the shelter of La Palma, working their way south to catch the trades, *Annyah* was becalmed.

They lost ten days.

Those are hard days on a sailing ship, rotting in place, the garbage thrown overboard yesterday still floating in front of the ship. There was some snapping and growling, but the crew managed to keep tempers in check.

Then they caught a shark. There's an old tradition, that if you fasten a shark's tail to your bowsprit, you'll call in the fair winds. They brought the shark alongside, and Melbourne sliced it open. A shower of fetal sharks spilled into the sea. He sliced off the tail and began tacking it to the bowsprit. Just then, the crew noticed a row of clouds heading their direction. And the wind came.

SET SAIL!

"It was a beautiful sail from then on," Melbourne recalled. Shark-following fish stayed with them for miles after. They made the crossing in about thirty days, taking it easy all the way under squaresail (painted boldly with a great maple leaf), using the jigger and forestaysail to steady her in the long tradewind swells.

When they eventually fetched Antigua, the hour was close to midnight. A small boat came out to guide them into Nelson's Dockyard. They had followed the route of Christopher Columbus, pretty much. In the stillness and dark, having come so far across unbounded seawater, they were startled by the unexpected shrill of crickets on the headlands. The sudden land, a shocking black presence against the night sky, seemed to push the familiar stars miles farther away.

Luffing his way into the prevailing wind, Captain Smith carried through the narrow, rocky harbor entrance, passing Fort Berkeley. He rounded up in the tight anchorage and dropped the hook. There were no lights in English Harbour in those days and no buoys.

Annyah's stern was pulled to the wharf.

IN ANTIGUA Melbourne renewed his acquaintance with Commodore V.E.B. Nicholson. This veteran of British naval command had once visited with Melbourne during the stay in Cadiz, and now Melbourne returned the courtesy.

In 1940, early in the Second World War, Nicholson had purchased a seventy-foot schooner named *Mollihawk*. His main intention was to strip her of linens and household wares, the type of goods that were rationed or unavailable during those hard war years. Even so, he sailed her at that time to Antigua, with his manly young sons as crew. Later, after father and sons had all served their country's war effort and survived, Commodore Nicholson decided that there wasn't much future for the family in England. They returned to the Caribbean and the ruins of Nelson's old dockyard. In 1950 he and the sons took their first guests on a charter excursion. From that start unfolded the charter industry that, ten years later, Melbourne hoped to join.

V.E.B. Nicholson congratulated the bold, young Canadian on his crossing. "I have work for you," he said. "But you have to get an engine."

How to afford it?

Annyah got some charters down to Martinique, a few Americans each time.

It was no stress to sail unmotored down and back again. But after a month or six weeks, the coming of the winter holiday season struck an emotional chord in all the crew, Melbourne in particular. He used his diminishing resources to fly back to Canada, partly for emotional contact with family, specifically his deceased wife's family, and partly to assess the odd situation he had created for himself in the Caribbean.

To do this, he had to repatriate much of his crew. The Spaniards stayed on board, hard at work with their sewing gear. Paddy Adam stayed too, picking up work as a handyman for the charter fleet. The rest were all paid off and sent off.

The mate from South Africa proved to be a pain—the last place he wanted to go was back home. But home was the cheapest ticket, and it was the legal extent of Melbourne's obligation. Still, the fellow flew back to Antigua and demanded a ticket to Cadiz.

Such bickering tarnished the brightwork, so to speak, of the beautiful sailing ship, as did (literally) the many idle days at anchor. After Melbourne returned from his winter excursion to Montreal, *Annyah* became increasingly a figure in decline and a focus of contention.

The American investor, Aubrey Young, flew down to see the vessel he felt he owned. He believed that he should simply sell her for value, whatever that value might be in a remote port. Like a true, red-blooded American, he also believed that all the profits from the sale should go to him. In that case Melbourne, who had done all the outfitting and reviving, would have been left with no reward for all his efforts. Melbourne protested. He claimed that, once the initial loan had been repaid, he and Young should divide the profits.

They were at stalemate.

Young ordered Melbourne to bring *Annyah* up to New York, where she would likely fetch a better price. And he left his two incorrigible sons in Melbourne's care, to be trained in the ancient disciplines of the sailing life.

The boys were out of control, ages eight and ten. No one had ever given them the smackings they deserved. Their idea of fun involved throwing things off the ship to see how much trouble it would cause to fetch them back again. Disgusted, Melbourne put them both on a plane back to the U.S. "They were terrors, idiots," he said later. "They would have just drowned."

He returned to contemplation of his dilemma—what to make of this beautiful vessel that was motorless, generatorless, and now almost crewless, tethered to the quay in a little-visited port of the British West Indies.

The very presence of this big, sleek three-masted schooner dominated the tight anchorage at Nelson's Dockyard. Everyone saw and asked about her. But you can't fill a luxury charter without the equipment, and you can't buy the equipment without the income of a few successful luxury charters. Melbourne returned to painting watercolor portraits of sailing ships. He peddled them to tourists. If Antigua had been as frequented then as it is today, he might have made some real money.

AROUND this time, Mick Philp showed up, mesmerized by the sight of *Annyah*. He was in his mid-twenties, a native of Tasmania, and he had interrupted his college studies to vagabond a bit. He came to Antigua as crew on a forty-foot ketch from England. He and another crewmember, Jane Henry—an adventurous young "trained nurse with a can-do attitude" (quoting Melbourne)—were hoping to sail back to Australia. But they were snagged by *Annyah*'s allure. Especially Mick. He made friends with Melbourne and elected to stay, to see what he could do to get this elegant ship back on her feet. "Her sheer size was fascinating," Mick wrote a few years later. "Whenever would I find another chance to sail such a boat?"

He signed on as mate. Night after night he, "Mel," and Paddy sat around the swinging table in *Annyah*'s saloon, passing around a fifty-cent bottle of Antiguan rum and concocting crazy schemes to get her back to work.

They raised some money by working on other boats in the bay, including a complete floating refit on a powerboat. The Spaniards helped with that work while they completed stitching and repairing all of *Annyah*'s sails. Mick managed to bring one of the two generators back from the dead by jury-rigging its fuel pump. "No one else ever learned how to start that generator," Mick recalled. "You had to heat up the air intake with a burning rag, then pour heavy oil in the decompression hole and squirt lighter fluid into the filter as you cranked." That way he managed to get some juice into *Annyah*'s ancient batteries.

Then they received a surprise charter offer—a group of six Americans who wanted three weeks on a big vessel at a time when nothing else in the harbor was available. These people were romantics at heart, and they fancied the idea of a great, fading ship with a crew of talented ne'er-do-wells. That crew, by then, was no more than Melbourne, Mick, and the two Spaniards. Paddy had a shore job and couldn't go along. But Jane Henry signed on as the cook. She proved that she could produce gourmet fare out of a camp stove and a pot.

"I don't think we slept more than ten hours a week," wrote Mick, remembering that cruise. "But we felt fine. *Annyah* was back at work. She thundered along in the lee of the islands, masts creaking, half the bulwark in the water, four thousand feet of canvas driving her south and four men to handle her. She lay in still harbors—Martinique, Portsmouth, Dominica, Monserrat. She ghosted quietly across the passages in the light sunset breezes. The guests never knew how much labor went into their comfort." For example, having no engine, the crew had to raise and lower the anchor by personal muscle power sometimes three or four times a day, twenty fathoms of heavy chain with a three-hundred-pound pick on the end. Unwilling to blow the weak generator by running a freezer, they would row for miles to buy ice that would melt within hours. The guests dined like royalty while the crew survived on Spam and sardines. On the last day the old generator overheated and seized up. They had to hire a motorboat to speed the passengers into Martinique in time for their return flights to the U.S. All that considered, the cruise was a great success. *Annyah*'s crew sailed back to Antigua exulting in a profit of fourteen hundred dollars.

One or two more such ventures could get them an engine.

Mick described their return with these words:

"We took the big schooner into harbor under full sail, just the four of us, and the trades were really blowing that day. With the cook at the wheel and Mel shouting orders from his perch on the deckhouse, we pinched into the bay and ran down very fast toward the stone wharf. It was two sets of halyards to each man, and the sails had to come down like clockwork in the crowded anchorage. We shot by the wharf, skimmed within ten feet of the Brixham mule *Georgiana*, and rounded up, letting all peaks go to scandalize everything. I threw the three headsail halyards off their pins, and they came rattling down around me as I ran to the anchor cat. I hit the slip stopper, and the chain ran out the back into the brown water. *Annyah* settled back, swung her stern past a visiting goldplater with three feet to spare while that yacht's anxious crew stood by with fenders and boathooks. (You don't stop a vessel *Annyah*'s size with a boathook.) The Spaniards had the small dinghy halfway to the wharf with a stern line as the anchor dug in, and in minutes *Annyah* was stern-to the wharf and all snug on her mooring again."

In retrospect, Mick wrote, "It was wonderful. I learned more about sailing in those three weeks than I had in the previous fifteen years."

Trade winds swell *Annyah*'s sails as she crosses the Atlantic. Note the yard fitted to the foremast for a "fortune" sail, also the twin raffees set as topsails.
To take this photo, the mate went overboard in the ship's launch.

But there were no new charters. They went back to picking up odd jobs and hatching schemes—maybe use *Annyah* as a training vessel for delinquent boys. Maybe strip her down for use as a trading vessel.

Around that time the Harbour Police came and removed the ship's compass—their way of confiscating the vessel. They arrested Melbourne as a thief. The charge emanated from a suit filed by the American investor, Aubrey Young, who claimed that Melbourne had stolen his valuable vessel.

And yet the authorities in Antigua proved to be much more sympathetic with the young Canadian, particularly because he was a British citizen, the boat in question being registered in his name and berthed in a British port. With a lawyer's help, Melbourne got away with a fine—one dollar—and returned to the dream.

It was a fading dream. Mick needed to move on. A big English cutter had stopped in the harbor, *Solace* II, and was leaving in a few days for Panama and California. This looked to be a good way for Mick to get back home, so he signed on.

In fact, it was his last evening in Antigua, lounging on *Annyah*'s foredeck and sharing a farewell rum-and-water with Melbourne in the hot Caribbean sunset.

Then a voice hailed them from the wharf. The voice emanated from a tall, slender man, a Scotsman it turned out. As he came aboard, this man inspired two very different impressions. One was that he was ill, perhaps with a heart condition, or at the end of his rope somehow. The other was an imperious sense of command. In every gesture and phrase of the conversation, he made it clear somehow that one man was fully in control of the present situation, and that special person was without a doubt himself.

His name was Ian Munn. He produced paperwork that proved he was no less than plenipotentiary extraordinaire of the national government of Guatemala. His exalted position—not that he mentioned it at the time—derived at least in part from the fact that he had married the daughter of the current *hefe* and *presidente* of Guatemala, Miguel Ydigora Fuentes. One of Munn's governmental duties—he made this clear to Melbourne—was to serve as Secretary of the Navy, also Special Envoy to the President of Guatemala. And since the Guatemalan Navy had almost no boats, and fewer still naval officers, Munn wished to purchase *Annyah* and commission her as a training vessel for the glory of the homeland—or at least for the satisfaction of his own appetites. For it was clear to Melbourne that Munn lusted after *Annyah*, her lines and her teak, her brightwork and her grandeur. And it was also clear to Melbourne, as he read Munn's body language, that Munn felt it to be his right in life, given his high office, to shove overboard anyone who might get in his way.

What is she worth? The price of twenty-five thousand dollars was established quickly.

"Now here's how we do it," said Munn.

He said that the Guatemalan Navy would charter *Annyah* for one year, paying twenty-five thousand dollars for a twelve-month period. During that year the Navy would provide the money for a new engine, new sails, everything necessary to refurbish the boat. The task of refitting *Annyah*, also of training Guatemala's cadets, would lie with Melbourne. After that year, Melbourne would secretly transfer ownership of the vessel to Munn. (The sovereign government of the country of Guatemala would hand over the promised purchase price of twenty-five thousand dollars.) Melbourne's ability to collect the monthly fee was assured when Munn offered him a commission in the Guatemalan Navy.

To confirm the handshake deal, Munn was prepared to deliver one thousand dollars cash "on the morrow"—certainly enough to enable Captain Smith to find his way from Antigua to Puerto Barrios, two thousand miles away, in a Central American country that the young Canadian had never even studied on a map.

As Munn's hard footsteps sounded on the companion ladder, across the deck, and over the stern, Melbourne grabbed his school atlas. He contemplated his potential future as *teniente-comodoro* in the Marina de la Defenca Nacional de Guatemala, a naval hero of a country he didn't know.

Mick later wrote, "This strange affair was bound to attract Mel irresistibly. He told me that he'd do it whether he thought it would work or not, just for the adventure. 'Anyway, I've never been to Guatemala,' he told me."

Melbourne figured that if the charter didn't work, he could pay his partners and his other creditors and come out ahead with just the kind of sailing job he had always dreamed about.

"What else do I do with this damned boat?" he said to Mick. "There's nothing else to do, is there?"

"This whole thing is crazy," said Mick, "even for Central America, where everything's crazy. If Munn can think up a scheme like this, he can just as easily double-cross you. These politicos have a lot of power. What's to stop him from seizing the boat as soon as you arrive, some fake charge? He could put you in the pokey forever. *Annyah* would be pretty cheap for just a thousand dollars. He'd probably take what was left of that, too."

Melbourne replied, "I'm not getting anywhere here. If I stay, this partner of mine will probably figure out some way to arrest the ship again. If I lose the ship in Guatemala, it's no worse than losing her here in Antigua, or leaving her here to rot. The thing may work anyway."

Melbourne added, "I think I trust this Munn."

Mick snickered.

But what could Mick do? He was set to leave the next day for "a very pleasant cruise through Panama and up the Mexican coast," for which he would actually get paid.

They arranged mailing addresses in Panama and Mexico so that Melbourne could keep Mick apprised of developments. If things went well, Mick knew he would be deeply tempted to rejoin the *Annyah*.

"But if you need rescuing," he said, "I'll go see the foreign service and raise a rumpus." ✷

Guatemala | 1961

*"Even if you're on the right track,
you'll get run over if you just sit there."*

— WILL ROGERS

MICK sailed out of Antigua's English Harbour aboard a new ship, *Solace*, bound for a tradewind-fast ride to the coast of Venezuela, then some rather tedious sailing through the Panama Canal and up the west coast of Mexico.

As *Solace* left Nelson's Dockyard, Melbourne stood on the wharf atop a stack of crates, waving. He had Ian Munn's thousand dollars in his pocket. Mick could see *Annyah's* crew—now reduced to the two loyal Spaniards, a Tasmanian cook, and one additional West India crewman—loading food and gear. He would be looking for Melbourne's letters in Colon, Panama, and in Mexico, and he was interested in returning to *Annyah's* service if this far-fetched Guatemalan deal actually played out.

Soon after, Melbourne and crew slipped out of Antigua and set sail for Puerto Barrios, Guatemala's only eastern port. They had a slow squaresail passage the entire two-thousand-mile, open-sea journey. Captain Smith had no charts, only a school atlas and a map of the harbor that Munn had sketched freehand. *Annyah* had no radio, so there was no contact with the Guatemalan Navy. A speedboat came out to escort them into the harbor. Otherwise, Melbourne realized later, he would have run aground.

He saw one large vessel in the harbor, a big gunboat called *La Frigata*, which Guatemala had purchased—second-hand from the Swedish Navy—using aid money from the United States. This was the Guatemalan Navy's only ship. But she was steam-driven and very fast. She was waiting for *Annyah* at Matias de Galvez, the harbor within Bahia de Amatique, a huge, deep bay fringed with palm fronds and dark green jungle hills. The port town, Puerto

Teniete-comodoro Melbourne Smith of the Marina de Defenca National de Guatemala.

Barrios, was a welter of mud streets, rough bars, and repulsive brothels. At some five miles distance from the throbbingly humid town lay the neatly trimmed and carefully guarded navy base, an institution with a history only a few years old. Besides the gunboat, the naval harbor included a cluster of small, planing-hulled speedboats with machine guns mounted on their bows. The bulk of the country's naval force comprised two officers and six midshipmen—eager lads ages eighteen to twenty who had transferred from the army because they wanted to learn about boats—and about a hundred seamen. The armed speedboats were operated by privileged Guatemalan lads who had joined the navy. They all spoke English quite well. Most had been sent to the U.S. Naval Academy, but were subsequently rejected and sent home, so the midshipmen were facile with Melbourne's native tongue. He was not wholly inadequate with theirs.

When he reached land, Melbourne was received as a visiting dignitary. He enjoyed a hearty reception with Capitan Sosa, the base commander. Sosa's business card read that he was "colonel of the artillery" in bold type, and under that in a much smaller face "captain of the navy." He was a hero of a former revolution. He wore a heavy caliber machine pistol—as did everyone on base—and though he knew almost nothing about ships was a very competent officer,

CHAPTER 6 | 57

a tall and powerful figure.

Capitan Sosa welcomed the nautical training that "Capitan Smeet" had come to provide. There was no contract yet, no formal agreement, but in respect of courtesy Melbourne was given a naval officer's uniform. In accordance with Munn's promises, the two Spaniards went to work at the naval base. The cook, Jane Henry, went on to California.

Melbourne wrote to Mick and suggested that his former *compadre* might want to come down to Guatemala. This letter got to Mick after sitting in a pile for two weeks in Acapulco, Mexico. Melbourne's message was this: "Things are good. Mr. Munn has visited aboard saying that everything was fine. In two or three weeks he will have the deal drawn up."

As requested, Melbourne had provided Munn with a list of the materials needed to refit *Annyah*, including quotes from the U.S. for a complete suit of sails, including square topsails. *Annyah* would be getting a topsail and topgallant to improve her downwind performance. In two or three weeks Melbourne would be officially recognized as a *teniente commodore*, lieutenant commander, and the refit would begin in earnest. The cadets would need intensive training. How soon could Mick join him?

Mick left *Solace*—she was close enough to her destination to finish her cruise short-handed—and flew down to Guatemala City, a pretty little town in the cool mountains. Then he made the hours-long, blasted-hot bus ride from the high interior down to the Atlantic coast. As the sun fell, a hot rain began to fall as well. Murky Puerto Barrios looked like a sty, shacks and muck. Mick got a cab to take him the five miles to the navy base. He found Melbourne there, waiting for him, standing under a big umbrella, lit by the guardhouse searchlight, flanked by sentries bearing machine rifles.

Melbourne grabbed one of Mick's bags, and they dashed along the wharf to where *Annyah* was lying stern-to and pitching wildly in the storm-tossed waters. She had a new name painted on the side—*Quetzal*, the name of Guatemala's national bird and national currency. Still no power on board. They ran across her heaving gangplank and huddled under a yellowish kerosene lamp in *Annyah's* deckhouse.

"I think it's going to work," said Melbourne, excited. Just a few days before this, he had breakfasted at the palace with the president's family in the Casa Crème in Guatemala City. He had signed a contract with the ministry and been given some charter money and wages, about eight hundred dollars altogether. Mick would go on the payroll. They would eat in the officers' mess. The refit materials would arrive shortly.

They made plans through the night. Three or four months should do for the refit. For skilled assistance they could hire the two civilian shipworkers whom Melbourne had observed doing tasks around the naval yard. A work period every morning would get the six midshipmen varnishing and painting. Then Mick would provide classes in basic seamanship—sailing theory, knots, and so on. Melbourne would continue training them in celestial navigation.

At dawn the gunboat crew mustered on the wharf for breakfast, and the two Anglo seamen followed them to the mess—corn mush with mashed kidney beans, graced with a tall glass of weak coffee. Melbourne introduced Mick to Capitan Sosa, and they learned about Sosa's heroic actions during the most recent revolution.

In that revolution, rebel army officers had suddenly begun shooting at the base from the surrounding jungle. All the personnel—about a hundred and fifty men—fled the buildings and gathered on the wharf. Capitan Sosa and a few key officers had famously run for *La Frigata* and moved her out of small arms range. From there, Sosa had shelled the base, also the Puerto Barrios airport, driving the rebels back into the jungle. Thanks to that counter-insurgency crackdown, the nation of Guatemala remained under the enlightened leadership of General José Miguel Ramón Laparra Samajoa Ydígoras Fuentes and his son-in-law Hugh Ian MacGarvie–Munn, who was an artist, a naval architect, and for now the Commander of the Guatemalan Navy.

The nation would remain safe and glorious in this way for a long time. For months, anyway. At least for the next eight months.

THE *ANNYAH* crew set up a productive routine. At ten o'clock, after Spanish instruction, the midshipmen came aboard for training. Mick issued gear and put them to work refinishing topsides, spars, and brightwork. After lunch Melbourne gave classes in navigation, and Mick explained the ship's gear, piece by piece. The Guatemalan lads learned to sail *Annyah*'s eighteen-foot dinghy. But the government continued to make no progress with the yard's main mission, which was to refit *Annyah* and put her to service as a training vessel for the Guatemalan Navy—or perhaps (the two Americans were beginning to suspect) as Señor Munn's purloined souvenir from his stint as the son-in-law for a soon-to-be-deposed Central American *hefe*.

As previously mentioned, the Navy was employing a couple of experienced civilian shipworkers to do various tasks around the yard, also to be on

CHAPTER 6 | 59

La Frigata, **the Guatemalan Navy's principal gunboat, came out to meet and pilot** *Annyah* **upon her arrival at the Matias de Galvez naval base.**

hand for the refit, when and if. These were British Hondurans who had been visiting relatives in Puerto Barrios.

The fact that they were British Hondurans merits some explication here. Their native land—and one of these shipworkers in particular—was going to play a significant role in the circumnavigations of Melbourne Smith.

British Honduras has been known since 1973 as Belize. Belize is now an independent nation and member of the British Commonwealth. But in 1961, the year of Melbourne's service in the Guatemalan Navy, the country went by its old name and was a colony. English language, law, and customs prevailed there and still do. In the grand sweep of Spain's New World empire, from California down to Tierra del Fuego, this was one bite of land that the Brits managed to wrangle for themselves. It's a small bite, about the size of Vermont. Essentially it is a stretch of fabulous shoreline facing the Caribbean, nearly two hundred miles of it, all naturally fenced behind a barrier reef studded with little mangrove islands called "cayes." Inland, the terrain rises into the inhuman thickness of Guatemala's jungle, rich with indigenous hardwoods, Mayan ruins, jaguars, and fantastic birds. Big rivers pour down from the highlands to the sea. Hurricanes trash the place frequently.

Today Belize markets itself as one of the world's last unspoiled travel destinations. In 1603, though, it was a damn fine place for a pirate's lair. That was the year a buccaneer named Peter Wallace, with six ships and a crew of eighty, found his way in through the barrier reef and set up shop on a river bank. They raided Spanish ships passing along the coast loaded with gold and silver from mines in Guatemala. Peter Wallace had been Sir Walter

Raleigh's first lieutenant and trusted pal. Or maybe this happened in 1638. Or closer to 1700. Such is the origin myth of Belize. It could be that Wallace never existed. But his name became, through lingual distortion, the word "Belize." Or maybe not.

For certain, British entrepreneurs with black slaves made excellent money during the eighteenth century by harvesting exotic timber out of this region's forests. They pushed into an under-populated, post-Mayan wilderness. Spain's territorial controls just couldn't extend far enough to stop them. In 1798 the British rebuffed Spain in the not-so-bloody Battle of St. George's Caye. The event has become the Belizean national holiday. British Honduras became internationally recognized as British. Thus ships of sail, ships like *Annyah*, once again determined the course of human history. Who can hoist the most sail? Who can come athwart the other? That significant savor of the power of sail still hung in the air in 1961. Sail still mattered, at least for characters like Melbourne and Mick. And British Honduras was still a rough outpost.

The concept of tourism did not exist there.

GUATEMALA, however, never surrendered to the surrender at the Battle of St. George's Caye. Guatemala remains quite *caliente* over the Belize problem. And a glance at the map shows why.

Guatemala—the heartland of Mayan history, roughly the size of Louisiana, situated just south of Mexico—looks as though it should naturally flow from shore to shore, from the Pacific to the Atlantic. However, a surveyor's line, an artificial boundary that runs right through one of the wildest tropical forests on Earth, keeps Guatemala from enjoying free access to its Atlantic face. The only turf that Guatemala controls on that shore is the southern part of one bay, Amatique Bay, and a single port there, Puerto Barrios, the naval base where *Annyah* was docked.

In 1961 Guatemala had just begun a long period of bloody civil war involving the military, squads of leftist guerrillas, and right-wing vigilantes who were secretly abetted by the U.S. government. Melbourne didn't have all the facts, but he understood the geography. If things got as bad as they seemed to be getting, perhaps he could have *Annyah* towed across the bay that separated her from British Honduras. Then she would be not only *not* in Guatemala; she would be back in the Commonwealth of Great Britain.

He talked about this with the British Honduran shipworkers. One of them in particular had caught his attention. This chap was wiry and small, not much more than a hundred pounds probably, and he looked Hindu. He was a supremely confident boatbuilder.

Simeon Young.

Melbourne watched with fascination as this man took a simple handsaw and, holding it backwards, cut a true line right down the center of a twenty-foot-long plank. The man knew how to use a hardwood pry-bar and a fulcrum to lift a boat off the ground and move it anywhere he wanted around the yard. He was part Mayan, part Hindi, part Spanish, and the full son of a Scottish boatbuilder who had made a life in the wilds of British Honduras. Simeon Young was a ladies' man, too. He played guitar and sang old-time cowboy songs that he learned by listening to Jimmie Rodgers tunes on a radio station out of Texas.

Simeon gave Melbourne a contact in Belize City, someone he believed could tow *Annyah* across the water.

By now *Annyah's* old gear and sails had been scrapped. Mechanics had taken away the old generators. The ship was stripped down and ready to go.

ABOUT SIX WEEKS later Capitan Sosa was obviously avoiding the *Annyah* boys. Whenever they went to ask about their list of necessary gear, Sosa would say, "It is not for me to say. You must speak with Señor Munn."

Melbourne wrote to Munn. His secretary answered that Señor Munn was away. She suggested that they wait and not try to communicate with him again.

Once again the charter money and wages came through. The painting was done, the spars were clean, the brightwork sparkled. *Annyah* simply waited for her new gear.

And waited.

No texts, no gear. The training program collapsed. The scent of "coup" began to drift over the wharf, the base, and the country. Melbourne decided that he had to get *Annyah* out of Guatemala somehow, stripped as she was.

Escape involved little more than towing *Annyah* across Bahia de Amatique to Punta Gordo. Such a border-crossing was not likely to set off an international rumble. No one really cared. After all, every year Guatemala attacked some small town in the British Honduras just to project a dose of Spanish swagger. The current Guatemalan president, Señor Munn's father-in-law, had already sunk two Mexican fishing boats and challenged the president of Mexico to a duel, *mano-a-mano*, at the border. The loss of an as-yet-unpurchased schooner would not rock the boats of such bullies.

So Melbourne went to the British Honduras to find the contact recommended by Simeon Young. He envisioned himself motoring south on this hired vessel, with Mick alerted and ready at the Guatemala base, then slipping *Annyah* into international waters within an hour or so.

In Belize City he located the man. His boat was smaller than Melbourne had imagined. The skipper swore his vessel could do the job. He just needed a larger propeller in order to pull a three-masted schooner. He said, the larger propeller would come quickly, and the job would be done. Melbourne gave the man five hundred dollars.

The boatman directed Melbourne to a Mrs. Brown, who maintained a *pension* in town. Melbourne could stay there until the new propeller arrived and the tow could take place.

Mrs. Brown's *pension*, like all the houses in the port town of Belize City, stood on stilts eight feet in the air to keep above the low-lying land. The walls didn't quite enclose her place. In the local style, spindles created a foot of open space both above and below the common walls. The wind blew through the house and through all the houses next door. Right across the street was the big wall of the town "gaol" (jail). Melbourne had diarrhea, so Mrs. Brown insisted that he use the public toilet in the street because hers depended on catching rainwater from the roof. "Must not flush too much," she warned.

Melbourne later said: "I was very happy to get in bed that night and just lie down. And then I started to hear giggle giggle, squeaky squeaky. Suddenly I realized—oh my, I'm in a whorehouse. Oh, this is marvelous."

He added, "I hope I feel better tomorrow."

THE NEXT DAY, Hurricane Hattie moved in and scoured away anything innocent, unlucky, or faint of heart.

The storm had formed weeks earlier in the Caribbean, then moved slowly to Central America. By the time it reached Melbourne, it was a category-four hurricane with sustained winds of one hundred and forty miles an hour, gusts of one hundred eighty, the biggest storm ever known to hit that country. The date was October 31, 1961. Weather-prediction systems were feeble in those days, and evacuation warnings ineffective. More than four hundred people died as a result of this storm, and thousands were left homeless.

Warnings came that morning. Suddenly everyone was told to leave town. Although the houses were built up high, the land itself was only a foot above

The aftermath of Hurricane Hattie

sea level. But Mrs. Brown refused to leave her house. Looting would be inevitable. She wouldn't have that.

Melbourne decided to stay, too. He had a will in his pocket, plus several thousand dollars, with his son's address enclosed.

Hattie surged in with biblical intensity. The sea began to rise. Corrugated zinc roof-sheets began flying through the streets, capable of beheading anyone stupid enough to be out and about. Then Melbourne heard a tremendous roar of male voices. The authorities had just opened the "gaol" across the street, releasing all the prisoners so that they could run for their lives. Mrs. Brown crouched under a table, clutching her silverware. The sea came in. Sea level rose twelve feet at the storm's height, which put the water level in Mrs. Brown's place at about four feet. Melbourne stood in a doorway. The house next door collapsed and sagged against Mrs. Brown's place. The family next door asked politely if they could step across into Mrs. Brown's.

At the end of the street down by the ocean, a big, iron tank cut loose. This was a fresh-water storage tank about twenty feet square and ten feet high. Because the tank was less than full, the rising sea picked it up and began shoving it up the street. Unfortunately the street was less than twenty feet wide, and across the street was the unmoving wall of the "gaol." So as the tank traveled up the street, it tore off the porches and front doors and walls. As it crushed Mrs. Brown's front porch, Melbourne tried pushing on it. The effort was ridiculous.

The next morning was bright and sunny. When the waters had subsided to about five feet above sea level, Melbourne ventured out. Dead bodies huddled here and there. The boat that had needed a new propeller—the one Melbourne hoped would tow *Annyah* to safety—no longer existed. He never saw the owner again, nor his deposit money.

Then the looting started.

That evening he was sitting in a bar. Most bars in Belize, this one for example, operated on the second floor and so had survived the destruction. Drinking beer on its verandah, Melbourne had a good view of the town. He watched a small squad of British soldiers move along the street clutching First World War-era rifles. One soldier used a big speaker to proclaim a curfew. Anybody found on the streets after seven o'clock would be shot. He wondered whether he should return to Mrs. Brown's place or stay in the bar all night. He chose the bar. Through the night he could hear shooting. In those days, no civilians in British Honduras possessed firearms. So every gunshot meant that a soldier was shooting a looter. The next morning he saw that nearly every shop had been broken into. He saw a house that was filled with so many stolen tires that the residents had to camp outside.

Melbourne tried to buy a car so that he could drive away from this mess, but no one would sell him a car. He wasn't a national. In the British spirit of civility during crisis, automobiles were to be reserved for the needs of the citizens.

Eventually he caught a refugee flight, no charge, to New Orleans. He found a car there at a dealership, a used Opel square-back with a lot of cargo room. He offered the salesman eight hundred dollars, saying that's all he had. The salesman said no deal. But when Melbourne returned to his hotel room, he found a message from the car dealer saying okay, the deal's on.

Mick flew to join Melbourne in New Orleans. When he arrived, he removed his trademark tinted glasses and said, "Look." His eyes were yellow.

A doctor in New Orleans told him he had some form of hepatitis and that he should eat red meat. In short, he (and Melbourne) were malnourished. "I had it, too," said Melbourne. "You want to sleep all the time, especially in that heat. Terrible food there. Much of Guatemala was beautiful, but Puerto Barrios was the end of the earth. There was no work. Lots of infected dogs. They were lazy people. They didn't even fish." In order to follow his doctor's prescription Mick had to eat hamburgers wherever he could—Melbourne was stuck with beans and a tortilla—as they drove that Opel all the way back through Mexico to their commitments at Puerto Barrios. The Guatemalan government had no idea that he had been away.

SHORTLY after this return, Capitain Sosa called Melbourne to his office and announced that the charter agreement was canceled, and that the midshipmen would not be coming to the ship any more. "Do not blame me, Capitan Smeet," he said. "I am your frien'. You must see Señor Munn. He ees een Guatemala Ceety an' he wan' to see you."

Melbourne and Mick took all the charter money and any unspent wages to a bank in Guatemala City and had the value converted to U.S. traveler's checks. The total came to three thousand dollars. They drove to the palace. Mick waited in the Opel while Melbourne had a showdown with Ian Munn.

Munn was angry. "I want you to turn the ship over to me right now."

"But you haven't paid for it."

"I'll pay for it right now." He had the palace guard search Melbourne. The guard confiscated the traveler's checks. "I'll give you these," said Munn, "as soon as you make out a bill of sale."

Melbourne thought about that deal for a moment—selling *Annyah* for three thousand dollars of his own money.

He said, "I can't."

"Why not?"

"It's a British ship. I have to get permission from the British Consulate."

Munn began poking Melbourne in the chest with his long forefinger. "You get your ass down there tomorrow morning, early, and bring me that paper!"

Melbourne looked at him and said, "What's going on here? I thought we were friends. Why are you doing this to me?"

Munn said, "Because I'm bigger than you, that's why." Poke poke poke.

THE BRITISH CONSUL told Melbourne to get out of the country as fast as possible. "Do you realize that they have you under virtual house arrest? You cannot go to an airport, nor to a seaport, not even a bus station. Perhaps you can get a bus ticket going south."

Melbourne checked with Mick on his own cash resources. They were far less than it would cost to tow *Annyah* out of the country into yet another remote anchorage. The two sailors decided to make a run for it on rubber tires. As Mick put it, "In Central America, you don't call the police when the president's son-in-law is on your tail—he does."

They raced down the hours-long route to the navy base in Puerto Barrios. The sentries waved them through as usual. Seamen cleaning *La Frigata's*

Mick Philp and Melbourne flee for their lives in a square-back Opel on the Pan-American Highway.

guns looked up and saluted. Their British Honduran shipworkers were playing volleyball with some of the midshipmen. Melbourne called them aboard *Annyah* and explained the situation. They were happy to get paid off and receive fare back home. They were nervous about the political situation. And they were homesick—they had missed most of the looting potentials in their home city.

Having paid the men, Melbourne and Mick possessed just enough cash to afford the gasoline it would take to reach California. They took everything they could take from *Annyah*—besides their own clothes and gear, the radio, the chronometer, navigational equipment, compasses, even the great copper running-lights and a pair of oak water breakers. They lashed stuff on top of the Opel, shrouding it with a piece of old sail. A crowd of seamen gathered to watch.

"Where you go, cappies?"

"We sold the boat to Señor Munn," Melbourne told them. "Going to Guatemala City for conference with him."

They went aboard *Annyah* for maybe the last time. They wound her out from the wharf a few feet. Mick doubled the lines. She would be safe for a few months. Then they climbed ashore along the stern lines. The four of them piled into the Opel. The two British Hondurans had to be dropped off in Puerto Barrios. They drove right past the *commandancia*, the office of Capitan Sosa. But no one shouted *"Alto! Alto!"*

They dropped the British Honduran seamen in Barrios, wishing them well and hoping for further adventures ahead. Much later, by letter, they learned that this hasty scramble had come none too soon. The national police had been informed that Melbourne and Mick were Cuban spies, and so armed authorities were waiting at every airport. Apparently Munn never considered the land border.

So the two sailors in their overloaded Opel drove the so-called Pan-American Highway through the center of Mexico, fording rivers, digging through foot-deep mud, banging over baseball-size rocks. Before, they had driven the Opel south at a careful pace along the Pacific coastal routes. But now they were afraid and traveling fast. They scrambled through desert mountains while hoarding their small stash of cash and imagining what it would be like to get hunted down. Or to blow their tires out here. Recent wet-season mountain rains had destroyed long stretches of dirt track. Sometimes they would come upon a modern concrete bridge built with money from the U.S., but the rotten road didn't connect with the fancy bridge. Once they almost collided with a sign that said, "This road is in bad condition." At the Guatemala-Mexico border, the sleepy guard seemed to be impressed by their old diplomatic visas issued by Munn, and he waved them through. As they traversed the hot plains of Mexico, the road steadily improved. But at night the pavement was full of people sleeping or camping or waving cars down for unknown reasons. They accelerated through. Mick had a revolver, just in case, jammed between his thighs.

When they reached San Diego, the gas tank almost empty, with a few bucks to spare, they got a hotel room. They stood in the shower for half an hour each, then splurged on steaks. Melbourne went to the bank and said that his travelers' checks had been stolen in Guatemala. Their full value was restored to him. They bought a new set of tires for the Opel.

They drove to Manhattan Beach to the home of Gisela's sister and scooped up Melbourne's son, Sean, age five. They took Sean to Melbourne's parents' house in Hamilton. Then he and Mick went to Montreal.

After all that, only one cylinder in the Opel's engine was missing its beat. The dream, the tedium, the boat itself all became like dawn's fading—something past and perhaps sad. ★

Ian Munn, son-in-law of Guatemala's President, lounges at the rail of *Annyah* with his daughter and Melbourne.

CHAPTER 6 | 69

Placencia | 1962

*Mick Philp returned to Central America
in a desperate attempt to rescue* Annyah.
He later published his account of this adventure in
The Skipper *magazine, January-March edition* 1964.
*We are grateful to Mick for letting us adapt his skillful narrative
for second publication here.*

FOR A WHILE both Melbourne and I were content to let *Annyah* sit. I think both of us had been disappointed a few too many times. Then Mel began a long and involved correspondence with marine lawyers, the Canadian Registry of Ships, the embassy in Guatemala, and the Guatemalan Defense Ministry.

At first he hoped for some compensation so he could at least repay his old partner in *Annyah* original purchase. I don't think he gave a thought to trying to rescue her again. There were too many problems and past failures. Too much effort and too much dreaming had already gone for nothing.

Negotiations for compensation went on for months and seemed to get nowhere. Lawyers' fees were high.

Then a letter came from the Defense Ministry asking if Captain Melbourne Smith were the owner of a Canadian schooner in Puerto Barrios and, if so, would he please come and take it away. The letter said Captain Smith could regard the vessel as officially released, and he could be sure that there was no claim against her.

I don't know what prompts these strange changes of attitude in Central America. Perhaps it's the changing of personnel in high places. Or maybe it's just a natural mischievousness—part of the comic opera.

The letter could have meant anything, but we decided to take it at face value. Not long after it arrived, Mel was offered a loan to finance an attempt to move the ship to British Honduran waters. A syndicate of ship lovers was willing to risk the rescue money. If we could get out, they would try to raise enough to recommission her.

It seemed worth the effort. In British Honduras she could be safely laid up. And she probably could be sold there for at least enough money to cover the rescue costs.

But Mel felt it was better if he stayed away from Guatemala until we found out what was really going on. Furthermore, he was sick of the whole venture.

But I was willing to take the chance. It did sound interesting. So I quit my new job in Montreal and flew south to try to tow her out of captivity.

I landed first in Belize, the capital of British Honduras, which is a hundred miles north from Barrios. There I questioned our two British Honduran seamen, who had gone back to work in their father's boatyard. They had good news for me. They'd heard that *Annyah* was still in pretty good shape but was deteriorating fast. The boys felt certain that Munn was in political trouble and had fled Guatemala. They said they'd go to Barrios with me and help tow her out. That was just as well, too. I couldn't have done it without them.

The fiight to Barrios took an hour. We traveled by cab to the naval base and walked into the commandant's office armed with the Defense Ministry's letter of release and an impressive embassy document covered with seals (really just a letter of identification and the power to act as the owner's representative).

I had a thousand dollars in five and ten-dollar bills.

Captain Sosa was still behind his desk. Evidently he had managed to stay on the right side for another year of chameleon politics. But Sosa had a surprise for me. He said the ship was free to go, so far as the Navy was concerned. But there was a civil case against her that must be settled. I would not be allowed aboard until I had brought him a release from the civil court in Barrios.

At the courthouse I discovered that Munn had presented claims for unpaid wages on behalf of the two British Hondurans. Apparently British registry had stopped him from seizing her, and he'd thought up the claim just to make things difficult for us if we ever came to take her away.

Of course, the seamen had always been properly paid, and they identified themselves and so told the court. But the judge wouldn't drop the claim. I suppose he was afraid of losing his job. It took me the rest of the day to find an anti-administration lawyer who spoke good English. Then we used two more days arguing with the judge and sitting in the lawyer's office while he prepared long written statements to absolve everyone of responsibility for any decision.

I was worried. I had hoped to surprise everyone and tow *Annyah* out quickly. Now everyone had time for second thoughts. Was Munn really out of the country?

The roll of bills got smaller as I paid fees and bribes. Finally the judge prepared a formal document of release.

The previous day I had optimistically paid a deposit for a powerful shrimp boat to tow me into British waters. The skipper was from Livingstone, a part of Guatemala that once belonged to British Honduras and where the people were still English-speaking and pro-British. I arranged for him to come alongside at ten a.m.

The court handed me the release at eight-thirty that morning.

I drove straight to the naval base with it. I was pretty nervous and expected something to go wrong any minute. I even imagined that I'd find Munn sitting in the commandant's office. But he wasn't.

Captain Sosa seemed surprised to see the release, but he said we could go. I told him a tug would be alongside at ten and we would take our departure immediately.

Up to that point I wasn't sure whether *Annyah* was still afloat. I first saw her when we walked around the corner from the commandancia and came within sight of the bay. She was at anchor. Her jigger mast was gone, but she was riding easily on her lines.

I found the big sailing dinghy pulled up on the beach, battered but still usable. The boys and I sculled out to the schooner with a broken oar. No one was aboard. We found her stripped below. Someone had splashed red and blue paint on the deck and houses. The rigging screws had been let go on the jigger mast, and it had broken off at the deck, carrying the bulwark with it when it fell, but going clear of the ship.

I wasted a few minutes sitting in the saloon staring at the veneer paneling. An arrow of sunlight came in through a broken skylight and cut a sharp circle in the dust of the cabin sole. I sounded the bilges, found them full, and tasted the water. It was fresh and must have come from the broken skylight.

Going on deck, I found the anchor winch rusted solid. I freed it by dousing it with kerosene from an old riding light and hammering on the handles with a boathook. The seamen manned the winch while I climbed out onto the rotten mancatcher under the long bowsprit and began bashing the kinks out of the chain with a lump of wood. The schooner had been swinging around her chain for months, and it was snarled. The chain came in link by link as the big winch squeaked and clicked. I became increasingly worried that we would be stopped at the last minute, and I smacked at the tangled chain in a half-panic.

President José Miguel Ramón Ydígoras Fuentes of Guatemala

The tug came alongside a few minutes before we broke out the anchor. We secured to a towline, the tug took up the slack, and we began to move slowly out of the bay. We were four miles from shore when I saw two of the navy's small gunboats racing out after us.

I called one of the boys to the wheel and jumped up on the companion house. One launch sheered off and trained a machine gun on us. The other came alongside. I stood there with my arms folded, too angry to speak. I was saying to myself, "The bastards are not going to stop me."

The tug slowed.

Then I recognized the little man standing in the launch. It was President Fuentes—Munn's father-in-law.

I jumped off the house and stood at the rail staring at him.

He said in English: "Is Captain Brown here?"

I said: "If you mean Captain Smith, he's not here. I'm representing him."

He shouted: "This ship cannot leave. Captain Smith owes my son-in-law much money."

I began to shout in return. I told him his son-in-law was a bandido. I told him in detail why the Captain and I had come to Guatemala. I described the deal Munn had made with us, and the troubles we'd had. "I'm just trying to get out of this goddamn country, and it's already cost a few thousand dollars," I told him. "Your son-in-law owes us plenty." I said the ship was still under British registry, and if he stopped us now, it would be very serious—at least an act of piracy.

I was almost incoherent with anger and, if anything, rude. But it must have been the right attitude. The launch was loaded with army officers, and some of them undoubtedly understood English. Fuentes must have been feeling a bit insecure by then—an army coup ousted him just a few months after this event. References to questionable dealings by his family were probably embarrassing.

Anyway, he interrupted me and said: "So you have no Captain Brown here. Then it is the wrong ship."

He signaled to his coxswain, and the launch swung clear and headed for the shore. The tug picked up speed.

I was shaking so much I had to lie on the deck for a while. You don't win an argument with a president every day.

It took us four hours to get out of the bay, and then the tug had to cut its speed because ocean swells were straining the hawser. We towed all night. About eight in the morning I estimated we were in British territorial waters. I found some paint and made a clumsy Canadian flag on a piece of canvas. A few hours later, with the flag flying from a stick aft, we let go anchor off the little village of Punta Gorda, British Honduras.

The tug ran up alongside, and I paid the skipper his three hundred dollars. The fee was high, but he earned it. He'd taken quite a risk towing a ship that was obviously in trouble with the administration—and he had kept right on towing while the president's launch was alongside.

The tug cast off and headed out to sea. I watched her leave, then went ashore to find the customs and immigration authorities.

After clearing the ship, I went back aboard and slept through the long hot day. It seemed to me I hadn't slept for days. That evening the district commissioner came out to see. He brought a big bag of food with him, and then he took me ashore to his house for supper.

The next day I arranged for a local tug to tow us the rest of the way—to Placencia, the only sheltered harbor on the long, open coast. The tow took eighteen hours. We ran several unlit channels in a stiff beam wind, At times had no more than two feet of water under her keel. I took soundings all the way and kept a sharp knife near the towline, but we did not touch. In Placencia I anchored just out of the channel behind a small island.

For a week in Placencia I squared away the ship, pumped five tons of water out of her, rigged awnings, and tried to protect her from further deterioration. She still seemed sound as a bell. There was no softness in the hull, and the bolts and frames showed no sickness. I swam around her and dived along the bottom. The sheathing was intact under its thick layer of goose barnacles.

I figured it would take twenty thousand dollars to put her in good working order again.

Mel and I exchanged cables. Then I flew back to the States to talk to the syndicate. I left the schooner in charge of the storekeeper at Placencia, a little man named Alvin Cabral, who said he would keep the anchor light burning.

As I rowed ashore the last time, *Annyah* was sitting quietly in her own reflection—a bird with broken wings. She swung easily to her anchor in the little tropical harbor. Great hanks of weed were streaming like hair from her rudder post. Her faded, black hull rocked gently in the calm water, lifting the heavy marine growth along her waterline and dropping it back again with a soft swishing sound. The rotten canvas awnings sagged tiredly between her masts. The clumsily painted flag hung sadly from her stern.

THE SYNDICATE was unable to raise enough money to start a refit. Mel was considering three low offers to buy the ship. He had to do something to pay back the rescue loan. I talked to two of the buyers, who wanted me to take charge of a refit and put *Annyah* back on charter. But I wasn't too anxious to start the whole heartbreak over again.

Then came the final blow. Mel's old partner sued for full ownership. He sued in a British Honduran court, so *Annyah* was impounded to wait for the trial date. The buyers withdrew, and we returned their deposits.

Mel's lawyer said his partner hadn't much hope of winning. But *Annyah* would have to wait for her case to come to the top of the list. That would be a few months yet. By that time she wouldn't be worth anything. Melbourne declined to waste his money in defending the suit.

A while later my storekeeper-shipkeeper in Placencia wrote me this letter:

> Dear Mik,
> We wiat now to her from you of concern the great ship. I keep always the light and everythin clean. I used the little saildingy as you say, an the sail tor, but my wife sew her. The big one she stay always properly to anchor till any big wind come and when she swing she cry sometime for you. tell us now what you do.
> —ALVIN CABRAL

In a few years I suspect Alvin will be able to add a room to his little store on the beach. He has eight children, and his house is small. He likes to add bits onto it when he collects enough good, straight driftwood. And drifting wood from wrecks is public property—even teak driftwood. ✶

—MICK PHILP

F ORTUNATELY Melbourne won the case in the British Honduras court, and *Annyah* was released again. He sold the vessel to Dr. Kelvin Minchin, a doctor practicing in Washington, DC. The sale price only covered the expenses incurred by Mick in his recovery of the vessel, including his hiring of Belize City lawyers.

In 1967 Aubrey Young sued Minchin and Melbourne Smith in the Circuit Court of Anne Arundel County, Maryland. Mick Philp gave witness for the defendants. Mick described his ordeal in claiming the vessel, and Young accused Mick of bribing judges and officials in Guatemala.

To the surprise of everyone in the courtroom, Judge E. Marshall Childs announced that he had once lived in Guatemala, and that he was intimately familiar with the corruption in that country's court system. The judge complimented Mick Philp on his resourcefulness. Then he awarded full ownership to Minchin. The judgment read: "Although a subsequent possessory action had been instituted by the plaintiffs in (British) Honduras, they had ordered the yacht released to Smith. Clearly, under the conditions then existing, the plaintiffs at that time had no right to immediate possession in that jurisdiction." ✭

PART TWO

Shipwright

Maryland | 1962

*"We both slipped quickly back into the rat race.
In a few weeks it all seemed very far away—big schooners,
Latin American politicos, border posts, beans and tortillas
—all quite unreal."*

— MICK PHILP

LIKE A WOMAN who has dealt and been dealt too many heartbreaks, *Annyah* inevitably lost the fervent commitment of Melbourne Smith. Although he conferred with marine lawyers and sent piles of letters to the Canadian Registry of Ships, also to the Canadian Embassy and the National Department of Defense in Guatemala, he was not going back to Puerto Barrio.

No way.

Mick had made a dashing rescue of the gorgeous abducted schooner, but he could take her no farther than a port of retirement in the British Honduras and certain deterioration.

The British Honduran court decided that Melbourne was the owner, and that he owed his partner one dollar. Because the court did not specify that the dollar had to be Antiguan, British Honduran, or American, the entire matter was suspended. And so it is today.

Melbourne's small children were now secure in family homes, being cosseted by relatives. He found work in wintry Montreal, basically the same commercial art production he'd been doing back when he first fell in love with a young bank teller. How little time had elapsed. Maybe six years. A man in his early thirties doesn't simply brush off the kinds of experiences that had fallen on Melbourne. Such experiences become the man. They become his defining adult armor, no matter how mushy or bristly or slick.

Melbourne had changed. For one thing, he had sailed too much and too far to give up sail. While he worked in art, he kept looking for a job at sea.

He succeeded in the Master's Exam, given by the Examiner of Master's and Mates in Montreal. During this six-hour exam without that aid of notes, manuals, or scratch paper, he proved that he could find the latitude by a star, determine the effect of a ship's iron on its compass, use the laws of tides in order to shape a course, compare soundings with depths marked on a chart, demonstrate how to construct jury rudders and rafts, understand the laws involving management of crew (including how to protect them from the threat of scurvy), and navigate the intricacies of invoices, charter-parties, Lloyd's agents, also the leading lights of any channel he chose. He convinced the examiners of his mastery of rigging, measurements by logline, glass, and lead-line, mortar and rocket lines in case of a stranding, and the proper reporting of such an event in a logbook. And so on. His license was for Master, Home Trade, and it included the waters on the East and West coasts of North America from the Panama Canal to the Arctic Circle.

Soon after, two offers of employment came. One was to deliver a supply boat from Montreal up to the Arctic Circle on Hudson Bay. The other was to deliver yachts for Coastwise Marine Service in Annapolis. Melbourne was determined to accept whatever offer ripened first and let his fate take him from there. Would it be the extremity of north Hudson Bay, or else the intricate gullet of Chesapeake Bay? The latter hooked him first. He traveled by train to Maryland.

THE VERY NEXT day he was sailing a chartered yacht to Nova Scotia and back. *Waltzing Matilda* was a famous forty-five-foot ketch that had once won a Fastnet Race in England. To win the Fastnet, a biennial offshore yachting race organized by the U.K.'s Royal Ocean Racing Club, is a great honor. It's a rough race, notorious for capsized boats and lives lost. So, to pilot *Waltzing Matilda* was a fine first assignment for a sailor craving to get underway.

The yacht had been chartered by a polite young couple, the Starbucks, who had two small children and some limited experience in small boats. The food was all cereal and white bread. They kept inquiring, "Are we going to see a storm?"

"I hope not," said Melbourne. Oddly, they weren't quite happy with the answer.

After a stop in the Cape Cod Canal, they did get hit with a storm, a little squall. "I really needed some help," Melbourne later recalled, but the couple disappeared below decks, leaving the children in the care of the captain. Quickly Melbourne realized that the charter contract had not stipulated everything his clients desired—for example, sex on the ship while it's getting thrashed at sea.

With these and other distractions, the charter never quite reached Nova Scotia, but the return was happy and all were satiated. On the day he got back to Annapolis, his next piloting gig was trim, stowed, and ready.

"For the rest of the year I was just moving boats, sometimes with owners, sometimes without, nonstop." A few of his assignments were charter excursions in the manner of *Waltzing Matilda*, but most were simple deliveries of purchased boats. His pay was a hundred dollars a week and all expenses. These days the same work pays up to seven times that amount, but in the early sixties Melbourne considered it good return. He rented a little house, but he was never in it more than a couple nights at a time with long intervals between.

After a year of this, he wearied of the pace. He had other ambitions. In 1963 Mick came down from Montreal to take over the job, which he did for a time until he married and decided to go back to college and cultivate some diplomas.

MICK'S RELIEF freed Melbourne to explore other opportunities in the city of Annapolis. And there were plenty. "America's Sailing Capital" had focused on transport and trade by windpower ever since its founding in 1649, advantaged by its position at the point where the Severn River meets Chesapeake Bay. Area merchants once made fortunes from the slave trade, and after the Revolutionary War the city was prominent enough to serve as the U.S. capital for two years. Those years began in 1783, when George Washington went to Annapolis to resign his commission as commander-in-chief of the Continental Army, and ended in 1784, when the perplexing debate over a proposed U.S. Constitution moved from Annapolis to Philadelphia. By then the deeper port of Baltimore, located about twenty-six miles to the northwest, had become the more capacious port of entry. Annapolis settled into a less glorious role as a center of oyster-packing, sail-making, and boat-building. The city preserved its historic presence—the cobblestone streets of old town, the little slave houses, quaint now, the old market with its ghosts of the auction block, and its gorgeous capitol building, the oldest American capitol still in use today.

In the early 1960s a young ambitious navigator and nautical artist would have seen Annapolis and its environs the way a young ambitious writer sees Manhattan—the place to be. There were a myriad of shipyards and harbors, plus the hefty presence of the nation's maritime history and institutions, also a market for ship-related book design and illustration.

He found work as a compass compensator for the U.S. Coast Guard at Curtis Bay, an outlier of the Baltimore urbanscape. "A lot of people in the Coast Guard know how to adjust compasses, but they don't want to sign their names to it," Melbourne commented later. "So they prefer to hire a civilian compass adjuster. I'd done it on my own boats."

He made it sound easy. But his ability to compensate compasses illustrates the level of mastery Melbourne had achieved from his intensive self-education in the math and mechanics of maritime tradition, especially his disciplined reading of the classic *Dutton's Nautical Navigation* and his experience with celestial measurements. In short: a ship's compass is susceptible to forces within the ship, not just its pitch and roll but also the influence of iron, electronics, and cargo. How can a ship stay on course when the ship itself is loaded with materials that have their own magnetic fields? Or (these days) if somebody hangs a camera near the compass?

"It's all in Duttons, how to do it," said Melbourne. "You take a bearing on different things, what the compass should be doing. I always took azimuth bearings on the sun, that was the fastest way. A little trick you learn, take the shadow of the sun. I thought when I got older, that's what I could do"—go hither and yon compensating compasses.

However, like so many of the arcane skills Melbourne has mastered, "It's all done by electronics now."

THE OTHER Melbourne—painter, illustrator, book designer, maritime artist—also rose to fertile opportunities. An important nautical serial publication, *The Skipper: Chesapeake Bay Magazine*, was headquartered in Annapolis. Even more compelling was the Naval Institute, cloistered and tempting behind the walls of the U.S. Naval Academy. Though he was a civilian—and at this point still a Canadian citizen with a green card—Melbourne found his way inside.

The USNA's 338-acre campus or "Yard," the undergraduate college for would-be officers in both the Navy and the Marines, is forted-off by high walls set against the Severn River. The river forms an unwalled waterboundary, a constant reminder to "plebes" that they are, above all, now men and women of the sea. The buildings within the compound are lavish and monumental, all done in neoclassical "Beaux Arts" style, and the Yard teems with symbols and relics of U.S. naval glory, including an exact replica of the great bell Commodore Matthew Perry brought back from Japan in 1855, also the mortal remains of John Paul Jones in a crypt guarded by Marines beneath a sensational (and non-denominational) chapel. More pertinent to Melbourne's ambitions was the Rogers Collection of antique ship models (second floor of Preble Hall), the Nimitz Library (Melbourne found a way to qualify for access there, too).

Situated within the Yard, the Naval Institute, or USNI, was and is primarily a publishing house. But it is not, strictly, a mouthpiece for the Navy. In fact, to its credit, some of USNI's publications have nettled the officials enough to get themselves banned. The Naval Institute is a nonprofit association established by professional military personnel. Non-partisan, it focuses on national defense and security. Its mission: "to provide an independent forum for those who dare to read, think, speak, and write in order to advance the professional, literary, and scientific understanding of sea power and other issues critical to national defense." An Act of Congress in 1936 gave this entity its own place in the Yard, where it produces magazines and books, about eighty titles a year, some of which serve traditional military functions (manuals and guides to ship-handling) and some of which are tailored to the popular market (for example, page-turners by Tom Clancy and Stephen Coontz).

In this setting, Melbourne returned to his design skills, especially his book-design experience acquired while living as a "super" in Manhattan. Mostly though, he returned to the expansive art project he had developed before purchasing *Sanspariel*—a sequence of nautically precise watercolor paintings, each one portraying a sailing ship of yore, a collection utterly lost in the midnight shipwreck at Cap de la Hague. Sensing the possibility of making his mark in the publishing world of Annapolis, Melbourne began producing a new edition of ship portraits.

IT had never bothered him, having that entire collection of original work flushed forever into the black maw of the swallowing sea. Or so he said

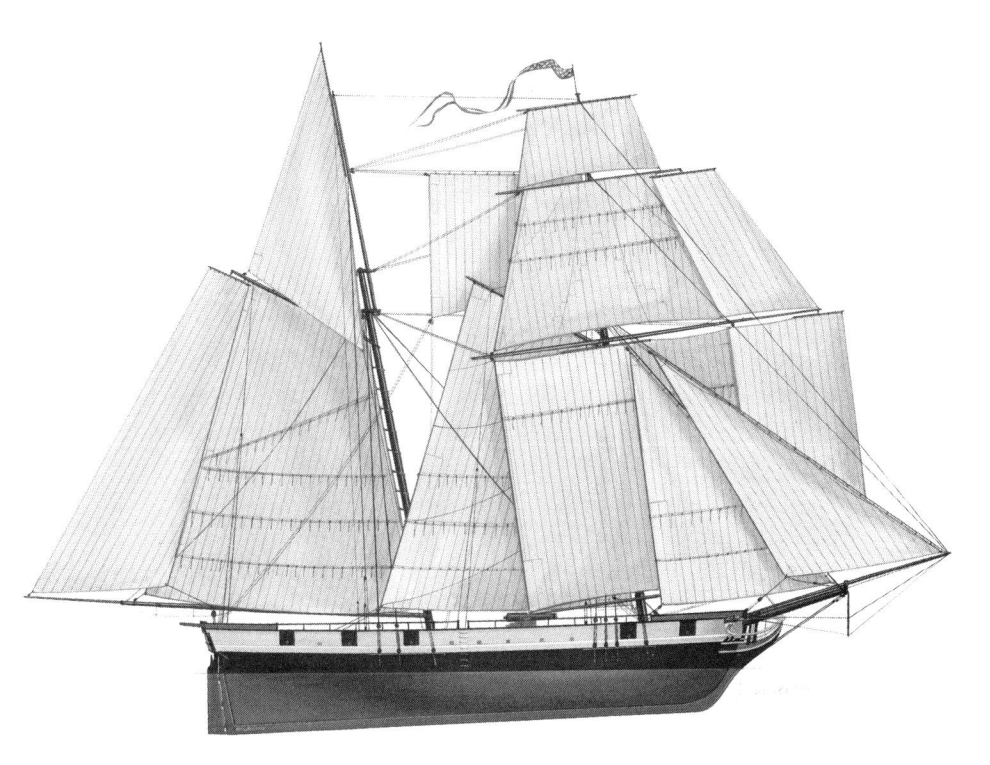

Melbourne created this illustration for his *Ships of the American Sailing Navy* collection—*Alligator*, a schooner of twelve guns built in the Boston Navy Yard in 1821.

much later in life, in his early eighties. "I always took the attitude that whatever happens must be."

Melbourne spoke this without a hint of piety, quick and matter-of-fact, like a high-energy mechanic with an amused look on his face explaining how to change a flat tire. "I always think, it will be better the next time. Same with my paintings. I lost them all. What the hell am I going to do? But then the next ones *were* better."

He said, "You might as well laugh because there's nothing else you can do."

Then he told a story about taking a girl to the high school prom in his Model A roadster and getting stuck in the mud. The roadster of course was a novelty in the forties, a beautiful mechanism to Melbourne but a silly old thing in the new age of electric starters and roll-up windows. He and his date were dressed finely of course, and it began to rain. In the darkness Melbourne took a detour that turned into a muddy slide into a grassy gulch. Like a gentleman, Melbourne lifted his date in his arms and began sloshing back up the slope to the road. Then he slipped and landed in thick mud with the outraged girl in his lap. He laughed. There was nothing else he could do. The laugh at the end of the line—that attitude brought Melbourne through innumerable failures on the way to some brilliant successes.

HIS NEW PORTRAIT SERIES had a consistency of presentation that allowed the viewer to learn something of the history of sailing design. He did not romanticize. Each was a stem-to-stern capture of a true vessel under perfect conditions, under full sail, rigging taut, brightwork shining, hull exactly rendered, sometimes with sailors on deck, perhaps a pennant snapping in the breeze. The paintings were more suited perhaps to a museum than a gallery.

He devised his style with the precision of a mechanic. Each portrait, after research, took him about a day to execute—four hours to begin, and four to finish. "I don't want to work it too much. Usually it's easier to just start over than to go back."

His medium was always opaque watercolors, gouache, in tubes that he kept in a lidless La Corona cigar box, applied with fine-pointed brushes. First he made pencil drawings on tissue paper, then he transferred the design in light pencil to illustration board. The hull went down first. The hull was the essence of the vessel. Then the sails emerged full-blown. Then he installed masts and spars. After that came the rigging, all done in brushwork freehand with the truest lines possible.

After he had executed several of this new generation of ship portraits, Melbourne took them over to the offices of *The Skipper* magazine, and the publication immediately purchased two. The editor there also suggested that he show his work to the USNI, the publishing house inside the walls of the Naval Academy.

That Melbourne did. He offered to create a series, comprehensive, one that would give broad tribute to "Ships of the American Sailing Navy." He conceived it as forty-eight works in this order:

6 | American **SHIPS-OF-THE-LINE**   6 | American **SCHOONERS**
6 | American **FRIGATES**   6 | American **SLOOPS**
6 | American **SLOOPS-OF-WAR**   6 | American **GUNBOATS**
6 | American **BRIGS**   6 | American **SMALL CRAFT**

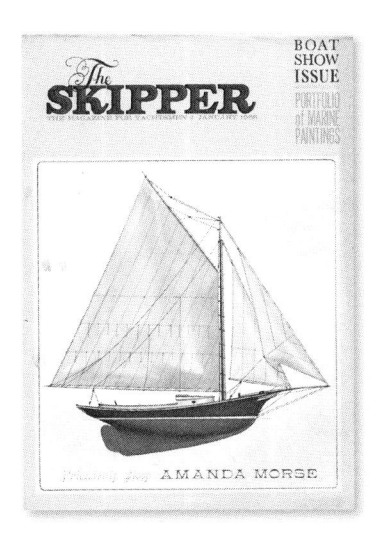

The USNI commissioned all forty-eight works, offering two hundred dollars each. Once the series was complete, USNI intended publish it and to mount an exhibit of Melbourne's work.

The Skipper magazine asked him to be its art director. The magazine thought it would be a full-time job, but Melbourne did his tasks at night, often in a single evening.

SUDDENLY this thirty-something, rascal Canadian had become a brand. His talents and obsessions had coalesced. He knew full well that, had things gone differently, he could be languishing in a Guatemalan jail. But now (he later reflected, using a nautical term that probably goes back to Vasco da Gama) he was "farting through silk."

Numerous maritime architects came to the Naval Academy to critique Melbourne's work prior to publication, even the renowned Howard Chapelle. Melbourne later had many conversations with Chapelle, whose books on nautical design and maritime history were both respected and rejected by people working in the field. Such controversy is endemic to the field, as Melbourne would come to learn. But at this moment, what dazzled him was that he had suddenly got himself *in the field.*

Years later he still said, "Not bad for a kid from Hamilton!" And he laughed his woodpecker-style laugh, which emerges by itself as he wonders over life's strange vagaries:

"Heh - heh - heh - heh - heh." ★

British Honduras | 1965

"I was going to make my fortune, sell them by the hundreds."

— MELBOURNE SMITH

KIDS who wander around a dull town, or a bad town, or any town that doesn't seem to them to be the right place to be, kids that aren't getting into trouble but are just searching for something to get into, these are the talented kids. You should help them, but maybe there's no helping them. Maybe the best help you can give is to make their lives as boring as possible so that they finally depart with jet propulsion.

Speaking of Melbourne, of course.

As a kid he used to walk around town all over the place. He walked way outside of town to Red Hill Creek, under a railroad bridge, very peaceful on the other side. Some years later he drove that distance in a car and thought, "Gee, it's a hell of a long way."

He walked around to see the Niagara Escarpment, a long cliff, ten stories high that encircled the city. He watched a mechanical railway incline as it raised and lowered automobiles two at a time. Unspoken message: it took some work to get out of town.

But the land there at lake level was fertile, no doubt about it, full of fruit trees and grapevines and such. Nevertheless, as Melbourne recollects, "I'd be gone all day walking around, finding places. Sneak into the movies. Being Baptist, I wasn't allowed to go to the movies. I'd walk up to town, the center of the city. That's a long way, too. With twenty-five cents allowance. They always showed a cartoon. I would keep sitting there and see the whole thing again."

On one such boyish wandering, he stopped to stare at the open doors of Farmer & Son: Carriage Builders on Barton Street near Emerald. The building was strong as a barn but just one story high, with big double doors to allow for the coming and going of horse-drawn carriages. The broad and shadowy interior of the shop had room for two carriages in its main space and a workshop in back with a hot forge and many sensational hand-tools. He heard the ring of the hammer on red steel, and he smelled maple wood that had just been turned on the lathe.

"The door was open, and I stood at the door looking in," Melbourne recalled. "The old man must have felt sorry for me. I would come every day. It became almost a job for me. Sometimes I would just stand there. If he had nothing for me to do, I would be satisfied just watching."

THE ALLURE was in the old tools, the practical brilliance of the old ways, of spoke shaves and draw knives, rasps and various hammers for different purposes, and with them the skills to make on site an entire market-ready vehicle without the use of electricity. At age twelve Melbourne learned to work a forge. He watched the old man, despite his rheumatism, take a swordtail paintbrush laden with white paint, spin a newly made wheel, and apply the brush to its rim, creating in one touch a perfect ornamental ring. The gratuitous flourish. Young Melbourne absorbed all this with the clarity and hungry wonder that comes with first sight.

Farmer & Son—the son knew all these skills, too, and worked with his father. But after the elder Farmer died, so did the brand. The son became an optometrist. The market for horse-drawn carriages was no more.

And yet something endured. That allure of hand tools and traditional craftsmanship lodged in the soul of Melbourne, and it still clung to thirty-something Melbourne. The more he learned about pre-industrial boatyards and the skills of the old days, the days of the wooden ships—the astonishing skills of coopers and caulkers, riggers and sawyers and blacksmiths—the more he wanted to build a boat. He kept remembering Simeon Young, the boatbuilder from British Honduras who could do so much with the simplest tools. He also remembered the great resources of that country, probably its greatest—the hardwoods of its dense forests, especially its mahogany and rosewoods.

Feeling now financially secure, even a wee bit prosperous, he went down to British Honduras and found Simeon. They talked about what kind of boat they could build together, a design that could be repeated, that could become a boating fashion and keep them both well employed indefinitely. Something simple but enticingly seaworthy.

They dreamed up a type of cutter—single mast, fore-and-aft rigged, with a couple of headsails, a gaff-rigged mainsail, and a jackyard topsail. It would have a deeper draught than a sloop and narrower body lines. Of course it would be constructed entirely of Honduran hardwoods there at Simeon Young's boatyard, which was little more than bare flat ground by the river, a shed, and a few small boats hauled up for repairs of an uncertain nature. Simeon made a half-model of the proposed hull—the traditional way to begin a boat design project—showing the ship's lines, the arc of its bow, the depth of its keel, the half-width of its beam. No need to build a full model because the port side exactly mirrors starboard. To make the model, Simeon glued planks of hardwood, alternating colors, into a single laminated block. Then he chopped thoughtfully at the block using an adze. Once he'd roughed out the design, he handed the block to a boy who did the sanding. In his world, sanding was always done by boys or women.

Melbourne carried the half-model back to Annapolis and showed it to Eric Steinlein. Steinlein said it was very good, but it needed some adaptations if these vessels were going into open sea rather than simply cut about in the coves and reef-protected waters of British Honduras. These locally suited designs were too sharp for big waters. The hull needed better balance. Melbourne offered to pay him something to draw up the design. They agreed on the ridiculous price of twenty-five dollars. Steinlein produced some line drawings, then was so slow in producing the construction plans that the original "Belizean cutter" was already built by the time Melbourne received them.

DURING the mid-1930s Eric J. Steinlein had done a great deed for the maritime history of the United States. With funding secured from the Works Progress Administration, a New Deal agency of the Depression era, he rounded up the best and brightest of the young maritime designers of his day. Together they created the Historic American Merchant Marine Survey (HAMMS), an eighteen-month search to identify and record vanishing historic vessels. The Smithsonian Institution was a cooperating sponsor. The complete published set of marine architectural drawings in numerous volumes weighed a total of one hundred and fifty pounds.

Most of the young designers that Steinlein recruited went on to respectable positions, even fame, some as heads of museums. Steinlein himself, not a good game-player, lived obscurely, any bitterness he might have felt now expressed as a curmudgeonly frankness. For example, during the 1980s, fifty years after the original Survey, a renewed interest in maritime history caused publishers to reissue the volumes. At that time Steinlein, age eighty-one, told a journalist, "It was information going down the drain, so I'm happy as hell that it's on record for those nuts who are interested in it."

When Melbourne got to know him in the 1960s, Steinlein was living on a small farm he'd bought in Galesville, Maryland, about ten acres on the West River. He had willed the land to the Smithsonian, so long as he could live the rest of his life there with a pension of four hundred dollars a month—a figure that unfortunately did not respond to the rate of inflation. He'd built the farmhouse himself and lived there with his wife—"wasting away with all that knowledge," said Melbourne.

Melbourne remembered Steinlein as "the local sage in Annapolis." He would show up at small-boat races and always win. "He was a marvelous small-boat sailor." Younger boating "nuts" like Melbourne would go out to the farm to visit, bringing a bottle of gin or rum. Melbourne brought him dinners sometimes, though Steinlein would object unless Melbourne pretended that the food was leftovers and not made specially for him.

"We loved him, a sweet old guy who was mad at the world, smarter than any of those he had hired." The youngsters clung to his simple but wise design principles. Here's one such: "Both ends of the boat should be designed to go the same speed." Obvious, maybe, but converse to the practice of the day. He was a small man, maybe five-foot nine-inches tall, who puttered around the farm with his dog as company. When he died, his sons buried him in a hole they dug behind the farmhouse. One of his protégés, Howard Chapelle, wrote ten excellent books about shipbuilding though the boats he designed were failures. Said Melbourne: "Eric Steinlein was only a failure at bringing in the money."

AT SIMEON YOUNG's boatyard, conditions were primitive for sure. Projects began with handsaws in the forest. Vessels were raised with a pry bar and quarter-inch wedges, one side at a time, till the ship would be three feet in the air. Melbourne paid Simeon a hundred dollars a week, which was the equivalent of two hundred British Honduras dollars. Simeon always gave half to his wife, then spent the other half, much of that given to young girls who would come to him saying, "I need some milk for my baby." When Melbourne asked him why he gave the money away, he said, "Someday I'm going to get old. They will take care of me." Melbourne would smile a little and tilt his head.

Simeon had many children out of wedlock, but not as many as his older brother, whom he idolized. The brother had over thirty illegitimate children and none by his own wife.

The design of the Belizean cutter called for five tons of lead ballast on the keel. While the carpentry work went ahead, the fitting of futtocks and floor-timbers and frames, Melbourne paid pennies for any pieces of lead brought in. Kids showed up with lead scrounged from old batteries and construction scraps. After five tons of lead had been accumulated, Simeon built a wooden mold and coated the inside with concrete wash to prevent the wood from bursting into flame. At every knot in the mold, he reinforced the outside so that the molten lead wouldn't blow out through the knot. They melted five tons of lead in a huge pot—the kind that cartoonists draw to show missionaries getting stewed. On the first pour, a neglected knot blew, and they lost a quantity of lead through a drainage system that Simeon had rigged. They reclaimed the cooled spill and did another melt. This time the pour went fine, but some quantity of the lead was unaccounted for and the mold wasn't full. They searched around the boatyard and found a big iron chain with one-inch-thick links. Figuring that the chain would make up for the lost lead, they dropped the iron chain into the molten lead. Iron, though, is quite buoyant in molten lead. The chain floated like water wings. They kept pushing it down into the molten mass with long boards. Eventually the lead cooled enough that the chain stayed under and the proper level was reached.

Such was Belizean seat-of-the-pants boatbuilding.

Another example: The washers for the bolts had to be bronze or copper. Galvanized washers would rust in salt water. So Melbourne began paying about four cents per brass washer. Then he realized that the four large copper pennies he was trading for one brass washer were each the size of a washer and even more resistant to corrosion. So in the end all the cutter's washers were made of pennies with holes drilled through them.

IN THIS WAY, and within six months' time, the first and only Melbourne Smith-built Belizean cutter went to sea. Its name, *Appledore*, reflected a plan to name each subsequent ship for a small British seaside town, working alphabetically. The Honduran premier came down to Simeon's boatyard to launch the new ship, smashing a bottle of three-barry rum against its bow. ("Three-barry" rum is the product of three barrels and so is superior to cheap "one-barry.") The sails had come from England as had the ship's bell. Total

Melbourne's *Appledore*, a 33-foot topsail cutter built in British Honduras and sailed home to Chesapeake Bay.

cost, about twenty thousand dollars, including the diesel engine. Melbourne sailed the new ship right up to Annapolis.

Eric Steinlein viewed the new ship with cautious enthusiasm. Then he saw that Melbourne had put a hatch in the stern. He shot Melbourne a you'll-be-sorry look. "You'll rue the day you did that," he said.

This hatch was a design point the two men had discussed. Because of the hull dimensions, *Appledore's* stern was capacious enough to provide additional storage. But the addition of significant weight back there would certainly throw off the sailing efficiency of the cutter. Melbourne countered, "I'll just put light stuff back there, lines and fenders."

"Sure *you* will," said Steinlein. "But the next owner will put a water tank back there. I wouldn't put a hatch there."

Sure enough. For the next couple years Melbourne kept *Appledore* on her lines and sailed her around the Chesapeake Bay area, then sold her for twenty-five thousand dollars. As predicted, the new owner immediately installed a fuel tank in the stern. In the decades ahead through five or six owners, she probably never sailed as well as she might. But when Melbourne and Steinlein took her out, spanking new, she was fast.

Steinlein was proud.

THE DREAM of wealth from a production line of gaff-rigged Belizean cutters quickly fizzled. "I could never sell more than one at a time," Melbourne said later. "Most people wanted more modern rigging." What he didn't say—and there could be some truth in this—is that he hadn't much stomach for making the same boat over and over again. His restless mind craved new projects.

Experience now told him that life was a lot easier if you sailed someone *else's* boat. That way you don't spend half your life fixing your own. Go as the navigator. Or, prophetically: "Don't build your own boat. Build somebody else's boat."

Besides, there were so many other opportunities for him in Annapolis, so much to do besides construct a line of *Appledore* knock-offs.

For example, the Naval Institute hired him to design the next edition of an important official textbook, *The Watch Officer's Guide*, a work that the publisher updates every two to four years. As the title suggests, the book describes exactly what the watch officer has to mind on board a ship belonging to the U.S. Navy. Melbourne got very close to completion of this task—the pages had been printed and bound, and the volume was ready for covers. He was working on the book jacket. Then he came to work and found his desk cleared out. All the copies were gone. It so happened that the officer responsible for the revision of the text had just been court-martialed. This occurred during the Vietnam War. The officer had taken his wife on board his ship and, just to impress her, had gone up the coast and lobbed some munitions into North Vietnam. "You really can't have that," Melbourne said later. But he still has one copy, probably the only one in existence, of the banned text.

There was *The Skipper* magazine. There was the occasional yacht race with need for a skillful navigator. In such non-routine ways his life was full and getting fuller. He married again, and brought the children together into a stable home in Annapolis.

D URING the early nineteen-seventies Sam Lorea's Tavern in Annapolis was a prime watering-hole for sailing types, and that included everyone from oystermen to faculty of the U.S Naval Academy. Beer was twenty-five cents a can. On Saturday afternoons the patrons spilled out the door and onto the sidewalk.

One day, Melbourne was enjoying the convivial atmosphere of Sam's when a man approached him, later he couldn't remember who, someone from the USNA sailing office he supposed. The man said that some wild Australians were coming to compete in the Newport-to-Bermuda yacht race, and they needed a navigator who was familiar with the course. The fellow already had a half-dozen academy volunteers, but would Melbourne be interested, too?

"Sure," he said. Then he promptly forgot the question.

So Melbourne was surprised by a cable some days later, It came from the syndicate owned by Alan Bond, Australia's most sensational business tycoon. Bond's yacht *Apollo* was being shipped to Philadelphia, and Bond hoped that Melbourne could meet it there and then deliver it to Newport, Rhode Island.

Later when Melbourne finally met Alan Bond and asked him, "Why did you choose me?" the British-born Aussie spluttered, "'Cause your name's Melbourne! So you can't be all bad!"

Apollo finished second in that race but was disqualified "for some design detail in the yacht," said Melbourne. Two years later he got another call from Bond, this time for the Newport-Bermuda race followed by a trans-Atlantic race from Bermuda to Bayonne, Spain. Melbourne knew from experience that "the secret to that track is to make a good northerly distance before turning east for Spain. I held that north direction until I was confident that all the fleet had turned."

Even so, they finished second. The Naval Academy's *Jubilee* had maintained radio silence, waited for Melbourne to turn, then held its northerly course a day longer and beat *Apollo* by an hour.

Second place was not okay with the indomitable Alan Bond. Some years later Melbourne helped Bond challenge America's Cup in his first two attempts. On the third challenge, Bond won. He became the first winner from outside the New York Yacht Club since the race's founding in 1851—the longest-held record in the history of sport.

Working with Admiralty Publishing House Ltd. in Annapolis, Melbourne actually published Alan Bond's biography, a book called *The Southern Cross* by Hugh D. Whall, in 1974.

Later Bond decided to build a re-creation of HMB *Endeavour*, the historic British Royal Navy research vessel commanded by Lieutenant James Cook as he discovered Australia in 1770. This grand replication project was generally viewed as Alan Bond's *mea culpa* to the Australian nation, his atonement for various corporate crimes. Melbourne located and had shipped the Douglas fir spars and decking for *Endeavour*. This project put him back in touch with the expert sailors he'd known from yacht-racing. One of these was John Longley, the foredeck man from *Apollo*, who was now overseeing construction of *Endeavour*. Longley mentioned in a letter that the ship's designers had chosen polyester for the standing rigging. Over a hundred thousand dollars had already been spent on polyester cordage. Melbourne wrote back a simple observation "that I had learned the hard way"—that polyester stretches, and it never stops stretching.

"I gave him a simple test. Hang a length of synthetic line and suspend a five-hundred-pound weight on the end a few inches off the ground. In the morning the weight will be sitting on the ground. Do this each day, same thing will happen. Soon your half-inch-diameter line will be a quarter inch. There's just no end to it." The rough natural fibers of manila or hemp, after an initial stretching, "fetch up" (to use riggers' slang), and that's the end of it. These fibers will hold as long as they're kept dry. For that reason they have to be tarred regularly. In Melbourne's experience, this laborious old-days technology could not be bested by resorting to synthetic fibers.

The *Endeavour* team saw the practical truth in Melbourne's advice and trashed its investment in polyester cordage. John Longley explained the development in a letter to Melbourne, presented here verbatim:

> "The rig was I suppose the nearest thing to making a complete fool of her. As you will remember we had built at great expense a complete rig out of polyester when we received your advice that polyester would be a disaster. What to do? I went back to my rope manufacturer at Kinnears and they said you were wrong—polyester would be fine. I then worked with my naval architect to build a mathematical model of the rig. The combination of stiffer masts than the 18th century and stretchy rig was a disaster. Even manila was dubious. The problem was that, as the shrouds stretched, the load on the caps would either break them or twist them off the top of the spars. We built a complete new rig out of pure manila. We pre-stretched it by hanging it from construction cranes overnight with five-ton concrete

blocks on the end of each shroud. We used Stockholm tar to (coat) the manila. It does not like sticking to it initially but after several goes it gives up and takes it."

With this traditional rigging the new *Endeavour* managed to travel one hundred and seventy thousand nautical miles and circumnavigate the planet twice.

I N 1971 the Hudson's Bay Company approached Melbourne wanting to commission five of his ship portraits, each depicting a vessel of great significance in Canadian history. The company hoped to issue sets of prints of these paintings.

Hudson's Bay claims to be the oldest commercial company in the New World and one of the oldest in the world. Its history goes back to 1668 when the English sent a plucky, little sailing ship called *Nonsuch* into huge, icy Hudson Bay to explore possible opportunities for trade. The explorers established a fort on the bay at the mouth of what they called the Rupert River, named for the expedition's sponsor, Prince Rupert of the Rhine. Two years later the company received a Royal charter and began dealing mainly in furs. Today HBC has well proven that it's possible to adapt and thrive beyond the demise of the beaver trade.

Nonsuch was the subject of one of the five portraits. She was a ketch, which is a two-masted vessel, fore-and-aft rigged, that spreads larger sail on the fore or main mast. This is a rig favored for coastwise trading. After completing the paintings, Melbourne approached the client with an idea grander than portraits. "Why not actually *build* a replica of that ketch," he wondered. Then he added, "And have *me* do it for you."

He sold the idea with all his persuasive powers. His proposal went all the way up to Winnipeg to the company's main headquarters. The top guys liked the idea very much, so much in fact that they went right past Melbourne. They went back to England, to the original shipyard, where in 1970 a new *Nonsuch* came to life, crafted with tools and materials that were familiar to the seventeenth century. This replica, vaunted by public relations, strolled like a peacock along the Atlantic coast of Canada and the U.S. Then she was trucked to the West Coast and did the same. Today, the *Nonsuch* "rests" eternally in an A-frame museum in Winnipeg, and there's no plaque proclaiming that Melbourne Smith had the idea.

STILL, the venture whetted Melbourne's appetite for a historic replication project. Such a project would bring together his precise observations of ships of old with his eagerness to use the tools of old, plus his drive to be original. Once a person gets a taste for authenticity and a feeling for a project that only he or she can do only once, certain people will just not let go.

That's when Melbourne got a call from the City of Baltimore, the mayor's office. "Somebody has donated a Baltimore clipper schooner. You know more about this than anybody. Can you go out there and look at it? A guy in California built it and said if we want it, we can have it." Turns out the boat, built of marine plywood, was in Baja California and had been confiscated by the Mexican government.

Melbourne reported to the mayor's office that the vessel in question was a sham and a wreck. Then he said, "If you want a true Baltimore clipper, I can build you one."

He proposed a one-of-a-kind vessel built with traditional tools and skills. The construction site itself could be an educational attraction. And the ship would be the real thing, not an amusement-park silliness. It would sail. It would sail as they sailed in those bold old days, on the kind of ship that had turned Baltimore into one of America's great epicenters. Wherever she went, this ship would write the perfect signature representing Baltimore's proud past and proclaim Baltimore as one of the world's great municipalities.

Melbourne's suggestion struck the city bureaucrats at a receptive moment, and it floated to the top, to Mayor William Donald Schaefer. His Honor, a Second World War veteran and then colonel in the U.S. Army Reserves, was no seaman. But he knew that authentic re-creations of historic sailing ships, done well, could attract honor and international recognition to the sponsoring municipality. As we shall see, the idea meshed with his big plans for the revitalization of Baltimore's Inner Harbor. So the request for proposals went out, attached to an advertisement that Melbourne had himself (most obligingly) written.

But the Mayor didn't know what to make of this Melbourne Smith fellow. Melbourne presented himself with no degree in naval architecture and no previous success with a shipbuilding project of this magnitude. At one point in the deliberations Mayor Schaefer collared Melbourne in a hallway and said, "Are you sure you know what you're getting into? Here, come into my office."

Melbourne's transition—from painting historic vessels to actually building them—began with this watercolor portrait of *Nonsuch*, created for The Hudson's Bay Company.

There he indicated with a hand-sweep a painting on his wall, a minutely detailed rendering of a Baltimore-built vessel called *Rossie*, an 1812-era topsail schooner of the type being proposed. The Mayor said, "Now *that's* an accurate portrait of a Baltimore clipper."

"I know," said Melbourne. He stepped up to the painting and pointed to the signature of the artist.

"I know because that's my signature. I painted it." ★

Baltimore | 1975

"We hold that no man can improve to any considerable extent either in ship-building or any other branch of mechanism, whose volitions are not the result of his own conceptions."

— JOHN WILLIS GRIFFITHS | 1849

IN FACT, it was Melbourne's paintings, his ship portraits, even more than his own sailing experience, that drew him into his great shipbuilding projects. The paintings gave him a reputation. To have the cover of *The Skipper*, whose tag line was "The National Sailing Magazine," was to imply that the artist understood historic vessels with detailed precision.

His first of many *The Skipper* covers depicted a Baltimore clipper, and this may have been the very image on the wall of the Baltimore mayor's office. She's a classic schooner, fore-and-aft rigged on two raking masts, the overlapping foresail slightly smaller than the mainsail, both sails gaff-rigged. The topsails are square-rigged, and she's flying two headsails. This basic design, subject to innumerable variations, was a mainstay of New England trading from the early 1800s onward. What's remarkable about Melbourne's painting is not so much its accuracy as its feeling of lightness and loft. Its taut cumulus of sail, fully spread with a slight curvature in every line, looks almost transparent against the painting's nearly white backdrop. No sky or seawater are indicated, and yet the rake of the masts and the slight upward sweep of the sleek hull suggest that the vessel is pouncing forward, surging under the joy of full sail. Two flags snap in the breeze, and a blue pennant snakes and whips from the top of the mainmast. Much more than a mechanical rendering, the painting evokes the rigor and pleasure of sailing, when economy and beauty, design and delight, are indistinguishable.

The Skipper published this image in 1963. After the magazine issue appeared, Melbourne learned that his image had been lifted by Bergdorf Goodman, the luxury goods department store on Fifth Avenue in Manhattan, and copied onto the back of a silk sport shirt. Later, Melbourne confessed, "I was so flattered I went to New York and bought one. I was unaware that I probably should have sued them for copyright infringement."

Not long after that, while sitting in an Annapolis bar, Melbourne was approached by another sailor, a fellow in his late twenties but already weather-faced and ropy in build, clearly someone who had reefed many a topsail in the teeth of a squall. He introduced himself as Fred Hecklinger. In a slow, rather hesitant manner—as though he was concerned about angering this accomplished maritime artist—Fred made it clear that he admired Melbourne's illustrations and design work for *The Skipper*. He just wanted to point out that the Baltimore clipper painting had a defect in its rigging. The stay for the forestaysail should have been rigged to the lower mast, not the topmast.

Not knowing what to expect in response—likely an arrogant huff or a sarcastic rebuff—what Fred got was a lifelong friendship. Melbourne thanked him, went back to his research, and later caught up with Fred again to tell him that he was absolutely right. Here was another fellow with experience in, and love for, traditionally rigged vessels. From that point, Melbourne involved Fred in nearly every project that arose. Fred said: "When he did a book of illustrations of America's Cup Defenders, he would have me look at the original paintings for technical errors. I used to get paid by liquid measure." That is, drinks at the bar. Fred also served as paid hand on the yachts whenever Melbourne went as navigator. In 1973 Melbourne got Fred involved in the *Peggy Stewart* project, the historic re-creation that never got off the drawing board.

LOOKING BACK, it's easy to see how a number of seemingly random challenges—the ship portraits, time spent with Simeon Young, the exciting idea of building *Nonsuch* for Hudson's Bay Company, and the near-hit of *Peggy Stewart*—all led to that ironic moment in Mayor Schaefer's office in Baltimore's City Hall, and indeed to the confidence Melbourne would need in order to confront the feckless aldermen of Baltimore and push his way to success in building and sailing a re-created Baltimore clipper, Melbourne's first great success as a shipbuilder.

Peggy Stewart was a cargo vessel whose destruction became part of the revolutionary-era history of Annapolis and Chesapeake Bay. October 19, the date in 1774 when *Peggy Stewart* was burned to the waterline by its owner, continues to be recognized patriotically as the anniversary of the "Annapolis Tea Party," a southern counterpart to the more famous "Boston Tea Party" of December 1773.

The burning issue (so to speak) of this historic incident was, of course, not the tea itself but the taxes that the British government expected colonials to pay when purchasing tea from the British East India Company. At that time no war had begun, but the colonies were full of seditious hotheads who were looking for a fight and enforcing a boycott against tea. And the colonies were just as full of British loyalists who wished everyone would settle down and get on with business. *Peggy Stewart's* owner was among the latter—a prosperous Annapolis merchant and loyalist named Anthony Stewart who got himself caught in the furious revolutionary squeeze.

In 1774 *Peggy Stewart* set out on her return voyage from England loaded with cargo. The bulk of the cargo was human—fifty-three indentured servants headed for work in the New World. Also aboard: seventeen packages, about a ton in total weight, labeled "linens." This was all, in fact, forbidden tea, the flashpoint merchandise. Stewart's British partners had set up a little scam that went wrong. After the vessel's captain found it out shortly after departure, he worried all the way across the Atlantic, not only about the incoming autumn storms, the leakiness of his vessel, and the deteriorating health of his human cargo, but also about the trouble that would explode once he reached Annapolis. To save his own hide, when he reached port he wrote "tea," not "linen" on the cargo manifest.

The Loyalist colonial merchant who had ordered the cargo, Anthony Stewart, realized that he couldn't just send the ship back to England—fifty-three souls on a leaking boat through the blasts of winter. Unconscionable. So he paid taxes on the cargo, violating the seditionary boycott, in order to get the passengers onto the shore. But he left the tea on board, wondering what to do next.

The bully boys of the coming revolution proceeded to build a gallows in front of the Stewart home. This apparition proved quite distressing to the merchant, his bedridden wife, and their children. In the end the only action Stewart could take that would satisfy the riled-up mob was to have *Peggy Stewart* towed to a crowd-pleasing location, let it be anchored under full sail, and then torch it himself, tea and all.

This act of mob coercion continues to symbolize the revolutionary fervor of Marylanders. Some two hundred years later, the Chesapeake Bay Maritime Museum* conceived the idea of commissioning a re-creation of the martyred brigantine as a history lesson to all its visitors. At that time, the early seventies, this museum was less than a decade old and hungry for a signature exhibit. It put out a call for proposals, and an ambitious upstart named Melbourne Smith won the contract. For the museum he drew a set of plans that captured the particulars of the lost vessel, from the details of its rigging to the design of the beams and futtocks constituting its hull. And he provided a fully rigged model, so that museum visitors could at least see the miniature version of *Peggy Stewart* in case the full re-creation failed to develop.

Which it did. The re-creation never happened. But Melbourne's preliminary work was perfectly successful, produced in the fashion of all his projects, however unprecedented and unpredictable they were—on time and on budget. And the *Peggy Stewart* experience simply sharpened his appetite for a big project, a project that would go all the way into the sea under sail, a dazzler, a wonder, a reversal of the extinction of traditional sailing ships.

He got that from the City of Baltimore.

The Baltimore clipper project, which came just a year or two after *Peggy Stewart*, had all the classic elements of greatness—a lack of precedent, daft but passionate ambition, the marshalling of every resource from skilled muscle to sharp-minded innovation to companionship and all-out personal drive, and then triumph that free-falls into loss.

IT WASN'T nostalgia that gripped the City of Baltimore, nor was it a passion for maritime history. The city had begun to rot at the center, and anyone with vision could see that—especially Mayor Schaefer. Odd as it may sound, a public display of throwback shipbuilding fit perfectly into his larger plans to heal his urban cancer.

At its heart Baltimore is a harbor town. During the late eighteenth century, Baltimore led the nation in shipbuilding. The City dodged the worst effects of the Great Depression on the strength of its active port. During the Second World War it boomed with the business of shipping munitions

---

* A popular institution located on eighteen waterfront acres, the Chesapeake Bay Maritime Museum attracts fifty thousand visitors a year.

Melbourne's model of the colonial ship *U.S. Peggy Stewart*, designed for the Chesapeake Bay Maritime Museum. He hoped to build the ship for the Bicentennial of the American Revolution in 1976.

where needed, also with providing jobs in manufacturing plants—Bethlehem Steel, General Motors. All of that changed during the 1950s and '60s as Baltimore's liveliness moved outward, leaving the Inner Harbor area to the unemployed and destitute.

"The whole downtown area became obsolete and decayed," remembered Fred Hecklinger, who served as yard manager for Melbourne's great Baltimore project. "The only people that lived downtown were... troublemakers shall we say." During the early seventies he called a friend who worked downtown and suggested that they go out to dinner together after work. The friend said, "Nobody stays downtown after dark any more." He recalled an incident in a downtown park in which the harmless gathering of a local garden club—floral bulbs, cuttings, and old ladies in broad-brimmed canvas hats—was violently disrupted by "a bunch of undesirable people."

Mayor Schaefer had begun implementing an ambitious plan to reverse this decline by turning Baltimore into a hub of national tourism. By the time Melbourne's proposal was getting attention at City Hall, Schaefer had already dedicated a public wharf for visiting ships, begun the construction of an Inner Harbor promenade, and hosted a new Baltimore City Fair. About the same time that Melbourne set up his impromptu shipyard on the shore of the Inner Harbor, the City was opening its new Maryland Science Center. Soon to come: the National Aquarium and the Hyatt Regency Baltimore. Given this civic context, Melbourne's proposal to resurrect one symbol of the City's sailing-era glory made perfect sense—especially the manner in which he intended to construct the thing.

He planned to build it Simeon-Young style, seaside on flat ground with no existing shipyard infrastructure. The blacksmith would set up his shop. The carpenters would erect a secure tool locker and a big open-air shed. Any passer-by could stop and watch the action, chat it up with the blacksmith, and learn something about wooden ship construction. A perimeter fence was necessary, but it would not obscure the drama of watching the hull rise, the seams get caulked, the masts being shaped. During the proposed ten months of construction, the site itself would be an attraction to tourists, journalists, and admirers from other seaside municipalities.

This transparency, of course, would place Melbourne's leadership under ruthless scrutiny by exposing any delays, disharmonies, or disasters. But it set a standard, a daring style, for historic re-creations that was admired by many and repeated by few. It established the Melbourne Smith brand.

THE CITY'S request for proposals, using words suggested by Melbourne, called for "an authentic example of a historic Baltimore clipper" to be built "using construction materials, methods, tools, and procedures... typical of the period." Only two bids came in, one being Melbourne's. The other came from a shipwright in Pennsylvania who planned to build it at home and deliver it fully rigged to Baltimore. Melbourne's had the advantage of touristic theater, also a substantially lower cost. The low bid would come to mean that nobody on the project made any real money. But the work proceeded without mutiny, seven days a week for ten months, and the job came in on schedule without cost overruns. On time and on budget—that too became part of the Melbourne Smith brand.

He claimed a stretch of ground between the bay shore and a three-story condominium complex. He summoned his key people. White-bearded blacksmith Gerry Trobridge set up the forge and became the respected elder of the project, the spine, the steadfast reminder that, no matter what, the work must proceed. Melbourne brought up Simeon Young with a select group of Caribbean shipwrights. Yard manager Hecklinger was thirty-eight at this time, recently married and therefore happy to have some work on shore. He and his wife had just honeymooned on a topsail schooner called *Shenandoah*, so he was quite familiar with the rigging and plan required by this project.

Around this nucleus, young carpenters and craftsmen gathered. Nothing was advertised. The word got around. Guys showed up in their trucks with tools and girlfriends or dogs or both. Most of them knew just the basics—how to make things square. But there's nothing square in a boat. They came to learn, knowing that the pay would be small and temporary. Some of these young guys learned a lot, and they went on to compete on their own for historical shipbuilding projects, sometimes bidding against Melbourne. (Later, Melbourne admitted, "They beat me sometimes. Pisses me off, but it's very fair.") In short, this improvised Baltimore shipyard became the incubator of a new spirit in heritage shipbuilding. In Hecklinger's words, the project has been "much respected, much imitated, and much criticized by people who didn't do it themselves."

BEFORE the shipbuilding could commence, one rather important mystery needed to clarified—What is "it"? What kind of ship is a Baltimore clipper? The word "clipper" just means speedy. How does that word determine just how a carpenter might cut a futtock? Or measure the length of a spar?

As a point of clarification, the term "clippership"—referring to the superships of the American 1840s, *Sea Witch* for example—constitutes a brand name. It's a design that each new individually built ship tested, teased, and tried to transcend. But the "Baltimore clipper" concept was loose. A variety of ship designs could fit the function.

Here is Melbourne's definition: "Basically they were fast schooners, some of them brig-rigged, all built for the illicit trades—smuggling, privateering, slaving. They were the slavers of choice, fast, cheap to build. Many were built like throwaways. A fast boat can get away when you are about to get caught. And they were built for the revenue marine, too—for the police who went after them to collect taxes or enforce the law. To catch a crook, you had to have the same kind of boat."

Melbourne added: "Baltimore clippers were never built for trade, unless you were smuggling something."

Pride of Baltimore **turned historic shipbuilding into a public demonstration, a spectacle that drew widespread attention.**

The city might not have viewed its heritage sailing vessel in quite such wickedly bright illumination. But it did want to know the name of the naval architect, the expert who would provide the *bona fide* construction plans. Melbourne didn't want a naval architect. He wanted to build it himself from his knowledge and nerve. But he had to admit that he had never built a ship of this size. *Annyah* was a much larger vessel, and he had sailed her without an engine for thousands of miles. Even so, he felt it was practical to capitulate on the point.

Melbourne suggested that the naval architect be Tom Gillmer, an obvious choice. Gillmer had established the department of naval architecture and marine engineering at the U.S. Naval Academy. He had taught there as a professor of naval architecture for twenty-seven years. He wrote books. *Modern Ship Design* was a standard textbook. He was interested in boats made with fiberglass. But he was not a practical boatman. He had never served as a seaman or deckhand. When he retired from teaching in 1969, he set up a private design practice. This Baltimore clipper oddity came right on cue for him. He resented Melbourne and the crew in the yard, their corrections.

Fred Hecklinger remembered Gillmer as "a difficult person to work with. He would not tolerate any question about what he did. Some of his ideas about rigging just didn't work." But he was always right regardless. He designed a metal facet on the tiller that bruised the pilot as it swung. Wouldn't settle for a soft knot instead.

CHAPTER 10 | 105

And yet he drew the plans, and they were fine.

Melbourne now had to learn quickly about hierarchies and bureaucracies. One early meeting with city administrators the question arose: what kind of a ship do we want? Someone said, "Give children rides around the harbor, and make it as authentic as you can."

Melbourne told them, "You can't have both. You don't give children rides on racehorses. You get a tired, old draft horse for that. Even the owner doesn't ride a racehorse. He spends millions, but he wouldn't dare ride on it."

The city leaders chose the authentic route. People would enjoy seeing it, but they would never ride on it. "I was very happy about that," Melbourne recalled. "Too many boats are just tubs going around the harbor, very safe."

And then there was the drama of choosing a name. After all, this was not a precise replication of a specific old vessel but the representative of a type. What shall we call it? Until anything has a name, we don't quite know it.

A S THE SHIPYARD was coming together, with tradesmen from diverse parts of the globe converging on the Inner Harbor, Melbourne was appearing at city council meetings over the question of what to call the new ship. Certain aldermen supposed that the vessel might carry their own name, or a favored colleague's name, though of course they hesitated to pose the nomination themselves. Prior to the key meeting Melbourne had heard plenty of suggestions for names. He knew from experience that ship names mattered. He had learned this from selling his ship portraits. People will eagerly purchase a rendering of John Paul Jones's *Ranger* but hesitate over the *Argyle,* or the *Tweed,* or the *Ann McKim*—even though the latter, a clipper, once sailed from Valparaiso to Baltimore in "quicker time by nine days than was ever made before" (quoting the *Baltimore Sun* in 1838).

Melbourne was determined that his vessel bear a dignified and memorable name.

He had learned another thing from his experience as a commercial artist. When he presented work to a client, he would often leave an obvious flaw front and center. That way the client could quickly find the flaw, correct it, and dispense with any further nitpicking—the client's job was, after all, to find *something* that needed correction. Melbourne was beginning to see that the same logic applied to city administrators. If they weren't impeding him, correcting him, second-guessing him, or in some way frustrating his progress, then they weren't doing their jobs as defenders of the public's self-interest.

Melbourne prepared himself accordingly. When the day came for the naming of the vessel, Melbourne appeared before the city council in its dazzling chambers. Baltimore City Hall filled an entire city block, a six-floor historic edifice built in the Baroque revival style with mansard roofs, white marble sheathing, and a massive cast-iron dome. Undaunted by such grandeur, Melbourne proposed three names for the ship, the third one—his intended—to be presented after two that he hoped would seem as ridiculous to the commission as they seemed to him.

First he suggested the *Johnny Unitas*, after a Pittsburgh-born quarterback whose prodigious passing abilities had made the Baltimore Colts triumphant through the 1950s and '60s. Imagine that, an eighteenth-century sailing ship named for a worn-out football star. Then Melbourne suggested a name honoring another Baltimorean legend—the *Blaze Starr*—after a burlesque star and stripper who went from headlining at the Two O'Clock nightclub to national fame and a scandalous affair with Louisiana governor Earl Long. Imagine that, an eighteenth century sailing ship named for a 1950s entertainer who worked with a combustible sofa.* As Melbourne presented this second idea, he deliberately gestured with both hands cupped towards his chest.

After the chuckles hushed, he pronounced the third name without suggesting that it would be the best choice. *Pride*. He said it again. *Pride*—of Baltimore. The city council fell over itself rushing to endorse this third name. The *Pride of Baltimore*, they called it.

"No, no," corrected Melbourne. The city of origin is always subordinate to the ship's name. When cut into the transom, the wording should read "Pride," then underneath that, "Baltimore." To have it read "Pride of Baltimore" and then "Baltimore" was redundant. Awkward. Dumb.

But the city wouldn't have it. After all, this wasn't just a boat. It was a marketing ploy. The longer name stuck.

Melbourne returned to the job site with a wry grin. "All right. We're building the *Pride of Baltimore*. Here we go." ✴

---

* At the end of her act, transported by ecstasy, she would fling herself onto the couch, which was rigged to appear to burst into flame.

Inner Harbor Baltimore | 1976

"I didn't make any money, but I was happy to get the job. Later, Wooden Boat *magazine called me 'the father of the industry.'"*

— MELBOURNE SMITH

THE TEN MONTHS it took to make *Pride of Baltimore* seaworthy included summer days as thick and hot as chowder, then a winter that people claimed was one of the coldest ever for Baltimore—not winter with arctic blasts of the sort that might cause Hollywood actors to wrap an arm around the mainmast and rattle a fist at the abusive forces of destiny. No, it was just damn cold. Every day a leaden sky. Every morning, clean the snow and ice off the deck, shake the stiffness out of your dirty jeans and return to the shoreline work site, maybe catch a few moments by the red fire of the forge, smoke a cigarette, joke and gripe, then get to work in a black-and-white world of ship carpentry.

The joining of timbers was done not with through-bolts or drifts but authentically, with trunnels. The antique and proper spelling of trunnel is "treenail," for obvious reasons. These were wooden dowels that had to be driven into holes drilled with a brace-and-bit. The trunnels, made from a local hardwood called locust, had the diameter of one inch. The prepared holes were deliberately fifteen-sixteenths in diameter. So the driving-in of trunnels was a torture of tension, often further tightened by the driving of hardwood wedges into the flush ends. (In practice, Melbourne found that a fifteen-sixteenth diameter wood bit was hard to come by. So he adopted a simple variation on the authentic practice: bore the hole with a common one-inch diameter drill bit, and have the locust trunnel diameter made one-sixteenth oversize.) The advantage of this pre-industrial technology over metal hardware is that wooden pegs swell when wet, further tightening their grip on the ship's timbers. Also, trunnels can be simply drilled out again if need be, not extracted with difficulty.

The naval architect for the project delighted almost as much as Melbourne in such "authenticities." The task ahead, as Gillmer read it, was to create "an authentic example of an historic Baltimore clipper in detail and possibly even in method of construction."

When giving sworn testimony a decade later, after the fate of *Pride of Baltimore* had played out, Gillmer itemized some of the gear that had been "forged on site in the ship smithy at the end of the building shed—rudder irons (pintles and gudgeons), trunnion straps and eyes for the six-pounders [*Pride* was equipped with four cannon and two martinets or swivel guns], rigging eyes and hooks, deadeye straps and chains and channel bolts down to the drifts for keel and deadwood and stern knees." The very process of construction was faithfully correct. "The eight-inch-sided and sistered frames were erected on the rough platen by fastening the futtocks with twelve-inch-long locust trunnels.... There were no cranes or gantries to lift the timber or frames to location. Sheer legs and roller ways were used to move these parts. The scaffold surrounding the hull as it grew was the simple pole plank structure universally familiar in old nineteenth-century building yards."

Because this vessel was never intended to impersonate a specific former historical vessel, only to represent the genus "Baltimore clipper," Gillmer was free to make some design choices. He went for an "extreme" vessel of the sort being manufactured near the end of the War of 1812—built for high-speed exploits and dashing escapes, so vastly topped with spars and sail that a reasonable sailor felt nervous just looking at her. After the Treaty of Ghent ended that war, Baltimore clippers adapted to peacetime activities such as hauling trade goods, so they became pudgier, slower, and safer. Gillmer favored the most archeologically intriguing kind of replica.

And yet "replica," even in this case, is a misleading term. As we shall see, in a concession to practicality, *Pride of Baltimore* was given a diesel engine and a propeller. She had navigational equipment (VHF radio/telephone, fathometer, hygrometer, clock), and a bilge pump that could be used for fire-fighting, as well as (fortunately) two six-person rubber life rafts and twelve personal flotation devices. Her galley possessed a traditional brick oven but also the rather more convenient three-burner kerosene type stove mounted on gimbals. Therefore, to be exact in diction, *Pride* was a re-creation not a replica.

From this point on, any new project of nautical archeology had to decide on the degree of its replication daring. Can Dacron replace proper cotton and flax sails? (Melbourne fitted *Pride* with the latter; others replaced those sails with the former.) Should the compass be the old dry-card type in a wooden bowl? Oil lamps conserve battery power—dare we go electric?

Compromise happens.

Nevertheless: with the building of *Pride of Baltimore*, a rigorous combination of authenticities—not only in design but also in tools and historically accurate construction methods—became the new controlling idea in every attempt to reincarnate the five-hundred-year-old heritage of handcrafted, pelagic sailing ships.

B EFORE any of this work could begin, Melbourne had to find the right wood. Without hesitation he went back to Belize.

That was another compromise with historical fact—going south to harvest tropical hardwoods. Baltimore clippers of yore were built with timbers pulled out the abundant North American forests of the area, often green wood. In the heyday, American shipyards would turn out their products so quickly and in such abundance that sometimes longevity was sacrificed. Two or three years of use often sufficed.

For example, the naval vessel *America* was still under construction when the Revolutionary War finally ended, and Congress, strapped for cash, opted to end the expensive construction project by giving the ship—little more than a hull—to the French. Three years later the French discovered that the vessel was riddled with dry rot, and they condemned her to be broken up. The official report stated, "This examination proves that the timber of North America can be of no use for ship construction, except perhaps for the highest parts of the superstructure." They were wrong of course, but unscrupulous builders who failed to dry timbers properly were at fault.

Such shenanigans would not do for *Pride of Baltimore*. Melbourne's decision: one can still be authentic without repeating mistakes.

Melbourne had learned the strength and durability of Belizean resources and knew he could get them cheaply, and that they were rot-resistant in marine environs. His access to hardwoods meant that the *Pride of Baltimore* had the potential to outlast any of its historic predecessors. He brought in

When USCG Bark *Eagle* needed a new compass and binnacle, the Coast Guard hired Melbourne to solve the problem. He did this as a side job during construction of *Pride of Baltimore*.

bulletwood—granadillo—for keels, sternpost, and lower futtocks, which have to be the toughest timbers in the vessel. And he brought a wood called Santa Maria for the ship's frames, and hard pine for planking and decking.

He was able to walk into the Belizean forest, point to a tree, and tell his woodcutters, "That one. That's our keel."

He watched the woodcutters fell the tree, strip it, and drag its beautiful timber up to the jeep road, set it on the roadside for tomorrow when they would return with a suitable flatbed truck. Then Melbourne and his cohorts went off to celebrate their feat with the aid of some one-barry rum.

That afternoon, feeling rather celebratory, Melbourne drove himself back up the jeep road to admire his capture and envision the sixty-foot keel it would become. When he got to the place, his eyes began an irresolvable quarrel with his brain. Someone had come along and chain-sawed the magnificent stick into eight-foot lengths.

It took a few minutes for the shock to wear off. Then Melbourne realized—this wasn't sabotage. Some stranger had tried to help. Most of the woodcutters in this forest were cutting railroad ties, eight-foot lengths that were then squared with adzes and hatchets. No doubt, a woodsman on his way home noticed a felled trunk that hadn't been bucked into chunks. Who knows, he could have been a line boss. Maybe tomorrow he would try to find a fellow to chew out for not getting the job done.

Around this same time, Melbourne found a sawmill operator who was willing to rip his logs into timbers and planks, but the fellow announced that in order to do the work he would need a new sawblade. The blade would have to be shipped from Florida. Melbourne took care of that. Then, pressured by developments at the Inner Harbor job site, Melbourne deposited his complete acquisition of Belizean hardwood with the sawyer and returned to Baltimore, where the shipyard was coming together and Mayor Schaefer was eager to make an official visit.

Two weeks later he went back to Belize and discovered that the sawmill fellow had gone away. So had the results of his work. The lumber had been shipped, but Melbourne didn't know quite where.

Eventually Melbourne found his timbers in a transshipment warehouse in Mobile, Alabama. The metal strapping had all rusted and failed, so the wood was scattered here and there. The materials finally arrived at the Inner Harbor site Sunday morning in late May the year of the bicentennial—nine truckloads of seven thousand board feet each.

The entire cost was less than a dollar a board foot, the sum of twelve cents a foot for the cutting and sixty cents a foot for the shipping. The lead truckdriver of the delivery caravan was irked because they'd been searching for the site since four a.m. he said, and now he wanted a certified check. It was nine-thirty on a Sunday morning.

Melbourne had a forklift ready to unload his timbers, and the forklift quickly bogged in the wet earth. They were off and running now!

FRED HECKLINGER said later, "To head up a program like this takes a very able person, and I'm not that. While we were working, Melbourne organized the finances and paid his people.

"Our site in Baltimore had very little heavy equipment. The bandsaw was not big enough, but we used it anyway. The blacksmith came in and set up his shop. We built benches, an open-sided building, a shed for tools, and we just did it. I've been involved in several projects over the years, where people will say you can't to that. Yes you can. How do you do it? Well, you just do it."

Melbourne gathered a select group of hand-tool extremists committed to ten-hour workdays for the ten months it took to get the hull floating. The term "committed" may be too general. There were three master shipwrights from Belize—Simeon Young, his son Joseph, and Aquilio Sandoval. Joseph left after a few days, frustrated because his wife was not available to cook his lunch. Simeon and the others tended to disappear now and then into the less respectable districts of downtown Baltimore.

When Simeon Young left permanently, Melbourne found Japeth Hazell, a shipbuilder from Bequia in the West Indies. Jay proved to be a master shipwright, and he continued working with Melbourne on other vessels.

Gerry Trobridge served as the master shipsmith and resident father-figure. There were four carpenters, three riggers, two caulkers, a few apprentices, and several boys, also a bookkeeper—fewer than two dozen workers total, including the comers-and-goers.

The bookkeeper was a kind and twinkly-eyed gent, a retired banker, who stopped by to ask if he could somehow be of assistance. His name was Jerome Batzer, or Jerry, and he hadn't a drop of saltwater in his veins. But he had wonderfully legible penmanship and a skilled public demeanor. So Melbourne wisely installed him as gatekeeper—the social interface—and a keeper of the daily records entered in the shipyard's log. Melbourne also employed Mr. Batzer to go hunting after Simeon Young, who would sometimes start at dawn with a cognac and coffee then disappear for days into the fleshpots of Baltimore, in the end claiming that he'd been somehow shanghaied and taken to foreign lands. Sadly, Jerry Batzer is no longer alive to recount some of his ventures in pursuit of the skilled but rather geographically confused Belizean. The headline of his much later obituary in the *Baltimore Sun* identified him above all as one who had helped build *Pride*—that's how much this single escapade had meant to him in the long course of his otherwise unadventurous life.

Hecklinger remembered the shipyard mood this way: "The Central Americans didn't get along with the younger boys. But they were always busy. We didn't have them working side-by-side. I thought the attitude of the younger fellows was remarkable. They all respected Gerry Trobridge. And they all knew they wouldn't be there that long. There was little money in it, but we knew that after a year or so we would have accomplished something. And gone on from there."

The pace gradually increased till it became relentless. "We worked seven days a week," said Melbourne. "Took Christmas and New Year's off." Everyone who worked was paid. No volunteers. "The problem with volunteers, they're not reliable and you can't fire them. Also, they want to do the *nice* things. The volunteer says, 'I'll paint that!' Then he takes the credit for it."

Circumnavigator and blacksmith Gerry Trobridge.

Sometimes they gave wood to visitors who offered to turn some belaying pins on their home lathes. Sometimes these visitors actually did what they said they would do.

"Reenactors" were hustled bodily off the premises.

FOR THIS shipbuilding crew, indeed for anyone who knew him, the character who most embodied the pre-industrial sailing era was Gerry Trobridge. "He set up his blacksmith's forge right on the building site," Melbourne recalled. "Gerry was a big, strong fellow who had a constant can of scorching hot tea on the fire. He had a white beard and always wore a pair of pince-nez glasses." The crew's gripes and grumbles went mute in his presence, partly because Gerry Trobridge's fundamental kindness acted as an emotional fire extinguisher. More significantly, he embodied the sailing life and the zeal that sustained the *Pride of Baltimore* campaign—a zeal much brighter than the city's official desire to bring more tourists to the Inner Harbor.

That zeal had compelled Trobridge to make the irrational decision to go to sea in the first place, despite the fact that he was born and raised in Johannesburg, South Africa, several hundred miles from saltwater. It was there he built a thirty-six-foot, steel-hulled ketch called *White Seal*, the ship that made him the first South African to circumnavigate the globe. He was as odd in this regard as Melbourne Smith—born under the spell that called him from the security of land to the wild promises of the open blue.

Even as a boy, Gerry Trobridge had such notions, claiming that someday he would sail away to an uninhabited island. Bedtime storybooks infiltrated his imagination. For example, Rudyard Kipling's *Jungle Book* tale "The White Seal" planted an image in his mind. In the story an odd child (a seal with white fur, not gray like the others) discovers that his uniqueness is his salvation as hunters slaughter the gray majority. Grown-up Gerry kept that story in his heart. When he went to serve in the Second World War, he carried with him the plans for the boat he would someday build, a boat that would let him circumnavigate the earth.

He had already dropped out of high school during the 1930s—his father's unemployment during the Great Depression forced that decision—and apprenticed as a blacksmith. When war erupted, he joined the South African infantry and fought in North Africa with the Rand Light Infantry. After the German/Italian front in North Africa collapsed, Trobridge enlisted in the British army and served in Italy. He ended the war with the rank of sergeant major.

He went back home and bought the lot next door to his parents, poured a concrete slab fifteen feet by forty feet, and enrolled in a correspondence course to learn the basics of boatbuilding. The vessel he had been imagining throughout the war was a variation of plans he'd purchased from a renowned Florida sailboat designer named John G. Hanna, a popular design called the Tahiti ketch. But Trobridge, being a metalworker, envisioned a hull of steel, not wood. He sent his revised plans to Hanna, who approved them. He also got a thumb's up from one of the leading U.S. designers of steel ships, J. Murray Watts. The actual construction of the ship stretched out over six years during which Trobridge must have seemed quite eccentric in the neighborhood, a next-door Noah building his Ark on weekends. When he fell and damaged his back, he used the downtime to learn celestial navigation. When he broke his arm later, he kept on building what he could with the other.

When the time came, he christened her *White Seal*. Then he and some buddies got the thirty-six-foot hull onto a lo-boy trailer and hauled it to Durban Bay. By 1952 or 1953 (reports vary) the ketch was rigged and seaworthy. So with four friends Gerry Trobridge, a man who had never sailed before, set out to sail the planet. For the next six years and nine months, with crew coming and going, and with necessary stops ashore to pick up temporary employment,

Trobridge wandered the world looking for the right place to live.

In 1957, while *White Seal* cruised the Great Lakes, he met and married a physical therapist named Marie Hickey. Years later Marie said, "It was either marry the man and his boat, or nothing." She chose the former.

That same winter, having nonchalantly navigated the Mississippi River into the Gulf of Mexico, the newlyweds wandered into disaster. At that point, the two of them were the ship's entire crew. A "Blue Norther" descended upon them, delivering forty-foot waves without pause for thirty-two hours. "We lashed ourselves on deck and rode it out," Marie recalled. Once that storm had spent itself, two others followed in short order. It was a hellish introduction to nautical living, but it also taught Marie something quite comforting—her husband Gerry certainly knew how to build things. *White Seal* with her tight steel hull outrode the wildest blasts.

In his 1974 book *The Navigators: Small Boat Voyagers of Modern Times* Donald Holm wrote: "*White Seal* proved to be a superb sea boat, easy to handle, dry and comfortable of motion, roomy, and able to carry astonishing stores of food and supplies, as much as six months' supply for four people. She was fairly fast up to seven or eight knots under the best of conditions (but carried an enormous cloud of sail, almost 1,200 square feet with everything flying). She was a gentle lady in a following sea, or hove-to, or even lying at anchor in a breeze. The mild steel used in the hull was of South African manufacture and proved to be completely practical and immensely strong in the face of sometimes crashing seas and occasional groundings. There was little difficulty with rust and corrosion, the only protection ever given the hull being paint and zinc sacrificial plates."

Seagoing trauma, though, did put some wear and tear on the new marital relationship. They needed to hide out and recuperate for a while, for three months as it developed, first in Grand Cayman for nine days, then after a quick six-hundred-mile crossing, in Panama. By the time they left shore again, Marie was pregnant. They came to an agreement: what's the point of being married if you only socialize while passing in the hatchway while changing watches? Gerry rigged *White Seal* so that she could steer herself. From then on whenever they could, they lay ahull at night, or let the ship tend herself, and went to bed together.

Their daughter Tracy was born in Brisbane, Australia, October 1958, and Trobridge found work there for nine months of life transition. Then they went back to sea with a baby and massive cartons of disposable diapers.

The shipbuilder/captain's erratic circumnavigation concluded November 24, 1959, in Durban Harbor at midnight.

But Trobridge couldn't stand being home. He despised the apartheid system, and as he put it, "the police state that is modeled on Nazi Germany." They went to sea again in 1963, now with a second child, a boy, Tom.[*] Soon after, they selected the U.S. as their haven. Trobridge settled with his family in Annapolis.

His landing there coincided almost exactly with the arrival in Annapolis of that fugitive from Guatemala, Melbourne Smith. Melbourne takes the story from here:

"I met Gerry Trobridge and his family when they visited Annapolis in *White Seal*. He got my number from Jack Higgins while in New York City. We were all members of the Slocum Society[†] and therefore bound to help each other. They had tied up in Smitty's Boatyard on Back Creek, a beat-up yard with rickety jetties, questionable electricity, old boats, but great characters. Gerry asked if I might know where he might find work, and I suggested Trumpy's Yachtyard on Spa Creek. He got a job immediately and worked there as metalworker.

"Gerry could make anything out of metal, and he became a most valuable employee until the company closed its doors many years later. When I built *Appledore,* Gerry made all the metal fittings that I took down to Belize City. His workmanship was beautiful and none of his fittings ever failed in service."

After *Pride of Baltimore* was successfully launched, Gerry went aboard as crew. "It was a great scene, departing Baltimore in the bitter cold. Gerry took his morning shower on deck in the nude. Then he rigged a roll of toilet paper in the shrouds and propped his bum overboard. Before retiring, he asked if anyone else would like to use the 'facilities.' Getting no takers, he quietly unstrung the toilet paper and took it below. He was a joy to sail with.

---

[*] Tom and his sister Tracy spent their childhoods living on *White Seal*. Tom later helped his father build *Pride of Baltimore*. He was a huge and strong lad, liked by all. At the building site, if a particularly large beam had to be hoisted, Dad would put four or five men at one end of the beam then say, "Tom, get the other." And he would.

[†] The Joshua Slocum Society International (JSSI) was formed in 1955 "to record, encourage, and support long distance passages in small boats." The namesake and patron saint of the society was a Nova Scotian who in 1895, at age fifty-one, departed Boston in his tiny sloop *Spray* and sailed around the world single-handed, a passage of forty-six thousand miles. The society was disbanded July 2011.

White Seal took Gerry Trobridge around the world.

One novice crew member once asked his advice about whether he should vomit or hold it back when he felt sick. Gerry thundered back that he would know exactly what to do when the time came!"

From this point on Gerry Trobridge was a fixture on as many of Melbourne's epic ship re-creations as possible. "We were fast friends all his life. He later sold his boat, bought a farm for his family, and purchased an old camping van for himself. After his wife died, he toured America, Mexico, Alaska, and Canada on both coasts several times with his small Belgian barge dog. He kept a log of his travels and sent me a copy every month."

Fred Hecklinger made the nameboard for the camper—its name was *Confidence*—and Melbourne added gold leafing. Trobridge mounted it on the stern of the camper and adventured with it up to the age of ninety, when he had to give up driving. At that point he became a volunteer guide on board the U.S.S. *Constellation*, docked in Baltimore's Inner Harbor.

He died from complications of a stroke in 2009 at the age of ninety-four. The official death notice in the *Baltimore Sun* newspaper read: "in lieu of flowers memorial donations may be made to *Pride of Baltimore*."

Said Melbourne: "They don't come any better than Gerry, and his many friends and shipmates will tell you the same."

T RUSTING in Hecklinger and the other key builders, Melbourne was free to endure necessary but long hours in meetings and city offices. He dealt with delays in money disbursement. In fact, he took out bank loans in order to pay his crew as promised. He knew that he had to keep the momentum of the work going nonstop. If the pace slackened, some of his workers would start drifting away and the very plot-line of the story would start to collapse. He had to defend his decisions before administrators who didn't know a hull from a hole in the ground. He had to adapt to bright ideas generated by committee. He began to feel that certain administrators were his principal impediments—that if things went smoothly with the project, somehow they would have failed.

One illustration of city dealings: the matter of an engine. *Pride* was designed without an engine. In a Baltimore clipper, of course, an engine would not be authentic. However, midway through construction, city officials decided that *Pride* would need an engine and a propulsion system installed. They voted to allocate another fifty thousand dollars to that end.

That sum was less than enough for Melbourne to install a cheap little diesel Jimmy, but he was determined to fulfill all his agreements.

One day a well-dressed fellow came to the shipyard and asked Melbourne, "Why don't you put a Caterpillar in?"

"Costs too much."

The stranger tipped his business card. "I represent the Caterpillar Company," he said. "Suppose I give you a Caterpillar engine for the same price."

"Why."

"All I want is a picture of it."

"You have a deal."

But officials of the city objected. "I don't know," they said. "The contract says something different. There's something fishy about this." They even asked, "How much are you making on the side by putting in a different engine?" They went to work investigating this possible threat to the wellbeing of the City of Baltimore. Only after they had compiled sufficient evidence of their exertions did they sign the papers.

Later, many of these officials remembered Melbourne Smith as being something of a grouch.

"W E LAID the keel in spring of 1976," recalled Fred Hecklinger. "We launched in '77. We were sailing by late spring."

Congresswoman Barbara Mikulski performed the launching ceremonies on February 27, 1977, ten months after the start of the project and eight-and-a-half months after the keel was laid. A huge crane owned by the Bethlehem Steel Company lifted the caulked and painted hull from its shipyard and swung it into the Inner Harbor at 2:47 pm. According to the log kept by Jerry Batzer, Mayor William Donald Schaefer told a shivering crowd of ten thousand onlookers, "During the years and months ahead, *Pride of Baltimore* will be a goodwill ambassador... a tribute to its port, its shipbuilding industry, the magnificent redevelopment of our city, and the sense of determination of all Baltimoreans to preserve the important traditions of the past."

She was floating but not finished. The crew went immediately to work loading ballast into the ship's hull. Masts were stepped the next day, and the riggers went above to rig shrouds and forestays. On St. Patrick's Day they were fitting the engine. On March 29, wrote Batzer, they "raised the foresail for the first time and painted the cabin trunk a cream color." On April 1 he wrote, "The City of Baltimore accepted the ship from the builder today with only a small amount withheld from the final payment for unfinished work, mainly the finishing of the cabin." The Mayor held a press conference at the site, then one month later, on May 1 he staged another ceremony, this time proclaiming "I, William Donald Schaefer, Mayor of the City of Baltimore, do hereby officially commission the ship *Pride of Baltimore* and call upon her and her crew to represent Baltimore and its citizens. Godspeed and may your voyage be a safe and prosperous one."

She then began her maiden voyage under the command of Captain Melbourne Smith. During the next nine years, *Pride* traveled over one hundred and fifty thousand nautical miles.

"WE HAD a great launching," said Melbourne, "a band, a congresswoman breaking a bottle of champagne on her. Then I asked to take her to Bermuda.

"They said, 'Well, we paid a lot of money for that ship. We really want to keep her here in Baltimore.'

"I countered, 'Put it this way—if you let me take it to Bermuda, they'll know it's a real boat that can really sail.' I shamed them into letting me take it to Bermuda."

Once he got that concession from the city, he kept pushing. "Can I take it to Halifax, too?"

After visiting Bermuda and Halifax, Captain Smith stopped at Boston, Newport, Mystic, New London, New York, Philadelphia, and Norfolk. "We had great receptions, keys to the city, an official visit almost everywhere we went." The mayor's office in New York City put up a hand-lettered sign "welcome to the city." He brought back a plaque from Philadelphia Mayor Frank Rizzo, an engraved silver platter from the Mystic Museum in Connecticut, and an "Old Spice Smart Ship Award" from New York.

"For Baltimore it was like sending a movie star to represent the city. When I got back, the first thing they said was, 'When can you go back out again?'"

MELBOURNE's contract to operate *Pride* lasted one year, and that was enough for him. It wasn't the sailing that brought him down. It was the city. The city presented him with a boss, a woman named Gale Shawe. She was a member of the Board of Directors of Baltimore OPSAIL, a committee established in 1975 to ensure that the Bicentennial celebrations would feature traditional "tallships." In 1980 she would be installed as executive director of Pride of Baltimore, Inc., a corporation charged with the duty to keep *Pride* afloat and on course. Her expertise (Melbourne felt) was more in the direction of marketing than seamanship. In his mind, she had come out of nowhere. During the maiden voyage, as *Pride* was sailing to Boston, he received orders to arrive at Constitution Pier at eleven a.m. on a given day and to arrive with all sails set. A big crowd would be waiting, along with the press. To arrive at a given hour is much easier for a commuter train than a sailing schooner. And the trim of the sails, of course, must depend on wind and weather. Nevertheless, Melbourne fulfilled his orders by laying overnight in the Provincetown bight, then sailing at midnight while carefully controlling the approach to Boston.

When they arrived, only a handful of workmen were waiting for them.

A similar embarrassment occurred at Washington D.C. because Ms. Shawe forgot to mail out the invitations.

The dealbreaker for Melbourne came with *Pride's* return from her triumphant first outing. "My budget for the year was a hundred thousand dollars, something like that. I planned to save twenty-five thousand of that in order to have her hauled out at the end of year, which I did. She needed painting and maintenance work."

But when the time came to haul out, Ms. Shawe stopped Melbourne.

"She said, 'There's no money to do that.' I said, 'Yes, there is,' and I showed her my figures. She answered, 'But you don't have my salary in there.'

"She was getting forty grand a year!"

As Melbourne said this, he shook his head as though trying to get an earwig out of his hair. "That's when I quit. The fun was over."

H‍ECKLINGER later said, "This *Pride* has been much criticized by people who didn't do it themselves. This was a unique program. Melbourne had not built a vessel of this type. When problems would mount up—the city or the weather, delivery failures, or the electricity at the site would fail, he was the one who had to lead the way out of it. He'd get testy, of course, everybody does in a situation like this. Some people in the city thought he was a terrible person. But I and several people I respect have made the observation that he can be considered a genius. His abilities are far-reaching—his ability to paint and write, naval architecture, the mathematics involved—and his drawings are beautiful. Very few people do this anymore. He is an artist. Compared to a trained naval architect, Melbourne's [ships] are just prettier to look at.

"That type of mathematics doesn't come easily to me, nor to most people. But it does come to Melbourne. He's read multiple books about it and done his homework. He has a good understandingj151

of layouts, the movement of people, and engineering. He can converse on many topics. And then he'll sit down and play honky-tonk piano."

In *Pride's* promotional booklet Gillmer is quoted thus: "I continually appreciate Melbourne's ability to understand the complexities of naval design. He is the only one I know who could undertake a project of this size, and carry it off. He is a true shipbuilder."

The relationship would not remain so cordial. ✶

Three Days North of Puerto Rico
1986

"Building a boat is like having a daughter.
Once she's on her own, you can't manage her any more.
If you try to keep track of her afterward, you only get upset."

— MELBOURNE SMITH

*P*RIDE OF BALTIMORE sailed on without its builder and first skipper. This separation caused no hesitation for Melbourne, whose inner fire for this kind of work was growing hotter. The greatest projects of his life were jostling for priority. He had more ideas than the slow machinery of social agreement could quite absorb. His third and greatest phase was rapidly seizing his attention. It can be difficult to look back under the force of such momentum.

But the full story of *Pride* cannot be left untold, even though the telling needs to skip ahead nearly a decade. It would be best to tell it now, then return to Melbourne's evolution. For the fate of *Pride* played out at some distance from his later occupations. This fate altered the lives of twelve mariners, shocked the City of Baltimore, and raised serious questions about the ethics of re-animating the windships of yore. For Melbourne it was a reminder of what he had already experienced—the terrible beauty of life and death under the forces of sea and sail.

*A*FTER MELBOURNE relinquished his command, Peter Boudreau, a charismatic lad in his early twenties, became *Pride's* second skipper. Boudreau had come to Baltimore not long after graduating high school, stumbled upon the little shoreline shipyard, and talked his way into a place on the work crew. His duties started with a broom. "I had no skills," he recalled in a 1996 interview with *The Baltimore Sun*. "I could hammer nails and push a plane." But he came from nautical origins on the Caribbean island of Santa Lucia. At Marigot Bay his father had created a thriving charter cruise business. His mother operated a small hotel there. Upon graduating, Boudreau used his nautical skills to find farther shores. He crewed and skippered "school" ships for survival-training programs such as Outward Bound. In Baltimore the sight of *Pride* under construction excited him in a fundamental way—ship construction interested him far more than open-water voyaging. "I took whatever they would give me, which was shoveling wood chips. I never even thought about things like getting to and from work, buying groceries, getting a place to live, needing clothes! I had a pair of shorts, flip-flops, and shades. It was an amazing experience. Actually building a boat was a brand new challenge. It was a learning thing for me, because I didn't have any real skills to bring to it, just brawn and a willingness to work hard. And we did work hard."

After the launch of *Pride,* he stayed with the ship as crewmember, then was tapped for skipper. For the next two years Boudreau and relief captain Fred Hecklinger sailed *Pride* into an A-list of sparkling ports—San Juan, St. Thomas, Caracas, Aruba, Grand Cayman, Houston, New Orleans, Tampa, Havana, Miami, Savannah, Charleston, and Wilmington North Carolina. Between runs the ship was constantly under revision. Naval architect Gillmer was busy with design changes, most of which further reduced authenticity, including changes that made sailors' lives easier (bunks, an upgraded galley). He also compensated for design flaws inherent in the historic model. In spring of 1979 the ship ran aground off Delaware, her radio knocked out with the loss of a masttop antenna.

Despite such problems *Pride* was pushed into ever more adventurous voyages of goodwill public relations. In 1981, under command of a later skipper, Jan Miles of Annapolis, she traversed the entire Great Lakes region, provoking festivals and mock sea battles in places such as Chicago, Detroit, Milwaukee, Cleveland, and Toronto. The mission control group back in Baltimore became more ambitious. At Christmastime in 1982 *Pride* became the first Baltimore clipper to pass through the Panama Canal, after which she made a mostly triumphal procession up and down the American West Coast. Upon her return she laid up in Baltimore Harbor for six months of maintenance and repair.

Pride of Baltimore **hard on the wind in the Straits of Florida.**

Her deck planking had to be replaced to recover from a design error by Gillmer. Melbourne reflected later: "Gilmer said to butt the fore and aft decks on a midship beam with a cross plank between to delineate between the maindeck and the quarterdeck. He argued that the waterways and carlins were sufficiently strong to maintain deck integrity in the vicinity of the line of butts athwartships. After several years he was proven wrong, as the cross seam began opening." Then in a manner most Melbournean he added, "The fault was not really Tom's, but rather my own for not refusing his directive."

For more than a year *Pride* loitered close to home, hosting corporate receptions, joining nearby gatherings of historic "tall ships," and flaunting her image on Chesapeake Bay for the three hundred fiftieth anniversary of the settlement of Maryland. Then Mayor Schaefer announced his most ambitious saltwater marketing scheme yet. At the end of March 1984, *Pride* would commence a twenty-month voyage taking her to twenty-eight European ports, during which she would log more than twenty thousand nautical miles. Captain duties would be traded between Jan Miles and New England native Armin Elsaessar. Thirty-one crewmembers (a couple of them women) would be rotated regularly.

On August 11, 1985, a mishap occurred in the Baltic that was not widely reported. A mishandling of sails in a brisk wind exposed the ship to the full force of a deck-sweeping wave. Seven crewmembers had to grab for their lives. Five succeeded. One deckhand flushed into the sea but managed to grab some sheets trailing on the water. The cook, Sarah Fox, disappeared astern. She was recovered with the help of the first mate, who climbed the rigging, spotted her with binoculars, then deployed the Dunlop inflatable. Evidently, Captain Elsaessar was as stunned as anyone.

This horrifying incident was just a harbinger.

ON MARCH 11, 1986, Captain Elsaessar took on six new crewmembers who had flown to Malaga, Spain, from Baltimore. Then the full complement—a dozen mariners, most of whom had little experience with vessels as demanding as *Pride*—set off to cross the Atlantic headed home. It was a voyage marred by sloppy shiphandling, but they reached the Caribbean safely.

On 9 May Captain Elsaessar made a phone call from St. Thomas that was broadcast on radio station WFBR in Baltimore. He made the friendly comment that the voyage's last leg, the familiar twelve-hundred-mile sail back to Chesapeake, was about to begin. He closed with the sentence, "I'll be home soon." That was his last message to the outside world.

On the morning of 14 May, after a day of good sailing, *Pride* was beset by rough weather and a mess of little squalls. During a bout of confused handling with Elsaessar at the helm, the ship was struck by what one meteorologist later identified as a "microburst." To the horror of all twelve people aboard, *Pride* was knocked down, her masts floating like sticks on the surface of the boundless ocean and her starboard beam now jutting straight into the stormy sky. And sinking. This was a freak occurrence, as quick as an auto collision. The wild blasts that had swatted her down dissipated almost immediately. As the inexperienced crew wrestled with faulty and tangled life rafts and safety gear, *Pride* performed as hoped by righting herself in the water. Problem was, she was under the water, not on top of it. Weirdly, the eight crewmembers now clinging to the one serviceable raft could see her down there, submerged, fully rigged, her emblematic flag, yellow and black, still flying from her topmast. Then she dropped into the abyss and was gone forever.

Three crewmembers were mortally injured during the mishap. Eight survivors, now climbing into a raft designed for six, vomiting, huddling in shock, saw Captain Elsaessar swimming away, about fifty yards off. They called to him, but he showed no sign of hearing their calls. Then he too was gone forever.

Though the desperate raft could have been sighted by several close-by cargo ships over the next few days, it wasn't till the fifth night of the ordeal, having drifted one hundred and forty miles on the open sea, that the survivors were rescued by a passing tanker. The 680-foot MV *Toro Horten*, of Norwegian registry, was bound for Venezuela. The fact that such a behemoth actually spotted the little raft, then turned in its own ponderous trajectory, was a stroke of rare luck. Ill, injured, emaciated, the survivors collapsed as soon as they hit the deck of the tanker. The Norwegians revived them with orange juice and Ritz crackers then put them into safe bunks. *Pride's* second mate Joseph McGeady tried calling his boss, Gail Shawe, using the tanker's radiotelephone, but Shawe's phone was out of order. So instead he called his uncle Eamonn McGeady, who was a member of the Pride of Baltimore, Inc.'s board of directors. The rest of the story is largely about public-relations damage control and a thorough Coast Guard inquiry.

OF COURSE, a portion of the post-disaster examination focused on the vessel's builder, Melbourne Smith. Twenty-five years after the inquiry Melbourne made the following summative observations:[*]

> "How did I find out about the sinking? I don't quite remember. Maybe on television. But even at the time I kind of understood why it happened. They were really not doing the right things—though I had no involvement with it any more.
>
> "*Pride* covered a hundred thousand miles, which was equal to

---

[*]Details of the disaster and subsequent investigations are fully reported in Evan Wilson's exhaustive study called *Epitaph for a Beautiful Ship*, self-published 2010.

four times around the world. Later they almost lost someone in the Baltic. You could have seen that something terrible was going to happen. There was never any oversight of the captains, and some captains just weren't very good. Boat operations need someone to give strong supervision—not the captain, but someone on shore.

"*Epitaph for a Beautiful Ship* puts the blame on Gail Shawe. She was still running the boat when it sank. When I was captain, she tried to put an inexperienced young guy on my crew. I sent him back home. I found there had to be twelve people on board and that every one had to be a good sailor. Your life depended on it. When they were lost, only three or four of the crew were good sailors. The others were dinghy sailors. Using bad judgment, Gail Shawe drove the ship into the ground.

"They had the big hearing. I testified. Everything came back on me. There were all kinds of speculations. One was that the ballast had shifted. But I knew the ballast [in *Pride*] could not shift. I had it locked in. All this speculation kind of made me mad. That's not what caused it! It finally came out that construction and design had nothing to do with it.

"They just didn't get around to understanding that a hatch had been left open. The squall only lasted a few minutes. *Pride* was knocked on her beam ends, mast in the water, then very quickly she righted herself perfectly upright, but sinking.

"The crew saw the squall coming. When weather like that comes, you have to take it on the nose, or else run off from it and take it on the stern. Running reduces the relative velocity of the wind. On the nose has its own advantages. But in this case the captain did neither. He let the sheets fly and sat dead flat to the sea. The storm hit them on the beam. Broadside. I had just received a card from him, how they had crossed the Atlantic, beautiful sail, full sail, never touched the sails for a week. Trade wind sailing is just beautiful. Once he reached Puerto Rico, though, he should have taken the top hamper down. Take all the weight down. Each time I went to Bermuda I always sent the topmast down. 'Sorry,' I always said. 'I'll put it up when we get there.'

"During the hearing Tom Gillmer said, 'That boat's strong

enough. That should never have happened.' He was implying that I had made an error in the building. But the risk of sailing such a demanding ship is inherent in its design.

"Tom Gillmer and I never spoke again.

"If the sliding hatch had been kept closed, the vessel would have never filled with water and sunk. It was as simple as that!"

IN 1851 author George Coggeshall (in *Voyages to Various Parts of the World made between 1802 and 1841*) wrote:

"These (clipper) schooners are built expressly for fast sailing, but require very skillful management and constant watchfulness; otherwise they are very dangerous. A captain only accustomed to sail a ship, is not always competent to manage one of these sharp and delicately-built schooners. They have often been compared to a racehorse with an unskillful rider, when commanded by a man unaccustomed to manage them. I do not mean to say a man thoroughly bred to the sea, and an able shipmaster, may not become a good schooner sailor, but I wish to be understood that it requires a great deal of practical experience to handle them properly in all climates, and all kinds of wind and weather."

ON October 21, 1986, the announcement was made in the Maryland Science Center in Baltimore that a new *Pride* would be built by Peter Boudreau, following a new design by naval architect Tom Gillmer.

To allay general fears of replica ships, Gillmer proclaimed, "She's not going to be authentic at all." The new ship would be heavier, longer, and beamier. She would have external ballast, higher freeboard, and watertight compartments. "She's going to be a Baltimore clipper visually." But the new *Pride* would qualify for a Coast Guard license to carry students and passengers.

Said Gail Shawe, "We decided that using Peter Boudreau would give us more control." Her implication: the younger builder would be more compliant than the increasingly opinionated Mr. Smith.

Melbourne shrugged it off. By then he had moved on to projects grander and, when possible, less encumbered by managerial interference. ✷

Skipjacks are built upside-down and need to be righted to be framed-out and decked.

Annapolis | 1978

"Shipbuilding is America's greatest pride in which she will, in time, excel the whole world."

—THOMAS PAINE
Common Sense | 1776

In 1978 *Pride of Baltimore* eased into Chesapeake Bay under the command of her second skipper, leaving her builder and maiden-voyage captain behind. Her wake left Melbourne standing alone in the lull of his own life story. He knew he would have to invent his next future. Now in his late forties, he probably felt more than he knew how much his life was changing.

For one thing, he would not go sailing again—not certainly in the spirit of *Annyah*-style, shoreless adventuring. What had his full attention now was not seafaring but the vessels themselves. He had become a shipmaker now, a completely self-educated expert in a field that no longer existed. What's worse, he had learned not to trust the plans of credentialed naval architects—their decisions often failed the test of use. He now suspected that he knew as much about historic sailing ship design—not the new, the advances in yacht technology, but the old ways, the gone technology—as just about anybody.

He was aware that he had pulled off a real coup—an audacious act of living history that could lead to an immensity of comparable projects. Now that Baltimore had her *Pride*, New York would want hers, and Massachusetts, California too, and so on. He couldn't have known for sure, but he must have felt the coming wave. Melbourne certainly wanted to top his own achievement by producing a masterwork, the greatest of all historic reincarnations—conceived, designed, and built by him—that would rip the hood of maritime amnesia from the American mind.

He was well situated now for success. He had earned U.S. citizenship, a requirement for registering as captain of *Pride of Baltimore*. And he'd created a company in order to manage the financial complexities of boatbuilding contracts, the temporary hires, and the acquisition of timber, rope, sailcloth, paint, and so on that any sailing vessel comprises. The International Historical Watercraft Society, he called it, incorporated 1975 as the *Pride* project was first beginning to clarify in the offing. The name derived from an exhibit he'd staged for his ship portraits—the International Historical Watercraft Collection. He changed the last word thinking of the French *Société* "not that it was a membership situation."

During this same period the Naval Institute in Annapolis occupied him with major tasks in book design. Melbourne's published projects from this period are beautiful works that combine a graceful sense of proportion with fanatical attention to minute detail. His treatment of *Junks & Sampans of the Yangtze River* by G.R.G. Worcester elevated obscure subject matter with precisely drawn schematics of Chinese craft, balanced by elegant applications of calligraphy and other traditions of Eastern imagery. Rare now, this artifact sells new for close to three hundred dollars.

Also, to his great personal satisfaction, Melbourne was hired to prepare a new edition of *Dutton's Navigation & Piloting*, the standard textbook of traditional navigation techniques first compiled by Benjamin Dutton in 1926. A much younger Melbourne had once struggled to learn this difficult text without the help of teacher or classroom, reading obscure passages over and over till they finally yielded their meaning to his driven brain. Some of its drawings or paragraphs had taken him a week to penetrate. That effort had enabled him to pass the Master's Exam in 1962. Now the Naval Institute wanted him to prepare the twelfth edition of *Dutton's*. Melbourne approached this challenge with a feeling of reverence, but also with the determination to clarify the text for the sake of anyone who "doesn't know the language." Essentially he intended: let no one suffer as I suffered. He created all new drawings for the book. Today *Dutton's* is in its fifteenth edition, and it still retains many of Melbourne's drawings.

"I made it like a bible," he recalled some three decades later. "I had great fun redesigning it, one of my pride-and-joys."

In short, during his post-*Pride* period Melbourne made a few big books (also, as we shall see, a couple of good-size boats). Coincidentally, it was a different book encounter at this time that pushed Melbourne's career into its next full acceleration—that is, the loan of a book or two, not a commission from the Naval Institute, just a simple life-altering surprise casually dropped by a bookish old-timer.

ERIC STEINLEIN continued to serve, whether he knew it or not, as Melbourne's mentor. "He became like my father," said Melbourne much later. "He was the greatest guy I ever met. I used to visit him all the time. Except he was kind of a grouch—I learned to avoid that part." The reclusive small-boat expert had previously created designs for the experimental Belizean cutter *Appledore*, and now Melbourne sat in Steinlein's small farmhouse talking with him about the history of American shipbuilding. It's not clear if the question actually arose, "What should I do now after *Pride of Baltimore*?" Nor will it be known if Steinlein decided to initiate Melbourne into the inner mysteries. Perhaps they were just swapping boat lore.

All we know is that Steinlein started talking about a certain other self-taught naval architect named John Willis Griffiths, who had done important work in New York during the mid-nineteenth century. "He was the first American to write about this country's shipbuilding practices. Otherwise, the entire tradition was illiterate," said Steinlein. "During the eighteen hundreds Americans invented ways to build sailing ships quicker, cheaper, and with less timber than anyone else, and these ships were the swiftest ever made. But without Griffiths, we'd just be guessing about what they were doing in those shipyards."

"Do you have any of his writing?" Melbourne asked.

Steinlein returned from a back room gripping two thick, old books. He set them on the coffee table. "Don't forget to bring them back," said the old man.

"Yes, sir."

Part One and Part Two of *The Progressive Ship Builder*, published in New York in 1875 by John W. Griffiths.

Melbourne opened the first and grabbed a few glimpses. One glimpse said, "The thinking man will discover that a system of proportions is needed, to which the *mechanic*, the *merchant*, the *mariner*, and the *underwriter*, can alike refer...."

"The thinking man," Melbourne said aloud.

"Nice phrase, isn't it?" said Steinlein. "That's Griffiths."

"'The *mechanic*?'"

"He means you. And he means himself. 'Mechanic' is an honorific. He doesn't mean just anybody who knows how to change a flat tire. He means someone who understands how all the parts fit together for optimal design and performance."

Melbourne read aloud: "'Chapter One—Different kinds of timber used in vessels, and in what parts; comparative strength, weight, season for cutting, modes of preservation and treatment.'"

"Very thorough. Thank God. He was the first and only. From the Revolutionary War onwards, and especially during the War of 1812, American shipbuilders broke all the rules while experimenting to create ships that were fast and daring. Speed and stealth were the only ways the U.S. could compete on the open seas against the European powers. For sixty years anyway the shipyards here and in New York, Boston, Philadelphia, Baltimore, they were all locked in a rivalry. They experimented and invented. But all their work was done by 'rule of thumb.' They wouldn't keep records. Here's the man who put it all on paper. He understood the science of it. You'll see."

"Long paragraphs."

"Super long."

"This one goes on more than a page."

"Hey, it was the nineteenth century. Dickens. Ralph Waldo Emerson. Trollope."

"Who?"

"I know ship designers who won't read this stuff. They complain that it's badly written."

Melbourne leafed through the pages. "The Bible's badly written, too," he remarked.

"Amen."

As Melbourne went to leave, books in hand, Steinlein handed him another. "You don't need to borrow this. Just read the dedication."

This next crackling tome, dated 1916, bore the gilt title *The Heritage of Tyre* by William Brown Meloney. Its dedication:

> To the memory of John Willis Griffiths, whose genius revolutionized the science of merchant shipbuilding and naval architecture and enthroned the United States as Mistress of the Seas. From his poet's brow the peerless American clipper leaped full blown to make a starred banner the talisman of the world's commerce. The

twin and triple-screw greyhounds of to-day are the posthumous children of his dreams. Ocean conqueror by sail and by steam, he sleeps as he died, unhonored and unsung—forgotten by a heedless people even as they have forgotten the sea heritage through which they achieved their national existence.

When he got the books home and bored into them, Melbourne had a revelation.
"Christ, now I see how it's done."
He never again built a ship that someone else had designed.

AROUND THIS TIME, the City of Baltimore, still glowing with the ardor to celebrate itself in historic watercraft, asked Melbourne to build a skipjack. To be more accurate, the City wanted a re-build of its mascot vessel the *Minnie V.*, which had been floating around for seventy years—an oyster-dredging boat.

Chesapeake Bay is the largest naturally occurring oyster bed in the United States. During the 1880s some fifteen million bushels of the meaty bivalves got lifted annually from Maryland waters. Today's harvests are less than one-tenth of that, thanks to pollution and overfishing. In an attempt to manage the resource, Maryland once forbade harvesting with powerboats and limited the industry to sail. (This restriction was eased in 1965.) The traditional oystering vessel, a unique regional workboat that's now represented by just a couple dozen working examples, continues to be the skipjack.

The skipjack is a single-masted boat of fifty feet or less in length. Usually it is sloop-rigged with a towering, triangular mainsail that sags down to a boom almost equal in length to the hull itself. The mast is dramatically raked—tipped back toward the stern—and a large headsail juts forward tacked to a long bowsprit. The hull, wooden of course, is beamy with a V-shaped bottom. Instead of a fixed keel cutting deep in the water, a skipjack comes with a centerboard that can be dropped or raised at the sailor's will. The bow is clipper-sharp, the stern square. The result is a small vessel—one person can handle it—with large baggy-looking sails and minimal penetration of the water, a good craft for maneuvering around shoreline waters in light winds. As formerly required by law, the skipjack is motorless, except for a power windlass to raise its scooped harvest. Now, little "pushboats" are employed to nudge the vessels in and out of the marinas.

Minnie V. sails *the* Potomac River.

Melbourne accepted the challenge of saving the city's mascot skipjack, *Minnie V.*, which had been first floated in 1908. But when he lifted the old gal out of the water, she hogged. That is, drooped at both ends. "Her back was broken." That was fine with Melbourne. In order to figure out how she was built, he was going to have to dismantle her anyway, measure every plank and scantling, precisely undo and analyze the process that had put her together in the first place. "I saved one piece of the rail so I could say, 'I rebuilt the old boat.'" Essentially he took it apart just the way he had stripped down that Model A Ford in his father's garage back in Hamilton.

For a bid of about one hundred thousand dollars, again working in the familiar harbor park but with a greatly reduced crew, Melbourne produced a new *Minnie V.* and launched it in 1980. By now, though, he had learned a few things about dealing with a big city bureaucracy, and he took some precautions.

For one thing, he asked Baltimore to okay the idea of his building two skipjacks at once, "one for myself on spec." He knew that committee squabblings, contract dickering, official timidity, and administrative buck-passing could easily—probably, predictably!—stall the process. He also knew that if a job shut down for more than a day or two, his workers would go away. Workers need work. So Melbourne decided that a second skipjack would give him a fall-back position when the city faltered.

The city said fine, and Melbourne found a buyer for the other skipjack right away.

This buyer was a new seafood pub in Annapolis called McGarvey's Saloon & Oyster Bar. When Melbourne began talking about the world-class novelty of an oyster bar that owned its own skipjack and harvested its own oysters, the owner bit the bait right away. He named the promised vessel after his grandmother—she would be the *Anna McGarvey*. Melbourne had a beautiful trailboard—the bright insignia that is mounted at the head of every skipjack— carved for him, and the restaurateur positioned the trailboard right over his bar. "That's the oyster boat I'm having built!"

MELBOURNE'S comment: "I was lucky that I had the second boat because, sure enough, the city stopped me about halfway through." The contract he'd signed specified "no sapwood" in the construction. Elsewhere it also demanded "no heartwood." No sapwood, no heartwood. That left nothing but bark and pith. Melbourne laughed about that silly error, but sure enough. "The city official came down and said, 'The contract says no heartwood!' I explained the error, and he said, 'I understand what you're saying, but that's not what the contract says. It says no sapwood no heartwood.' The guy knew this was absurd but he was helpless." Things would have to be suspended until the next committee meeting.

The skipjack is a simple construction, something that a skilled farmer could knock together working behind the barn. Melbourne built his skipjacks upside down in the traditional manner, bending one-inch loblolly pine planks over three molds. He secured the bottom planks in herringbone fashion about a sawblade's width apart. That way when the boat went into the water the first time, it would sink. At that point the planks would swell. A few days later he would pump out the hull and the craft would be water-tight. After he'd shaped the hull, Melbourne flipped the boat using a simple A-frame hoist that his trusty blacksmith Gerry Trobridge concocted, then he installed the frames. He used cheap paint on the hull bottom. That caused more friction with the City. Administrators wanted high quality paint. Melbourne insisted on cheap paint for the first six months so that water would seep into the hull planks and further tighten the craft. When the city refused to listen, Melbourne went on strike. "It was almost two months before they said, 'You were right.' Meanwhile I took the skipjack up a back creek and used her myself for a while. We—Fred Hecklinger and I—took her out racing and won every race. She was fast."

When pressed for more information about her speed, he just said, "I did some sneaky stuff in there." For example? "I made sure the bottom was the right shape." The role of the skipper was paramount, of course, in the performance of such a small craft. The new owner never did get the knack. "A skipjack is not easy to sail. It's a workboat. Different boats have different approaches, especially workboats."

In 1985, five years after Melbourne's successful constructions, despite piloting challenges, sapwood controversies, and the depletion of the oyster beds, the State of Maryland designated the endangered skipjack as its State Boat.

Today *Minnie V.* is part of the fleet of the Potomac Riverboat Company and is used for sightseeing and private charters. The company's website acknowledges that its historic skipjack was once re-built by a fellow they call "Lebourne Smith."

ALL THIS WHILE, Melbourne was deep in study of the writing of John Willis Griffiths. He grew increasingly fascinated with the documented designs for Griffiths's, and America's, fastest wind-driven ship, *Sea Witch*.

At the same time as if by coincidence—how could such a thing be coincidence?—the Naval Institute hired Melbourne to design the third edition of *Greyhounds of the Sea*, written by Mystic Seaport founder Carl C. Cutler and first published in 1930. Told with verve and elegance, *Greyhounds* presents an exhaustive study of the evolution of American clipper ships. It praises *Sea Witch* as the brightest of many stars. Melbourne's sensational design choices included a vivid jacket painted by the famous Richard Linton—depicting *Sea Witch* under full spread of sail on a shining sea—an inspiring new foreword by his friend Peter Stanford—founder of South Street Seaport and the National Maritime Historical Society—and an appendix of Carl Cutler's earlier work of *Five Hundred Sailing Records of American Built Ships*.

And somewhere about this time, Melbourne began to conceive the greatest project of his life. He intended to re-build *Sea Witch*. ✶

New York City | 1841

O to sail to sea in a ship!
To leave this steady unendurable land,
To leave the tiresome sameness of the streets, the sidewalks and the houses,
To leave you O you solid motionless land, and entering a ship,
To sail and sail and sail!

— WALT WHITMAN
A Song of Joys | 1860

IN 1841 the members of the American Institute of the City of New York for the Encouragement of Science and Invention gathered in a lecture hall* to hear a presentation by an obscure fellow, son of a Brooklyn shipwright, who claimed to have new, scientifically based ideas about the design of sailing ships. Although John Willis Griffiths had not yet made himself known by any particular innovation or notable achievement, he had published a series of articles in Virginia's *Portsmouth Advocate* that set forth many unconventional ideas about naval architecture. Unlike many in the audience he came with no academic credential. He was self-taught. He dressed in simple attire like a journeyman or a mechanic—no frock coat, no walking stick, no silken top hat. But the audience was aware that Griffiths, at the age of nineteen, a little over a decade earlier, had laid the lines for the U.S.S. *Macedonian*, a three-masted frigate built at Gosport Navy Yard. At the time of this speech, the *Macedonian* with its thirty-six guns was serving the nation (and its merchants) by hunting the Caribbean for pirates. Griffiths was employed as naval architect with the renowned Smith & Dimon, the

---

* We know that this event took place, but we have no record of the details. What follows here is a simulation of the probable.

shipyard at South Street, Manhattan, on the East River. So he merited a listen.

The audience included many businessmen hunting for the newest gadget to be turned to profit. These were heady days for investors. The young country had been at peace for a few decades now, and its boundaries were plastic—you could push them and they would stay pushed. Even here in New York, where the focus had always been toward the Atlantic and Europe, conversations kept turning toward developments in the West. Newspapers reported that a band of emigrants was preparing to leave the United States and cross the Missouri River with an orchestrated team of wagons, wagons covered with canvas, then work its way across the vast, wild continental interior to settle in the uncontrolled terrain called California.

The State of Illinois lay on the Western border. Just a few years prior, an Illinois blacksmith named John Deere had created a new sort of plow that he'd fashioned from steel. In general, you couldn't do much with steel. The difficulty of casting this slick metal limited its use to small, more precious items such as sawmill blades, which is exactly what Deere had repurposed to make his plow. People were saying that this shiny new plow was self-cleaning, that it could cut through the tough prairie clays with ease, and that John Deere was selling them as fast as he could make them.

Of course, no Midwest plowman could have attended the American Institute meeting in New York. But an inventor from Springfield, Massachusetts, was present, Charles Goodyear. He claimed that he had finally discovered a way to stabilize elastic gum into a lasting product, rubber, and he was in New York seeking financial backing. Poor fellow, he had bankrupted repeatedly in his mission. You could see suffering in his bearing, his proud posture, his hurt-looking eyes.

It is likely that William Howe was also present, a brooding, heavily bearded man. A Massachusetts farmer by history, he had built a bridge for the new Boston and Albany Railroad three years before. To make the bridge, he created a truss design that made sense to him—diagonal timbers absorbing the force of compression while vertical iron rods maintained the tension. This truss had proven so effective for long spans that William Howe had come to New York to register patents. With him came his nephew Elias, who affected a monstrous mane of wild-looking hair and who was said to be struggling over the challenge of inventing a machine that could sew. Both the Howes were prone to scowling.

John Willis Griffiths

There was talk in the room of marvels as yet unrevealed, especially the rumor of a new gas that, if inhaled, would eliminate the sensations of pain during dental or surgical procedures. The members couldn't have guessed at the creations to come in the next few years—the hand-cranked "ice cream" freezer, the safety pin, the rubber band, tape that could stick of its own accord, the rotary printing press, and the formalization of a popular boys' game called "baseball"—but they all sensed that they were living in an age of wonders.

No doubt there were scientists in the room, too, that is, true scientists. True scientists worked in the ethereal realms. They didn't worry about the best way to cut the clay of unbroken farmland or catch speed under sail. True scientists never took out patents.

One man in the room, the charismatic Charles Grafton Page, scoffed at the division between science and invention. Though Page was a physician and a professor of chemistry, he had also worked as a patent examiner. He moved through the room talking enthusiastically with everyone, his curly hair trimmed short in the modern style, but his beard of biblical proportions. The energy in his eyes suggested to some of the wits that he was perhaps spending too much time poking into electromagnetism, his favorite mystery. Five years earlier Page had patented what he called the "circuit breaker," a device that somehow sensed whenever electrical forces exceeded the limits of safety. Now he was obsessed with the idea of building electromagnetically driven trains and ships.

Whether scientist, inventor, or investor, every man in the room felt he was part of a circle of magic-handlers. Each had a grip of some kind on the pure forces of the universe—including the economic forces that can turn gumption into bucks. It was not their purpose to popularize their wizardry. Each was a driven egotist. Each lived to publish, patent, or capitalize on the secrets they so uneasily shared with very few. They were elite.

The shipbuilders present, and there were dozens, were the worst of this sort. Never mind a few covered wagons shaking their way along the cruel trails of the savage West. American shipbuilding was dominant and largely covert.

U.S. shipyards were producing new vessels at a dazzling pace, each ship a singular creation, each launch a bit of front-page news. The speed and cunning of these shipyards had helped a start-up nation fumble its way through two founding wars. But shipyard practices were kept in-house, passed from person to person, not promulgated, not publicized. Of course, the frenetic pace of shipbuilding could have been a factor in this silence—no time to reflect, nor to regulate. And there is always the American love of competition. (Those present did not regard each other as colleagues but as potential thieves.) For whatever reasons, the later motto "A slip of the lip can sink a ship" echoed a Yankee habit.

THE GAVEL STRUCK. Those murmuring took their seats in the lecture hall, finding their peers nearby, looking left and right. Then Griffiths walked to the podium. Good-looking fellow but plain in presentation, piercing gray eyes, and a big voice—probably used to shouting across shipyards.

Griffiths began. "Since the days of Platonism, it has been the custom for the most scrupulous of scientific men to destroy all traces of their investigation in physical science." He scanned the room picking out certain faces. "Others, having less rigidity in their mental constitution, concealed the key to the great laboratory of Nature within an envelope of mysticism." Then with a slight gesture he seemed to indicate himself. "While others, of still more enlarged views, have had *ebullitions of wrath* heaped upon them for applying science to sensible things, or to the everyday labors of life."*

What was this? The speaker's rhetoric was more than dignified. And yet as his mirthful eyes studied the room, his mouth a firm slit, his statements suggested a kind of moral judgment against members of the audience, many of whom considered themselves "the most scrupulous of scientific men."

And he went further.

"While thus the shadow of perplexing doubt hung over the time-honored traditions of the philosophers of yore, *mystery*, as a consequence, brooded over the genius of commerce. And the ocean was regarded as the charnel-house of fate—the depository for the victims of superstition, as well as for the mysterious traditions of commercial art."

Another way to say that: You scared people with your "commercial art," your big talk, and so you drove up your profits, but you never shared your technology. You have never told the world how exactly you make your fine ships. You have never submitted their design conceptions to any real test.

Griffiths said, "It was an era in which the novitiate could only be inducted into the perplexing labyrinths of nautical science through the channel of secrecy." The word "secrecy" caused everyone in the audience to squirm.

Then the speaker spread his arms in welcoming fashion and smiled. "That fatal shoal in the stream of time has been passed," he said. "The present is no longer an era when the mechanic, the mariner, or the merchant can profit by the *concealment* of commercial knowledge. The true spirit of progress is being infused into all the channels of industry. Commerce, the great engine of civilization, has borne the world onward to the threshold of an era in which *things as well as books* are to be regarded as valuable in the ratio of their *utility*, and not their antiquity."

Yes. Progress and practicality. Those were great virtues in the young republic. And yet the speaker continued to suggest that the true reforms had not yet come. He widened his attack to include scholars and statesmen. He said, "The commercial historian, the chronicler of science, and the recorder of maritime pursuits have all surveyed the ocean as the world's battlefield—the mirrored arena for the accommodation of contending foes. But the false

---

* The quoted statements have been adapted from Griffith's published works and are used here solely for the purpose of dramatization.

glare of national glory at the expense of human life is passing away. As the morning cloud wanes at the approach of the rising sun, even so the light of mechanical science is beginning to dispel the relics of a barbarous age."

Everyone in the room, of course, hoped that the decades of warfare on both sides of the Atlantic had finally stopped, along with the practice of capturing and sinking vessels that were purely commercial. But national glory—a "false glare?" This—a "barbarous age?" Perhaps it seemed so to such a fellow, whose relentless enthusiasm, inflated self-confidence, and naivete were starting to chafe most of the men in the room.

Griffiths pitched his voice higher. "The ocean is Nature's great theater for improvements. Freed from the noxious vapors that belong to the stagnant pools of earth, whose slimy depths exhale a nauseous stench, where hatch prolific noisome reptiles and dire disease, this lubric mass of matter, this boundless mirror, should be regarded rather as a healthful resort than as the dread charnel-house of the shipwrecked mariner, or the confiding traveler." He smiled and included everyone in the room as he proclaimed: "The ship should be the *life buoy* of the world."

Then came a direct attack on the members of his own trade: "With due deference for the opinions of others"—he nodded meaningfully toward certain heads in the room—"at least one-half of all the suffering from sea sickness and shipwreck arise from the scientists' inattention to the form and construction of vessels."

A gasp went up. Placing the blame for shipwrecks and even seasickness on the "most scrupulous of scientific men?" After such a provocation this fellow had better set forth, and clearly, his design for a ship that would be free of all such failings, both structural and commercial.

And Griffiths did.

But the modifications he proposed were apparently foolish. He described a radical alteration of a sailing ship's hull. The audience looked around with arched eyebrows. It hooted and scoffed. A ship such as the one proposed could never stand upright. It would sink at the dock.

Prevailing wisdom about hulls put the greatest width in the front of the boat. Broad bows were good ones. It didn't matter, people believed, how the ship entered the water, it didn't matter how much force the ship used against the sea, so long as the wake behind was clean and slim.

But this young man argued for a slicing, thin bow, even concave, with the beaminess (the width) and the greatest deadrise occurring amidships.

He wanted to reduce the keel—the great fin that runs along he bottom of the vessel, its very foundation. Griffiths claimed that a wide shallow hull would cut down the rolling and spilling in the wind. He argued that these simple adjustments would make a ship faster and drier. The boat's sheer should be minimal, keeping on the general plane of the water. The result would be less, not more, crashing of water on the deck.

Scoffers said this: such width with a reduced keel would have the vessel skidding over the water surface and capsizing off the pier. Only the harshest driver would dare captain such a one, or else a crew with a death-wish.

But the most offensive part of this fellow's presentation was his poetic philosophications and his irritating use of reason, his verbal swiftness that seemed like cleverness but only if you couldn't meet him on the level of thinking. "It must be evident to the thinking man," he kept saying.

"It must be evident to the thinking man that a given amount of power, when applied to proper vessels, will counteract an amount of resistance equivalent to that power. Also that as the resistance is diminished, the speed is increased with the same power." As he spoke, the implications came clear. He was saying that if you build a big fat front on your ship and smash it against the ocean with a high wall to protect you from the sea's retribution, then you are one of those "theorists" who have "committed an error that has proved fatal to the commercial world."

By now he was verging on blasphemy. He had certainly gone beyond mere insult.

"By an ingenious mode of reasoning, these theorists have, upon false premises, drawn absurd conclusions. And mankind, ever ready to believe that which their interest leads them to desire, has adhered to the dogma without having even claimed the right of thinking for themselves."

Then twenty-two-year-old Griffiths began discoursing on the mathematics behind center of gravity, center of buoyancy, center of effort, and their physical relationships. He said, "While a vessel is at rest and upright, all is well, because the center of gravity and the center of buoyancy are in a vertical line, and the one directly operates on the other. But at the least inclination, the influence is lost, and each central point has a separate interest to attend to."

He used an illustration that even a child could understand—provided that the child could decipher Griffiths's ornate verbal style. He said that if a man goes in the water and stands on a flotation device, he's okay only as long as he stays perfectly vertical. But if he tips, he has to fight to regain balance, and that fight consumes a lot of his energy. However, if a man holds a flotation device in each hand, he can ride out any wave, surge, or wobble. Hence the argument for a hull that's beamier amidship. "The stability of a ship does not depend upon the altitude of the center of gravity, but upon the distance between the center of gravity and the center of displacement. And the shape determines to a very great extent that distance."

Perhaps the crowd booed him just to get him to turn off the faucet. Too damn smart. Enough already. Leave it alone.

THE NEXT YEAR Griffiths returned to the American Institute. He presented a detailed plan for a complete vessel of his new design. After considering his plans and reasoning, the society urged his employers, Smith & Dimon, to remove such a dangerous person from their design rooms.

The same year, 1842, Griffiths delivered a series of lectures on ship design, the first such presentations ever in the United States. He announced that he was opening a free school for instruction in shipbuilding.

Some forward-minded members of the Yankee establishment actually did listen to Griffiths. Some actually developed a positive hunch about his ideas, a hunch based on his almost unbearable intelligence and the compelling enthusiasm of his vision. One of these was William Henry Aspinwall. In spring of 1843 Aspinwall signed with Smith & Dimon to build a ship of one hundred seventy-five tons to the specifications of John Willis Griffiths.

The New York papers reported this development as a scandal.

But Aspinwall was a businessman who had room to be visionary in those days. For over ten years he had been president of the merchant firm Howland & Aspinwall, and he wanted to move merchandise.

In the 1840s, China tea was making excellent money for American businessmen. The product was light and it was best when fresh, so the marketplace for tea favored the employment of speedy American ships. In fact, to the delight of patriots, the American colonies had gone, within a lifetime, from dumping British tea into Boston Harbor to getting rich by marketing tea to the British. A Griffiths-designed ship could possibly capture that market.

Aspinwall had a knack for good choices. Five years later, in 1848, he would create a steamship line with service to California—the year before gold was discovered. His Pacific Mail Steamship Company would eventually become the renowned American President Lines. Later he promoted the

Panama Railroad. He helped found the American Society for the Prevention of Cruelty to Animals as well as the Metropolitan Museum of Art.

Thanks to the financial backing of Howland & Aspinwall, John Willis Griffiths seized the challenge of creating the vessel his own science had predicted. Normally a sailing ship of that size would have taken four-plus months to build. Griffiths took two years.

Meanwhile both Aspinwall and Howland fretted. They suggested compromises. They sent to England for a sail plan, which Griffiths shoved into the back of a drawer. Journalists called the project a disgrace, built against the laws of nature. People joked that she'd be better sailing backwards. Her name was *Rainbow*. Griffiths's career and his life depended on this project. She was certainly one of the greatest calculated risks in the history of Yankee ingenuity.

Rainbow launched at the South Street site on the East River. It was a bitterly cold January morning, yet a crowd gathered. People came because Aspinwall was always lavish with refreshments and spectacle at his launchings. But this one had an extra draw because the crowd expected to see the vessel capsize and the nutty designer disgraced. Morning papers predicted that five minutes after the launch, the "dreamer's rainbow" would lie at the bottom of the East River. The crowd feasted at Aspinwall's expense, but it was disappointed to see the vessel settle properly on her lines.

In February *Rainbow* sailed for China. She was back in September. With that one voyage, she rewarded her owners two hundred percent on what she had cost. One month later she left again for China. This time she returned so fast she was carrying the news of her own arrival in China! The route out, against the monsoons and the headwinds as she beat her way up the China Sea, took ninety-two days. After three weeks of discharging and loading, her return took only eighty-eight days. The round trip totaled only six months and fourteen days. This sailing record caused a national sensation.

As soon as *Rainbow* had proved herself, Howland & Aspinwall commissioned *Sea Witch*. She would be one hundred tons bigger than *Rainbow*. Her captain would be Bob Waterman, a known "driver." On shore, Waterman was known for his wild, sometimes socially unacceptable behavior. At sea, though, his hyperactive madness turned to genius. He had been setting records with *Natchez*, an old "cotton wagon"—a feat comparable to winning a horse race with one of those westward-bound covered wagons.

Waterman was "a product of the North Atlantic packet service," where sheets were cleated down and halyards secured to the pin-rails. Nobody was allowed to touch them, "to prevent faint hearts from shortening sail when an officer's back was turned."

THE PREVIOUS references come from William Brown Meloney's 1916 *The Heritage of Tyre*. Meloney was a journalist with a maritime background. (He had run off to sea at age eleven.) Writing seventy years after the launch of *Sea Witch*, he avers that the United States of America lost its soul when it turned away from the sea to build railroads and to mine the continent. Then came the disruptive Civil War, mostly fought on land. As the country's focus turned within, boats clad in iron were fighting boats clad in iron, both driven by steam. (The ironclads were a new warfare technology that had just been developed in Europe.) Meloney felt that the U.S. had simply abandoned the sea to face its interior obsessions, and nothing would bring it back but global conflict—yet never back in the same way. There had once been thirty shipyards, he wrote, where there was only one today—that is, in 1916, right before the U.S. entry into the First World War. Some of the Griffiths story has been adapted here from Meloney, whose fervor perhaps exceeds his reliability. But Meloney was a career journalist. He knew facts.

Ship records, for example, are facts. After a huge send-off *Sea Witch* cleared Sandy Hook on Christmas Eve 1846, the tallest ship afloat. When she returned from China in seventy-seven days, the commercial world and the newspaper-reading public were astonished. In 1849 she made the same run home in seventy-four days, fourteen-hours. These records have never been beaten under sail, not even by ships twice her tonnage.

All the "China houses" of Boston, Philadelphia, and Baltimore were compelled to change their practices in order to compete with the well-calculated designs of the model "thinking man," John Willis Griffiths.

Two years after the launch of *Sea Witch*, Smith and Dimon signed a letter endorsing their star employee with ungrammatical praise: "Having known Mr. John W. Griffiths for many years, a number of which has been in our employ, during which time he has obtained celebrity for honesty and industry. It affords us pleasure to testify to his ability and moral worth. We have no hesitation recommending him as a 'Marine and Naval Architect' of the first order. A gentleman who has reached an eminence in the line of his profession rarely attained, and whose skill in this branch of Mechanism we believe to be unsurpassed."

How odd this sounds in our own time—that a person could achieve celebrity status by becoming a mechanic of high moral value.

Even his rivals praised him. Donald McKay in East Boston, his most successful competitor, sent his own endorsement in 1859: "In this testimonial I am happy to state what I believe all the Commercial World knows, that you are a Master of your profession, have no Superior in it—a Scientific and practical Ship builder—& an illustrious Citizen."

In fact, *Rainbow* didn't last long. After five successful runs she was lost off Cape Horn.

Griffiths wrote that the ocean is "Nature's great theatre for improvements." The utter loss of a fine ship and her crew was certainly greater "theatre" than he intended to celebrate. However, truth is, clipper ships tended to live fast and die young. And American destiny was surging at the same pace. Just after *Sea Witch* set her speed records between New York and Cathay, grubbers in the new State of California started finding gold. The resulting market for transportation of people, tools, and goods to the Golden Gate was huge and instantaneous. Three hundred thousand people moved almost immediately to the West Coast, half of them carried and supplied by sail. In fact, most of the famous family fortunes of America's "Gilded Age" began with clipper ships, later moving to railroads.

Sea Witch set the pace. Returning from China in April 1850, she was put on the berth for San Francisco, with Waterman relinquishing command in favor of his equally hard-driving first mate George Fraser. The average time for other vessels making that run was a hundred and seventy-one days; *Sea Witch* did it in ninety-seven. She was the first to beat one hundred days.

Now the race was on. Seven months later, Donald McKay of Boston bested his admired New York competitor. McKay's *Flying Cloud* proved that she could move at over fifteen knots an hour. (New steam-powered ships wouldn't reach that velocity until 1874.) When another Boston ship, *Surprise*, beat *Sea Witch's* time by twenty-four hours, lost wagers on that bet totaled some twenty thousand dollars.

Then *Oriental*, of the New York house A.A. Low & Brother, took tea to London in ninety-seven days. (While she lay there in dry dock, the British Admiralty tried to learn her secrets by copying her lines.) In 1853 Donald McKay produced *Great Republic*, the largest clipper ship ever, 4,555 tons, with

Sea Witch, depicted in an oil painting by Richard Linton, 1982.

four masts—the fore, main, and mizzen being square, the jigger fore-and-aft. Unfortunately, this blockbuster caught fire while being loaded at a New York pier. She never got the chance to live up to her promise. Technological and historical forces eclipsed the clipper ship phenomenon scarcely more than a decade after it had begun.

That revolution can be summarized in two words: metal and steam. First iron, then in the 1870s steel, utterly supplanted handcrafted wood in the making of hull and spars. Steam power vanquished the wind. At the same time America's attention followed the lines of transcontinental rail. Though bizarre in appearance, ironclad battleships made a fool of the age of powder and sword and sail.

Sea Witch herself was gone well before the last spike of the transcontinental railroad was driven at Promontory Summit in 1869. She was gone before the attack on Fort Sumter. A lightning strike in 1853, just seven years after her launch, split her royal and topgallant spars and seemed to forecast her decline. Two years later, on a run to Hong Kong, she stopped at Rio de Janeiro to offload the corpse of her captain, murdered by his first mate. She wrecked twelve miles from Havana, Cuba in March 1856, just over ten years after her triumphant launch.

JOHN WILLIS GRIFFITHS outlasted the era he had helped to create. Clippers of his style were already in decline by the time Grant and Lee met at Appomattox. And yet throughout his life he moved with the changing technology, true to his vocation as a mechanic.

Griffiths was creating designs for steam-powered vessels well before 1850, which is the year he submitted a model steamship to the World Exhibition in London, where it was much admired. Three years later he was constructing a steamer that would cross the Atlantic in seven days. In 1858 the U.S. government appointed him to the task of creating a new style of gunboat. The *Pawnee* resulted—the widest, lightest-draft vessel of her displacement that was ever built. Griffiths fitted her with not just one but a twin pair of screws, and he provided other innovations (a drop bilge, for example) to increase stability and efficiency of propulsion. She drew only ten feet, yet she carried the shooting power of a frigate. *Pawnee* served the Union cause during the Civil War and served the nation thereafter, not decommissioned until 1882.

In 1864 Griffiths invented a machine that could bend timbers—another application of steam, one that could create as-if-natural curves in frames as thick as ten inches in both dimensions. With it he could build a ship whose futtocks were single sticks from the keel to the rails. His invention eliminated the complex joining procedures that shipwrights had always used to make curved hulls from short flitches. In effect, he eliminated pockets of joinery where rot tended to eat into a ship's framework. As a side effect, he also eliminated the squeaking "eee-ooo-eee-ooo" noises that had always been part of shipboard living. In 1870 Griffiths built an entire ship using this timber-bending technology (*New Era* out of Boston) while scoffers predicted that the sticks would snap straight again as soon as they hit the water. (They didn't, of course.) Griffiths created timber-bending machinery for the U.S. government in the early 1870s, then used the technology to construct U.S.S. *Enterprise* at Portsmouth, New Hampshire. His machines received two prize medals at the Centennial Exhibition of 1876. Almost immediately, new steel manufacturing techniques replaced the product (wood) but not the design principle.

Griffiths also originated the idea of lifeboat steamers, and he presented a model and plans for these at celebrations of the country's Centennial. His other inventions: iron keelsons for wooden ships (1848), bilge keels to reduce rolling caused by water sloshing about inside the vessel's shell (1863), triple screws to increase the speed of steamships (1866), and improved rivets (1880). Meanwhile Griffiths wrote and edited. He was a natural-born teacher who worked in print journalism. For example, in partnership with shipbuilder William Wallace Bates, he published *The U.S. Nautical Magazine and Naval Review* from 1853 until 1855 and the *Monthly Nautical Magazine and Quarterly Review* from 1855 to 1857. From 1879 to the year of his death at the age of seventy-three in 1882, he edited a New York City-based weekly journal called *American Ship*. His books (especially his *Treatise on Marine and Naval Architecture, The Ship-Builder's Manual,* and *The Progressive Ship-Builder*) are American classics for those so inclined. And yet John Willis Griffiths died a pauper, and his grave is marked by neither stone nor monument.

Writing in 1916, William Brown Meloney nobly opined that Rome would have voted the man riches, Greece would have honored him as they did Archimedes, and the British would have buried him at Westminster Abbey. Americans responded in typically American style—by moving swiftly ahead to the next sensation.

And yet it's impossible to think of Griffiths as becoming bitter about any of these evolutions. He possessed the more-than-brash confidence of the new American man who sees that he lives in a "wonder-working age." He embodied the radical surge of American pragmatism and capitalism. There is no debate here. Griffiths simply sweeps the crumbs off the table and clears the boards for a new order, a new reality, a new world understood by "the thinking man." It's a secular view, even a nihilistic one, but it's not gloomy in the slightest. On the contrary, Griffiths's view is enthusiastic, brimming with confidence, liberated, joyful.

In terms of American mythology Griffiths was part Ben Franklin and part Johnny Appleseed. He was a visionary. Unlike other visionaries, though, his math was accurate and his ships the fastest and best that ever cut the "boundless mirror." ★

PART THREE

Designer

Revenue cutter *Californian* cuts through the fog of San Francisco Bay.

Spanish Landing | 1983

"But the money was soon spent, while the glory is everlasting."

— SAMUEL ELIOT MORISON
John Paul Jones | 1959

ONE DAY in the early 1980s a Southern California sea dog named Baron Thomas read a piece in the local newspaper that seized his attention. It said that a fellow named Steve Christman intended to raise funds to establish a nautical museum, and that the museum's first project would be the construction of a historic sailing vessel. The ship would be built in public view, and its design would be something along the lines of a Baltimore clipper. If the City of Baltimore could have its own official sailing ship, then the State of California certainly deserved one, too.

It's an inexplicable phenomenon, the widespread surge of interest in historic ship interpretations that followed the launch of *Pride of Baltimore*. The surge continues despite the often unstable condition of the U.S. and global economies over recent decades. People have built no fewer than seventeen versions of Columbus's *Nina*, at least two replicas of HMS *Bounty*, an excellent copy of Cook's *Endeavour*, a poor version of Drake's *Golden Hind*, and of course the *Mayflower*. There is a Greek trireme as employed by Jason and the Argonauts in 1000 B.C., and at least a dozen Viking ships. Most self-respecting islands have their indigenous vessels, the most dramatic being the voyaging canoe *Hokule'a*, which re-enacts the epic passages between Hawai'i and the Tahitian and Marquesan homelands. In a sense, these are all the offspring of Melbourne's breakthrough production for the City of Baltimore.

Such projects attract a rare kind of builder—impractical people caught up in the muscular romance of old tools and old methods, men most of them. They grab a hammer and chisel, a drawknife or rasp or plane or handsaw, maybe even a stone adze, and feel they are clasping onto a hundred generations of fellow builders. Many, though not all, are salt-soaked, wiry-muscled sailing fanatics who show up at a building site in search not of money but of the adventure of a lifetime. People such as Baron Thomas.

Baron and his brother Drake, a year younger, had grown up sailing schooners in and out of crowded Newport Beach Harbor in Southern California. As soon as the boys were out of kindergarten they were helping their dad compete in the annual Encinitas Race, which always finished north of San Diego with a bacchanalia on Cinco de Mayo. When the boys got older, they began racing against their father, whose schooner *Artemis* was tied up six slips from *Sirocco*, which was owned by his good buddy Erroll Flynn, the actor. (Baron's father and Flynn used to practice fencing together.) As adults, the boys stayed with the sea. Drake chartered and skippered around the Pacific—Hawai'i, Tahiti, New Zealand. Both he and Baron got involved refurbishing an old Baltic trader that had been square-rigged for the Hollywood version of Michener's *Hawaii*. That vessel, re-christened *Carthaginian*, (and its successor *Carthaginian II*) later served for many years as the town emblem of Lahaina, Maui, where Drake keeps a boatyard today.

Baron remained in California. Despite an early accident that turned him into a "pegleg," he has lived the nautical life unswervingly. He worked for Scripps Institute of Oceanography. "I spent a lot of time plowing ocean in research ships," he says. He also taught himself to fabricate deadeyes and bull's-eyes—complex-shaped wooden blocks essential for old-style rigging but difficult to find on the open market. The allure of building an interpreted Baltimore clipper hooked him right away.

Baron drove south to San Clemente, a wealthy coastal city at the southernmost end of Orange County, to introduce himself and to learn more about the shipbuilding plans.

Christman, it turned out, had ideas about the ship but no clear plans. He was a small, frail-seeming man with glasses, a closely trimmed beard, and a serious almost sour demeanor. He and his investors had already started construction of the museum, and they were working with a respected design firm to develop the right positioning. As to the boat, Christman said they were talking about a ketch, a coastwise trader type, something about forty-five feet long.

"Oh, a little guy," said Baron Thomas.

Christman looked at him.

At Spanish Landing, builders work on *Californian's* drilled iron ballast keel (L) **and timbers** (R).

To Christman, Baron appeared to be something out of Dickens. His beat-up captain's hat had apparently survived too many dousings. He wore a little sailor's coat, smoked a pipe, and his whiskers waggled when he spoke. At one point, talking about his skills with the fashioning of blocks and gaffs, he raised a pantleg to show his prosthesis.

If Christman had dared to ask, Baron would have gladly told him about the accident. It hadn't happened on the high seas but right off the freeway in San Diego. A driver, confused by off-ramp construction, missed a turn and flipped his car. Baron, coming behind, stopped to help. As he knelt by the overturned car worrying about two passengers hanging upside down by their seatbelts, he heard the scream of brakes coming from behind. Then he was crushed against the overturned car by a second speeding driver. Baron barely remembers clawing his way across the asphalt in order to deposit most of his blood into the thirsty soil of the freeway roadside. The Good Samaritan got screwed. He's one of the few living people who has experienced reading his own obituary in the newspaper.

All Christman could think upon meeting Baron Thomas was, "Holy crap, put a parrot on this guy's shoulder and send him to Disneyland." But he could see that Baron was for real, both earnest and competent. He found the whole package rather unnerving.

"I'll put you on the list," he said. "When the project gets rolling, I'll get in touch with you."

As Baron left, he said to Christman, "Have you considered San Diego?"

"What do you mean?"

"Well, you said you wanted to have her built at Dana Point."

"Or somewhere farther north, but definitely in Orange County."

"You're missing some real opportunities if you don't...."

"San Diego is too far away. It's just not feasible."

"Okay then. Give me a call when you get things going."

As he swung-stepped back to his car, Baron suddenly thought of Gene Autry, the romantic cowboy who'd never been on a horse.

"I TOLD MY DAD ABOUT IT," Baron recalled. "We agreed that sticking to Orange County was kind of a bummer because San Diego would be the perfect spot." They both knew San Diego well. In fact, his father had spent years there as the regional manager of sales for the triple-A automobile club. (These days even sailors need day jobs. Especially sailors with families.) So his father had a lot of connections in San Diego. He understood how the city worked, and he had some real clout in its nautical community. Both Thomases, father and son, knew that the San Diego Harbor layout was perfect for such a project. They concurred that the finest building site would be Spanish Landing.

Spanish Landing's sandy seaside curve is certainly one of the most protected coastlines on the planet. The hefty, right-arm hug of the Point Loma peninsula absorbs any force the sea might throw from the north and west. Any turmoil from the south gets blunted by the left-arm Coronado peninsula, which almost fills the bay. What remains is a full-rainbow curve of seaway within natural baffles, like an infant with two mothers. Not only that, the Spanish Landing site at the peak of the curve sits just across Harbor Drive from the San Diego Airport and the heart of the city. For Christman, the only inconvenience would be the hour-long straight freeway drive from his home to the construction site, passing through the vast Marine base at Camp Pendleton and down along the populous and congested coastal towns.

So Baron took his father to meet Christman and bend his ear. In that meeting Christman realized that he could benefit from the Thomases' connections and advice. He visited the site. He agreed to it. The relationship was collegial.

Soon Christman announced that he had found his shipwright. "He was a small-boat builder," recalled Baron. "He was a white-hull, fine-kind-of-skiff builder, East-Coast style. I could see that this project was beyond him."

Next development: a celebrated shipbuilder named Melbourne Smith was scheduled to give a talk in the Point Loma area near the Spanish Landing site. Melbourne's talk impressed the San Diego nautical community, especially those associated in any way with the rather nebulous clipper-building project, and most especially Steve Christman himself.

Melbourne remembered it this way: "I had been working with Steve Christman for about a year. Communication was all done by mail in those days. He wanted a forty-five-foot ketch. He didn't want to spend any money. I wasn't too interested. But finally he sprung for the money for me to come out. I took some sketches with me."

At that point Melbourne was soundly immersed in challenging projects. One was his complete re-design of Carl C. Cutler's classic volume *Greyhounds of the Sea*. Also, he was drawing up the complete design plans for a new ship, a re-creation of an old Gloucester schooner on the *Fredonia* model, to be called *Spirit of Massachusetts*. This vessel would be the historic emblem of its namesake and, for Melbourne, the natural sequel to *Pride of Baltimore*. After drawing the plans, of course, Melbourne bid on its construction. He was taken aback to find that his offer had been rejected by the promoter in Massachusetts in favor of a bid that was two-thirds the price. Two-thirds! Melbourne knew the work couldn't be done well so cheaply. What was worse, the competing bid had come from a boat-building rookie who had learned his core skills by working on Melbourne's crew with the *Pride of Baltimore*.

"I bid seven hundred and fifty thousand. Andy Davis bid five hundred thousand. I knew he couldn't do it. Out of curiosity, when that job was almost finished, I went up to Massachusetts and asked to see the books." Such inquiry was perfectly legal, a matter of public record, and Melbourne had legal representation. "I discovered that he was at a million four and not finished. And the ship wasn't built that well. For example, I had designed her with single frames made of laminated pine. My laminated frames would have been much stronger and lighter than traditional double frames. But this builder took the easy route and substituted the old-style frames, and his decision certainly knocked off the ship's calculated weight." He added, "I didn't mind so much because I was off in San Diego building the *Californian*."

1 March 1983
AS CONSTRUCTED 30 JUNE 1984

	SAIL AREA	MATERIAL*	NOTES
MAINSAIL	1738.F Sq.Ft.	#4 CANVAS	CLOTHS VERTICAL CUT. 2 ROWS OF REEF POINTS. LACING ON HEAD & FOOT. 14 MAST HOOPS ON LUFF.
FORESAIL	1492.0 Sq.Ft.	#4 CANVAS	CLOTHS VERTICAL CUT. 2 ROWS OF REEF POINTS. LACING ON HEAD. BRAIL CRINGLES. 14 MAST HOOPS.
STAYSAIL	752.2 Sq.Ft.	#4 CANVAS	VERTICAL CUT. NO MITRE. 1 ROW OF REEF POINTS. IRON HANKS ON LUFF.
JIB	830.5 Sq.Ft.	#6 CANVAS	VERTICAL CUT. NO MITRE. IRON HANKS ON LUFF.
FLYING JIB	474.4 Sq.Ft.	#8 CANVAS	VERTICAL CUT. NO MITRE. #6 SNAP HANKS ON LUFF.
MAIN TOPSAIL	457.6 Sq.Ft.	#8 CANVAS	VERTICAL CUT. LACING ON JACK YARD.
FORE TOPSAIL	772.0 Sq.Ft.	#6 CANVAS	1 REEF BAND. 4 BUNT BANDS WITH 2 BUNT THIMBLES EACH.
TOP GALLANT	308.7 Sq.Ft.	#10 CANVAS	4 BUNT BANDS WITH 2 BUNT THIMBLES EACH.
STUNSAIL	256.0 Sq.Ft.	#10 CANVAS	LACING ON HEAD

* ALL SAILS TREATED WITH VIVATEX

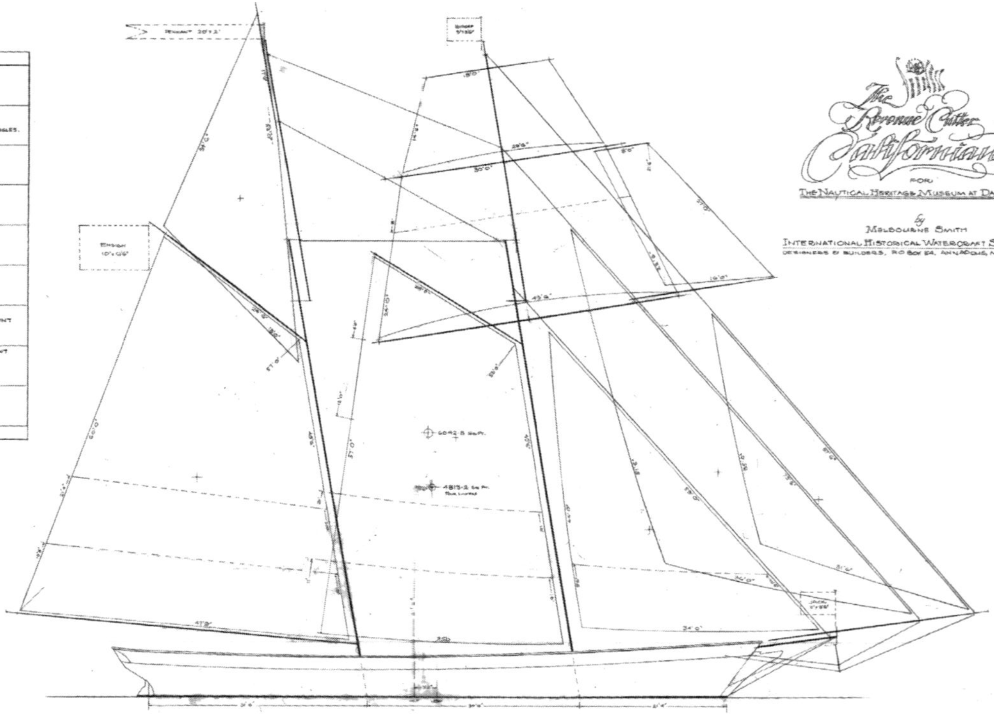

The Revenue Cutter Californian
FOR
THE NAUTICAL HERITAGE MUSEUM AT DANA POINT
by
MELBOURNE SMITH
INTERNATIONAL HISTORICAL WATERCRAFT SOCIETY, INC.
DESIGNERS & BUILDERS, P.O. BOX 54, ANNAPOLIS, MARYLAND 21404

DESIGN NO. 831
1:64 SCALE
3/16" = 1 FOOT

PLATE V: SAIL PLAN

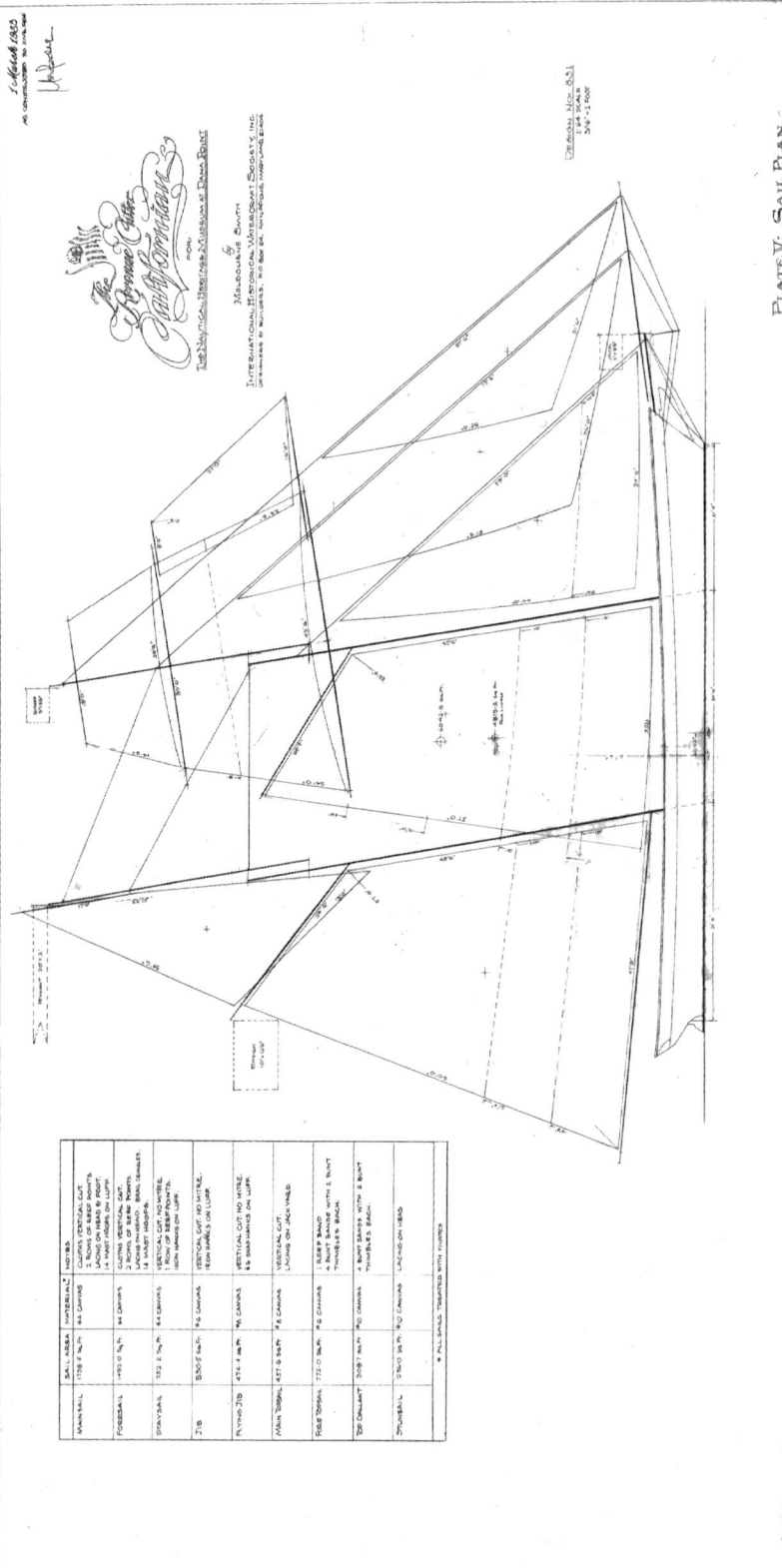

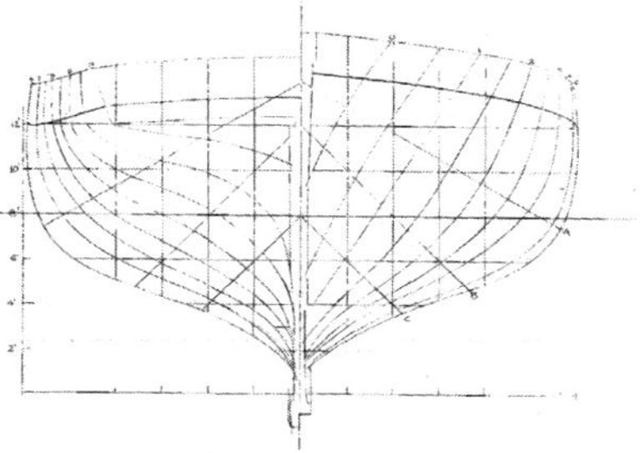

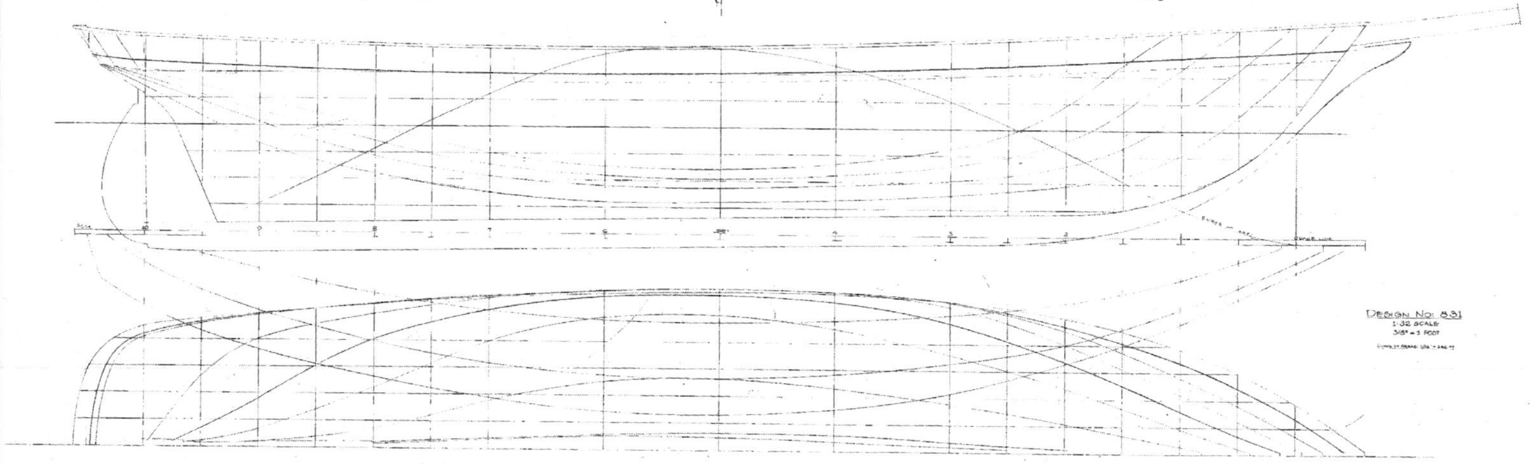

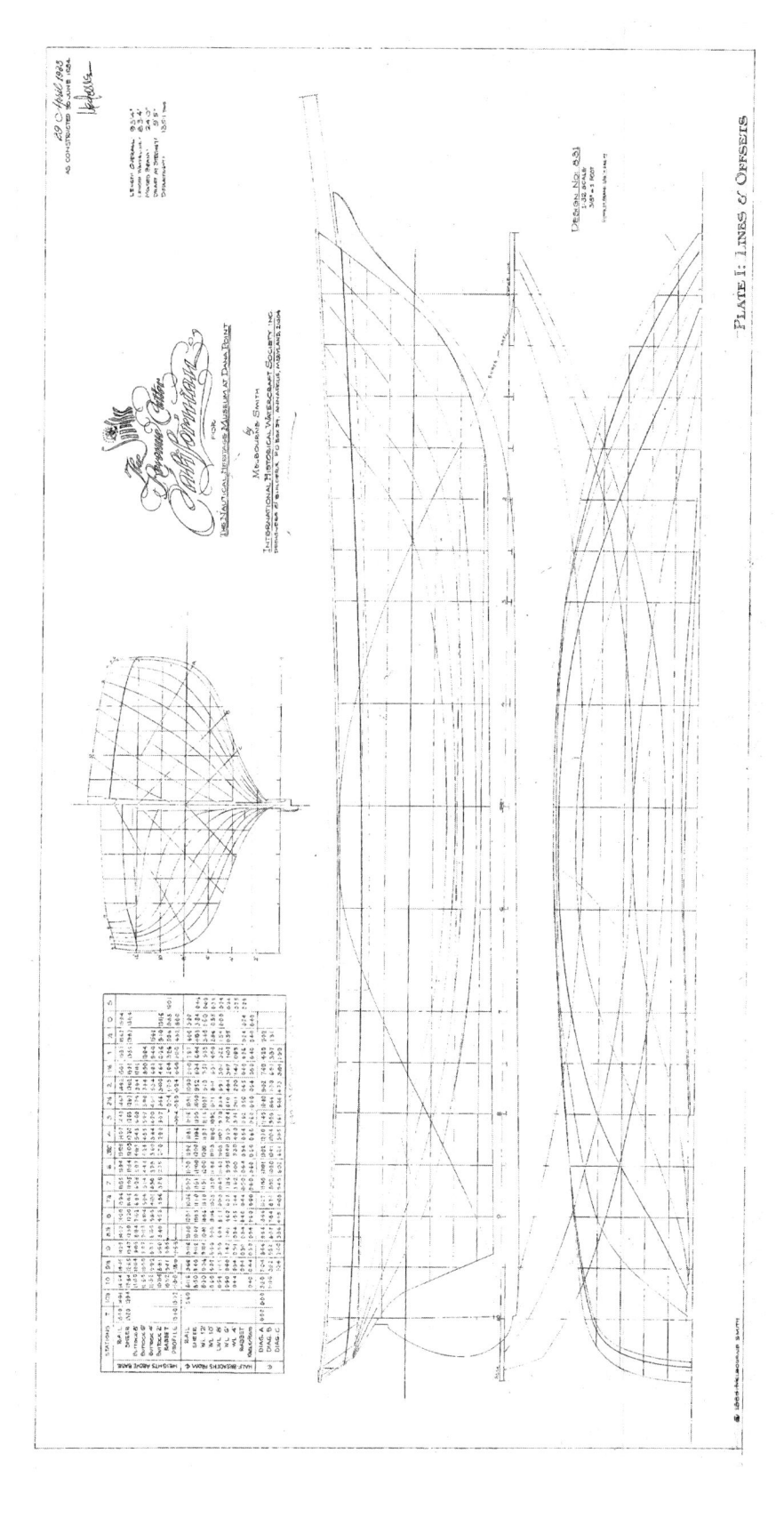

I N FACT, the *Californian* project came off very well, despite some grievous setbacks and emotional bloodletting. Today, decades later, the vessel still serves its present owner, the Maritime Museum of San Diego, as a lively attraction and educational experience. The ship was used by director Stephen Spielberg as the location for much of the action in his film *Amistad*.

According to Melbourne, the design of *Californian* derived from two comments he made to Steve Christman during the early 1980s.

Melbourne said, "I just built a ninety-foot boat for the City of Baltimore, and you want only a forty-five-foot boat for the State of California?"

Christman said, "How about ninety-five?"

Of course, enlarging the dimensions called for enlarging the fundraising goals. Melbourne said, "Someone once told me, Steve, that it's easier to raise a million dollars than thirty-five thousand. Come up with a million, and I'll build this ship for you within a year."

Pushed by Melbourne's clarity and determination, the project reshaped itself. The investors got excited and within a month had pulled together the million. Quickly thereafter, the commissioners of the Port of San Diego approved the use of Spanish Landing Park as the construction site. Then in June 1983, California State Legislature adopted Assembly Concurrent Resolution No. 69, designating the as-yet conceptual *Californian* as the "Official Tallship Ambassador of the State of California."

Melbourne went to work in several directions at once—designing the ship, rallying a crew (with Gerry Trobridge again at the hearth), constructing a large pavilion to protect the site at Spanish Landing, and locating the timbers they would need, most of which would come from Belize.

As Melbourne hoisted sail, so to speak, to launch this year-long creative expedition, he couldn't help remembering now and then an odd comment made by his client. Steve Christman let him know that he had previously financed the construction of several homes and the nautical museum. Then he added: "I have never done any work with any contractor that didn't end up with our becoming enemies."

Melbourne replied, "Maybe it will be better this time."

T HE PROJECT moved ahead smoothly because Melbourne knew exactly what sort of ship he intended to create. His model would be *C.W. Lawrence*, a revenue cutter that arrived in San Francisco at the end of October, 1849— the first year of the California Gold Rush—then was fatally grounded just

Californian **framed up**

south of Monterey Bay two years later. Those two years of service had given the long-gone vessel its place in national and state history, therefore qualifying it for legislative recognition.

The first revenue cutters were built from necessity just after the conclusion of the Revolutionary War. Their initial purpose, and priority number-one for the fledgling nation, was collecting taxes. Eventually the revenue cutter service would be elevated (in 1915) with a new name, the U.S. Coast Guard.

When Alexander Hamilton became its first Secretary of the Treasury, the fledgling United States was laden with seventy-five million dollars in war debt. Hamilton called this debt "the price of liberty" and was determined to pay it down. Seaports provided the readiest source of national income in the form of tariffs and taxes. But smuggling had become an established practice from colonial days. Merchant ships would dodge the payment of customs duties by offloading cargo into little "coaster" vessels offshore, or by finding unofficial ports. In 1790 U.S. Congress enacted a Tariff Act calling for the construction of "revenue cutters" to patrol coastlines and intercept approaching vessels. The term "revenue cutter" originated in England during the seventeen hundreds, when such ships were cutter-rigged—that is, single masted with two or more headsails. But these U.S. vessels would be Baltimore clipper types, two-masted schooners "light, fast, easily managed, seaworthy vessels, handy in beating in and out of harbors and through winding river channels." They had to be agile in close conditions and yet fast and weather-hardy in open-sea navigation.

36-inch galvanized steel drift-bolts being driven through *Californian's* tropical hardwood keel assembly.

Congress commissioned ten of these ships and positioned them at strategic locations along the Atlantic seaboard. Over time the service grew. Its duties expanded to the enforcement of all maritime laws, such as quarantine restrictions, neutrality and embargo acts, and prohibitions against piracy and, after 1807, slavery.

Once money and goods began flowing along the West Coast, along with U.S. acquisition of territories in Oregon and California, the Revenue Service dispatched the new *C.W. Lawrence*. She'd been named for Cornelius Van Wyck Lawrence, a successful merchant who had been the eleventh Collector of Customs at the Port of New York. Mr. Lawrence was also president of the Bank of New York for two decades, the first elected mayor of New York City (three terms), and a U.S. Congressman. He died in 1861 at age seventy, the country having received considerable more service from him than from his namesake vessel.

C.W. Lawrence was pierced for ten guns and carried two thirty-two-pounders, one long eighteen-pounder, two six-pounders, plus carbines, percussion pistols, Colt revolvers, boarding pikes, and cutlasses. She set sail in November 1848 and took almost a full year to reach San Francisco. Her voyage included a five-week ordeal trying to round Cape Horn plus stops at Rio de Janeiro, Valparaiso, and the Hawaiian Islands. Then for two years she patrolled the Pacific Coast as far north as Port Orford, Oregon. When an anchor cable parted under perilous conditions one night, she was driven into shoal waters near Point Lobos. She ran aground, the seas crashing across her deck, the entire crew terrified of drowning. In the morning she was hove up onto the shore. The crew methodically stripped her of all moveable properties.

Though the *C.W. Lawrence* ship's log survived, actual design plans did not. But Melbourne's research into other vessels of the same generation gave him the confidence that his plans were authentic. After all, his goal was not to make an exact replica but to create a fully functional interpretation.

He made a number of strategic adaptations that have proven to be smart. For example, the original *C.W. Lawrence* was rigged as a two-masted brig with square mainsail and topsails. But others of her generation were rigged as topsail schooners, with masts in a fore-and-aft arrangement, and Melbourne favored the simpler design. He also reduced the ship's dimensions proportionately, but not by much, in order to accord with present maritime regulations.

Melbourne introduced a new approach to framing one of these classic ships, an innovation inspired by Griffiths, who had used steam to bend large-dimension timbers. Without access to Griffiths's steam technology, Melbourne came up with an idea for making precision-curved timbers using lamination.

Lamination involves the splicing of many shorter-length boards in order to make full-sized planks by clamping and gluing. Lamination can produce a fused unit of any shape or design—could be a monstrous boardroom table the size of a roller rink, or maybe the dome-like entry to a well endowed country church. In fact, it was an architect of churches who told Melbourne—at a party—about a Greenville, Alabama, company that specialized in large custom lamination jobs. When Melbourne asked, the company said that they'd never made ship-framing timbers, but they were certain that they could. "They knew how to treat the wood so it would last forever." The secret is using resorcinol adhesive that makes a permanent bond. Melbourne had them make keelsons for his two skipjacks in Baltimore, and those succeeded. "Expensive," Melbourne said, "but they saved a lot of construction time in the yard."

"I lofted it all in Annapolis," he said. Lofting is the traditional design process that enables the architect to transfer the dimensions of a half-hull model to full-scale templates for each hull timber. Obviously, that chore requires a capacious flat surface, such as the floor of an empty warehouse, in order to work in the actual dimensions of the finished vessel. "I sent the full-sized drawings, with the bevels clearly marked to accept the planking, on Mylar sheets to Alabama, who then shipped the finished beveled frames to San Diego. Boy, it was perfect and it's still perfect today."

"THE NEXT THING you know, the word was out that Melbourne Smith was coming to San Diego to build the *Californian*," recalled Baron Thomas. "I shot right up, made a few phone calls, and went to introduce myself. Melbourne was renting an ostentatious place in Point Loma [a posh and woodsy residential area close to the building site]. I knocked on the door and he answered. Immediately he showed genuine interest in my sailing history. He talked about the project for a bit. Then he jumped up and started playing the piano. He played really well, too, some sad song, and then he started crying. At first I was pretty concerned, then I realized it was all a put-on. He started laughing. Then he turned to me and said, 'Yeah, your background sounds good. Do you drink?'

"I thought to myself, how should I answer this? But I said, 'Yes.'

"He said, 'Good. You're hired.'"

Another key shipwright who discovered Melbourne Smith through the *Californian* project and who worked with most of Melbourne's subsequent creations was Bill Elliott. When Bill heard what was happening, he loaded a "ton of tools" into a U-Haul trailer that he pulled with an old Ford Maverick sedan all the way from San Francisco Bay area to Spanish Landing, an eight-hour drive at best. It was New Year's Eve 1983, and Bill almost burned up the Maverick going over the Grapevine (the long grade of I-5 as it reaches the Tejon Pass).

"By the time I got down there, they were just starting to plank her. The frame wasn't quite complete." Bill was drawn right away to Melbourne's leadership presence, "his extreme intensity, his knowledge of the rigs, and his ability to put a project like that together, to generate interest, to get a guy like Steve Christman salivating, then to deal with pricing, funding, then to get the people involved. A lot of people have that fantasy, but not everyone can bring it to fruition. That was Melbourne's unique ability."

Bill appeared at the worksite and introduced himself as a shipwright. "Let's see what you can do," said Melbourne. He put Bill at the task of "dubbing"—touching up the beveled faces of the framing timbers so that the hull-forming planks will lie on them flat.

This work is traditionally done with an adze. Adzes, scarcely to be found these days in any hardware store, are the oldest of shipbuilding tools. They enabled Noah to build an ark and the early Polynesians to carve their masterful voyaging canoes. An adze consists of a wooden handle with a sharp blade lashed or otherwise affixed to one end, similar to an axe. However, the adze

The *Californian*'s building crew takes a pre-launch pose. Melbourne is center, arms crossed, with Jay Hazell to his right. Gerry Trobridge has the white beard; Baron Thomas to his right. The dark hat and T-shirt to Melbourne's left indicate Bill Elliott.

blade isn't parallel with the handle but fixed ninety degrees athwart. Instead of splitting the wood along its grain the way an axe does, the adze cuts cleanly across the grain. It's a sharp hacker.

Bill Elliott was delighted to discover that the shipyard supervisor, a lanky old Caribbean named Japheth Hazell, was a born-and-raised master of the adze. He was the calm soul of the shipyard, industrious, with high integrity, and honored by all the young rowdies and lunks who signed on for the job. "He worked all by eye," Bill later reflected. "His serenity and his demeanor— it was just great to be around."

JAY HAZELL became a sort of adze-wielding guru for the period ship movement. His native land was Bequia (pronounced "Beck-way"), which is the second largest island in the Grenadines, which are north of Grenada, which is north of Trinidad-and-Tobago, which is just north of the northern coast of Venezuela. Bequia is an S-shaped island enfolding big Admiralty Bay in seven square miles of decidedly unsquare verdant terrain. Population: approximately five thousand.

Melbourne Smith first met Jay in the mid-1970s when the lean old Bequian arrived to take over the shipwright role for *Pride of Baltimore*. After that, Japheth helped Melbourne build his two Maryland oyster skipjacks and then he became the guiding figure at Spanish Landing.

Melbourne's summary: "Simeon Young [*Pride's* original builder from Belize] was getting drunk all the time, then actually went home. He came back and we had to send him home again. So here we were in the middle of this huge project and I didn't have a good shipwright.

"I asked around, does anybody know somebody from the West Indies who can work big timbers? Someone said, I know this guy Jay Hazell. Then I found out that Jay was in living in New York City. One of his sons was a successful doctor. The other was an engineer. Jay had sent them to America to get training. He was a simple man himself, but he worked very hard and paid for their education. By then, the sons were already successful and so had moved the parents to America.

"I managed to reach him, and he came down in three days. He said, 'I need a job.'"

Bill Elliott met Japheth years later at the *Californian* site. He said, "Jay was the opposite of Melbourne—very low-key, calm, gentle. He was older than the rest of us. Extremely likable. And he came from Bequia, which is famous for its boatbuilding, especially double-ended boats known locally as 'two-bow boats.' These people built whaleboats and hunted whales. Jay worked with the adze and axe all by eye. He was extremely skilled with the adze. Melbourne had a lot of respect for him, for his serenity and his demeanor. The crew respected him in the highest."

Baron Thomas described him as "a real boatbuilder of the old school. Jay had built schooners with his father right on the beach. For the *Californian* he did most of the caulking—he was a master." Some of the local caulkers supplied by the owner tried to pour hot pitch into seams without caulking. It was an age-old trick to avoid work while still being paid. Fortunately Jay caught the trick seams before they launched. And Jay stepped the *Californian's* masts— that is, got them raised and secured in their proper, towering vertical position.

"Also, he was very religious," said Baron. "I'd go up to Melbourne's place at Point Loma. Jay [who was living at the house] would disappear right in middle of a conversation, go in his room, and read the Bible. He must have been pushing sixty-five years at the time.

"Jay didn't have time for beginners and guys that were saying how good they were. This one guy had been hired originally to build *Californian*, but he just didn't have the knowledge [so he had to be replaced with Melbourne]. The fellow used to come around the site, and he was always kind of irritated. One day at lunchtime we were eating sandwiches, and he asked Jay, 'How long do you think an adze handle should be?' Jay looked puzzled then said, 'Well, the length that it doesn't hit you in the nuts.'"

Melbourne: "I always thought of him as a real Judas Goat [a naturally charismatic leader of the flock], inasmuch as he worked so hard and was such a straight-arrow guy—and everybody loved him. The crew all worked twice as hard just because they were around him. At lunchtime he'd always get up five minutes before the bell rang. 'Come on, boys.'

"They would say, 'But the bell hasn't rung yet.'

"Jay would answer, 'The Captain's paying you to work, so you got to be ready when the bell rings.'

"He knew how to drive steel drifts into wood. In shipbuilding, when you're not using trunnels you use metal rods, or drift bolts. These used to be made of iron, but you can't get that anymore. Now it's galvanized steel. The one-inch-diameter bar has to be driven through the keelson into the keel, sometimes two or three feet. The hole drilled is always a hair smaller than the bar itself. The strong guys would always hit the drift too hard and it would bend. Jay would come up, 'No, no, go slow and steady.' He'd hit the bar four, five times, it didn't move. 'I'm teaching it that it got to go.' Slowly it would start to move. By the end, the head was all mashed over, then it would reach the clench ring and fit perfectly, forming a perfect seal. It's all about finesse, not banging away like a carnival contest.

"He would say, 'You got to teach the drift where it got to go.' When the seal fit, all the guys would let out a cheer and give him a big back-patting.

"He taught everyone how to caulk. He taught them how to sharpen tools. He was a God-fearing man who never worked on Sunday and sent all his money back home. He didn't chase women. The guys would take him everywhere, take care of him. They would say, 'This is Jay Hazell. He's our friend.'

"When we went to work on the *Niagara*, he was too sick to come up and join us. He had cancer of the testicles or something. They had to cut his nuts off. But he wasn't going to let them cut his dick off. Even when he was sedated he kept his hand clenched on his dick. I got that straight from his own son, the doctor.

"They loved him in Bequia. One time, he built a schooner, sailed it to Venezuela, and brought back a shipload of lumber. When he died, they had a great write-up in the paper. He was the hero boatbuilder on the island. Well deserved."

Melbourne fusses with *Californian*'s spectacular transom carvings.

BILL ELLIOTT quickly proved his dubbing skills and took leadership of the planking crew. In time he became the "nuts and bolts guy" who freed Melbourne to "tend to anything he needed to attend to, such as the customer and the design." A shipwright by trade, he enjoyed Melbourne's trusting approach. "He sees what you can do, and he establishes a good relationship quickly. Then he turns you loose and gets on to other things."

This was a work style well-suited to bohemian boatbuilder types, free spirits who were often highly skilled. Intelligent people were attracted to Melbourne's freewheeling style. These people longed to stop painting teak finish on plastic boats. They craved the experience of making a period sailing ship. According to Bill, Melbourne's perfectly pitched attitude was always, "Don't take it too seriously, but get it right."

He said, "Melbourne is never intense but he is very focused. He jumps right in and expects people to get after it. But he keeps on the light side, cracking jokes, not so darn serious. After all, we're just building a ship. He's a lot of fun to work with. He loves it, like we all do."

The *Californian* gig was " One of the best times I've had in my life."

TODAY if you fly over Oakland's Inner Harbor along the Alameda waterway, just before the coastline gives way to the eastern shore of San Francisco Bay, you will see Jack London Square and the Port of Oakland on one side. Directly across the waterway is Bay Ship and Yacht, a yard vast enough to match its eminent location. Automated systems there can lift twelve hundred tons of nautical apparatus and haul it by rail to individual dry-berths. BSY repairs and builds military vessels, commercial seacraft, and superyachts.

Bill Elliott started the company in Sausalito in 1977 with focus on wooden ships. Six years later, when Bill drove south to join the *Californian* crew, "he didn't have two nickels to rub together," according to Melbourne. "But god he worked hard."

Melbourne recalled visiting him in those days. "He lived in mud flats north of San Francisco. In a slough. He had a trailer that he and his lady-friend lived in, just big enough for a kitchen table, which doubled as a bed. He had established a boatyard, a bunch of wrecks. I was very surprised when I saw where he lived. He is a very good boat-builder, a jewel. He really knows his business."

Bill describes himself as an "army brat" who grew up on a series of U.S. Army posts but was "always attracted to the water." He worked around boats in Boston, then Penobscot Bay, Maine. While crewing on a schooner in Greece, he fell in love with the ship's cook, Vicky, who was from Sausalito. They moved together back to her home territory and "somehow I ended up with a shipyard."

His first break came several years after the *Californian*. The U.S. Navy hired him to resurrect some mothballed minesweepers so that they could be reactivated and sent to Vietnam. (Minesweepers are commonly built of wood because wood doesn't attract mines.) With the profits from that contract, Bill moved ahead in the industry to meet the needs of his era. But he never lost his foundation in "big wooden shipworks," practicing traditional skills such as caulking, blacksmithing, and dubbing.

Today BSY maintains the historic fleet of the National Park Service, and in 2004 did complete rebuilds of two historic ships *C. A. Thayer* and *Alma*, which is the last active scow schooner—a flat-bottomed sailing ship from the late nineteenth century. Bill's replicas sail out of San Francisco Maritime National Historic Park at the west end of Fisherman's Wharf.

Although he now operates the biggest and busiest shipyard in San Francisco Bay, a true Navy shipyard, Bill Elliott will take off to build the next Melbourne Smith period ship. "It's a driven or misguided fascination," he said. "You know when you run into someone with the same affliction.

"There are a bunch of guys, if they heard that Melbourne had the funding to build a ship on the moon, they would all be lining up to get on the space shuttle. He's kind of like a Pied Piper."

Baron Thomas worked on the *Californian* for a full year. He took on the task of making the cannon—their carriages, that is. The guns themselves were cast in bronze by a foundry in New England. Melbourne added a safety touch of his own invention by having the barrels sleeved with stainless steel. "The trouble with bronze," says Baron, "after a number of firings the powder made wormholes in bronze. Then you got explosions. You never knew. But Melbourne's idea really worked."

Cannon carriages are major works in themselves—massive lumber pinned together with fifty feet of bolts, several of those running from side to side of the contraption right through the cheeks and the axle tree. Blacksmith Gerry Trobridge manufactured the ironware on his forge ten feet away, a modified barbecue, while he complained, "I'm not here to build cannon, I'm here to build a ship." Even so, he made the bolts, fastenings, and the rest in half a day.

"Melbourne is a master of organization," says Baron. "He built the *Californian* the way they would have built it a hundred and fifty years ago—lining up the people, following a schedule just like building a house, everything so well regulated. Melbourne is a very, very accurate man who doesn't miss anything. He has a way of getting things done properly. He always had a smile on his face but was always busy, constantly in motion. It's fun while you're doing it, you know? We all worked hard and played hard."

After every workday they all gathered, with spouses and pals, in a favored bar that, after a year of regular patronage, they began to feel that they owned.

"Building *Californian* was the best job I have had," says Baron Thomas.

Launch day was a disaster. The ship looked beautiful—little rigging yet, but both masts erect, her lines so sleek she looked eager to slice into the blue home that was waiting at the other end of the beach. Her sexy figurehead, representing the mythical Queen Calafia of California, had been modeled after actress Catherine Bach, the Daisy Duke of the hit television series *The Dukes of Hazzard*. Prior to this event, Steve Christman had interrupted the workday by appearing in an elaborate antique Revenue Marine uniform and two rows of uniformed sideboys, who whistled him aboard to occupy his trophy vessel. No one on the crew knew quite what to expect next.

It was Memorial Day 1984, wonderfully sunny with a very cool sea breeze. Spectators filled the beach. Gloria Dukmejian, California's First

Lady, sat with numerous dignitaries on a stage under the forefoot of the new ship. There were the necessary speeches and broken bottle. Baron had all six cannon fired in succession. Then the wheeled launching cradle began to move across the beach toward the sea.

When you build a major, full-scale, dazzlingly big sailing ship next to water that is immediately deep, like at the edge of a commercial harbor, getting the boat in the water takes little more than a good shove. But on a long, gradually sloping beach you must roll the ship forward on a cradle and coax it into the sea, as you would a child approaching her first swim. *Californian* had been constructed on just such a cradle, and now as the cradle rolled forward it broke through the firm surface of the beach. The top sand of the beach lay on a lithified crust that snapped under the ship's weight like the top of a fresh apple pie. The wheels of the launch cradle sagged into even more sand below the crust. The boat laid over five degrees and stopped. The sound that escaped at that moment from several thousand spectators is not a sound you can expect to hear more than once or twice in your lifetime.

They were stuck in the muck.

After the crowd dispersed, Baron Thomas said, "Master builder Bill Elliott took this on. It was a real puzzle. He called over some Navy divers and started putting some big iron plates to support the ship on the next high tide. That didn't work. But Bill had a friend named Trost in Novato in the heavy moving business, a family operation."

The heavy movers came down to scratch their heads. Soon there were two enormous tow trucks, the kind used to haul semis out of holes, plus a bulldozer, and a big sea anchor, tines clasping higher ground, pulling with braided cable. "The tension on the wire was unbelievable. We had to move people way back. During all this, Melbourne was not flustered. He took this all in stride, leading. She finally started to move."

While the crew worked to get *Californian* onto a truck rig, the kind used to move entire houses, Melbourne went to locate another launch site. The most obvious choice was the Coast Guard station about two miles up the road, and the Coast Guard was agreeable. The problem was how to get the masted vessel to the new site despite low bridges and highway overpasses. Melbourne found an obscure side route. Baron remembers driving ahead of the boat, right under its jib boom, while six men standing in the bed of his truck used chainsaws to clear the way.

Then the ship was easily launched from the Coast Guard's tarmac.

Anticlimactic, certainly. Baron remembers looking around the gigantic steel architecture of the military base. The ship they had worked so carefully to build now looked "like a little model."

O NCE the ship was floated and rigged, Melbourne gave her several trial runs. The hull balanced and moved perfectly. The next stage was to sail her up to the 1984 Summer Olympics in Los Angeles. Melbourne chose a crew and made it clear that Christman and family would be on board for the maiden voyage. As supplies were loaded, Melbourne watched for a break in the weather. He posted a notice that the crew had to be ready to sail at eight-hour notice. Christman turned snarly. He insisted on two-hour notice. Melbourne protested. Many of the crew had obligations ashore, he said, and for them eight hours would be a simple courtesy. But Christman changed the notice and dismissed Melbourne. He, the owner, was now in charge. Thanks and goodbye.

A few days later, Christman announced an immediate departure, two-hour notice. The crew, many of whom were still working to finish details of *Californian*, scrambled to get ready. Because of the rush, the Spanish Landing shipyard was left wide open, the office unlocked. Recalled Melbourne: "A lot of gear left in the yard found its way into local garages as souvenirs of the construction."

Standing on shore, Melbourne watched her sail away. "She looked beautiful." Then he joined Baron at their favorite bar and watched the televised news of her departure. They toasted her success. They learned later of *Californian*'s dramatic arrival in Los Angeles, where she poked her jib boom through a window at a waterfront marina.

As Baron remembers the hasty departure, Melbourne's attitude was entirely philosophical. "It's Steve Christman's ship. That's just the way it is. This has happened before." In Melbourne's mind there was only one problem: "He never gave me the last month's draw."

M ELBOURNE did finally collect that last ten thousand or so dollars, but not until two years had passed. It so happened that Christman hoped to be introduced to some Sacramento insiders because Melbourne was in Sacramento building another official ship, the *Globe*. Melbourne said, essentially, "Okay, but you owe me. I came in on time and on budget, and you never finished paying me."

The beautiful topsail schooner *Californian* sailing to weather in San Diego harbor.

Californian continues to be a much-used nautical classroom and the ceremonial "Ambassador Tallship of California." But under new ownership. Christman's Nautical Heritage Society sold her in 2002. Then she was donated to the Maritime Museum of San Diego. The Museum chose to replace her Luke automatic feathering propeller with a much larger fixed-prop mechanism. According to Melbourne, the resulting drag under sail has curtailed *Californian*'s speed considerably. ✯

Furling the course on the U.S. Brig *Niagara*

Erie | 1987

*"The material results were not very great,
at least in their effect on Great Britain, whose enormous navy
did not feel in the slightest degree the loss of a few frigates and sloops.
But morally the result was of inestimable benefit to the United States....
I doubt if ever before a nation gained so much honor
by a few single-ship duels."*

— THEODORE ROOSEVELT
The Naval War of 1812

ERIE is arguably the only city in Pennsylvania with a right to have the state's official historic flagship. A glance at the map shows why. Except for a short stretch along the Delaware River in the east—which made Philadelphia an important seaport during the War of 1812—the Commonwealth of Pennsylvania is landlocked. However, a tab of land juts up from the state's northwest corner and claims a length of straight shoreline on Lake Erie. That's the only place in Pennsylvania aquatically grand enough to properly float the two-hundred-eighty-one-ton U.S. Brig *Niagara*.

In 1792, not long after the conclusion of the Revolutionary War, the federal government sold that tab or triangle of acreage to the later inhabitants of Penn's Woods, now ennobled by the name Pennsylvania. The fledgling state paid seventy-five cents an acre for the land, totaling $151,640.25 in what was called "Continental currency." About that same time, the settlers also paid their Native American predecessors for exclusive rights to the land. The Iroquois received two thousand dollars, and the Seneca nation cashed out for only eight hundred. For those sums the Commonwealth of Pennsylvania gained access to the potent transport systems of the Upper Lakes.

Over the next twenty years a new town developed, called Erie, right on the lakeshore. The inhabitants, mostly immigrant farmers and salt traders, numbered fewer than five hundred. The town had just fifty or so clapboard houses.

Then the United States went to war again with England.

This was 1812. British forces crouched just on the other side of Lake Erie, in Canada some twenty miles away. The city of Detroit, at the far west of the lake, with three times the population of Erie, had surrendered without a fight to British General Isaac Brock and his native ally Tecumseh. Clearly Britain had no respect for the boundaries claimed by its former colonies, and certainly it intended to push into the not-yet-exploited middle of North America. British Commodore Robert H. Barclay, who had fought at Trafalgar and lost his left arm while boarding a French convoy, was now patrolling Lake Erie with six warships. The people of Erie were sitting ducks. So were all the settlers to their south.

There at Erie the scarcely adolescent United States of America took its stand. U.S. forces confronted Barclay's flotilla and beat it utterly. On September 10, 1813, Captain Oliver Hazard Perry shifted the momentum of the War of 1812 and secured his country's northern border. He flew a battle flag that the women of Erie had made for him, emblazoned with the dying words his close friend Captain James Lawrence had uttered four months earlier: "Don't give up the ship." Perry famously wrote the following message on a ripped-up envelope: "We have met the enemy and they are ours." He was twenty-eight years old, and he achieved his victory aboard a ship that had been built in haste from green timbers cut in the nearby woods—U.S. Brig *Niagara*.

Now fast-forward to 1987, when a facsimile of *Niagara* stood on the roadside of State Street, right in the heart of Erie near the lakeshore. Kids could climb into it and wiggle the steering wheel, even though the original ship had operated with a tiller, not a wheel. Most of the deck was broken. The sails were actually canvas bags that had been bulked up with Ping-Pong balls—until a storm ripped up the rotted canvas and spilled Ping-Pong balls all over State Street. Despite its condition, the ship was an icon of civic pride, the single emblem of Erie's great moment in national history.

That year, Melbourne Smith came to Erie and had the thing chain-

On the Erie waterfront a new *Niagara* comes to life.

sawed down to splinters. "It was rotten as a pear," said Melbourne. "There was nothing in there but a hive of bees."

He had been charged by the Pennsylvania Historic and Museum Commission to replace any parts of the vessel that weren't original. And he had learned from his old friend Eric Steinlein, who had studied the ship back in the Thirties, that literally nothing in the facsimile was original. A few salvaged timbers had been stashed separately in a storage container—mostly natural crooks (curved tree trunks) that had been fashioned into the ship's framing. "I found close to sixty pieces of the original vessel in storage," Melbourne recalled. "I photographed and documented each one." Later when Melbourne and his crew were constructing a proper re-creation of the historic vessel, they placed in her bilges about twenty of these historic fragments—like pieces of the True Cross, documented evidence that the copy contained something of the 1813 original. But the town icon just had to go.

"The thing was built like a barn," said Melbourne. "It never could sail. One time, I think, it was towed around the lake." After that it became strictly a roadside attraction.

So Melbourne put Bill Elliott to the task. "Bill Elliott," said Melbourne, "you can't stop him. He is a very fast and thorough guy. Before you sit down, it's done."

SAIL AREA

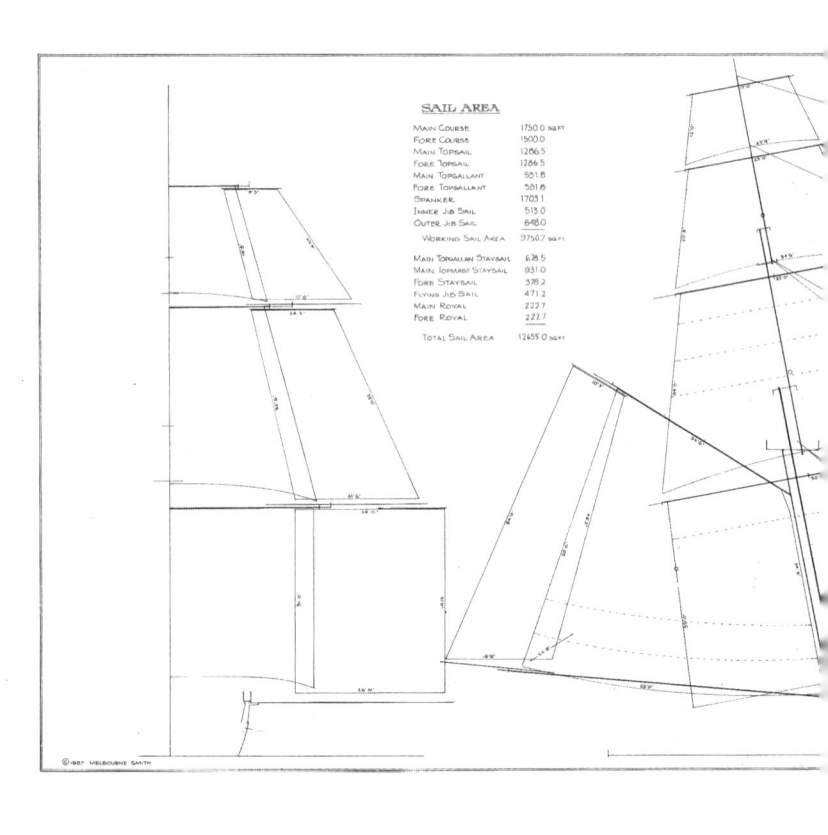

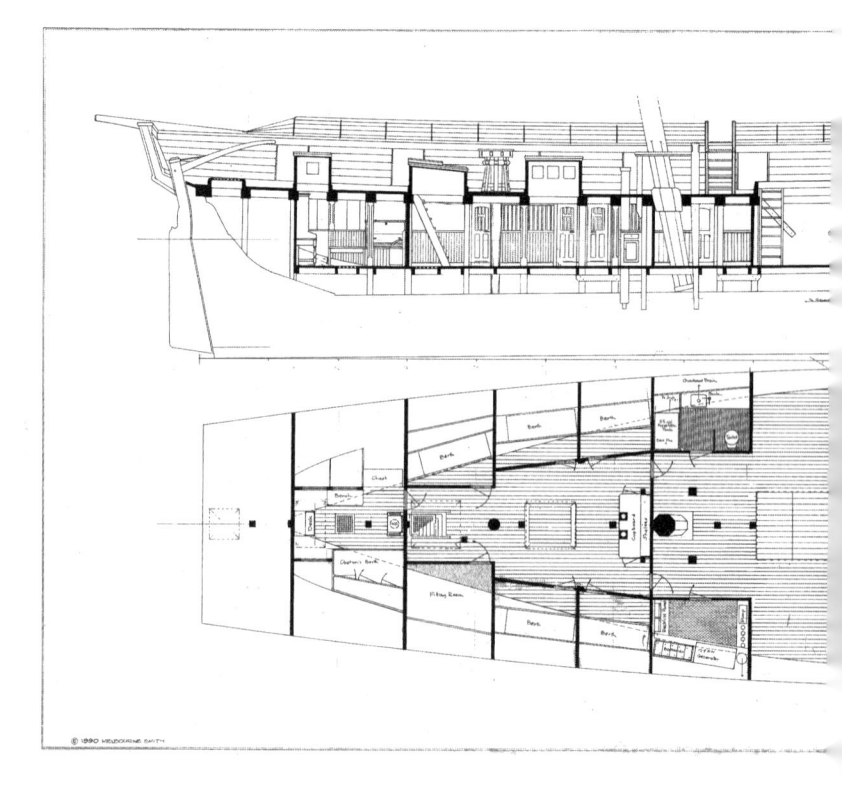

Sail	Area (sq ft)
Main Course	1750.0
Fore Course	1500.0
Main Topsail	1286.5
Fore Topsail	1286.5
Main Topgallant	581.8
Fore Topgallant	581.8
Spanker	1703.1
Inner Jib Sail	513.0
Outer Jib Sail	648.0
Working Sail Area	9750.7 sq ft
Main Topgallant Staysail	678.5
Main Topmast Staysail	931.0
Fore Staysail	378.2
Flying Jib Sail	471.2
Main Royal	222.7
Fore Royal	222.7
Total Sail Area	12655.0 sq ft

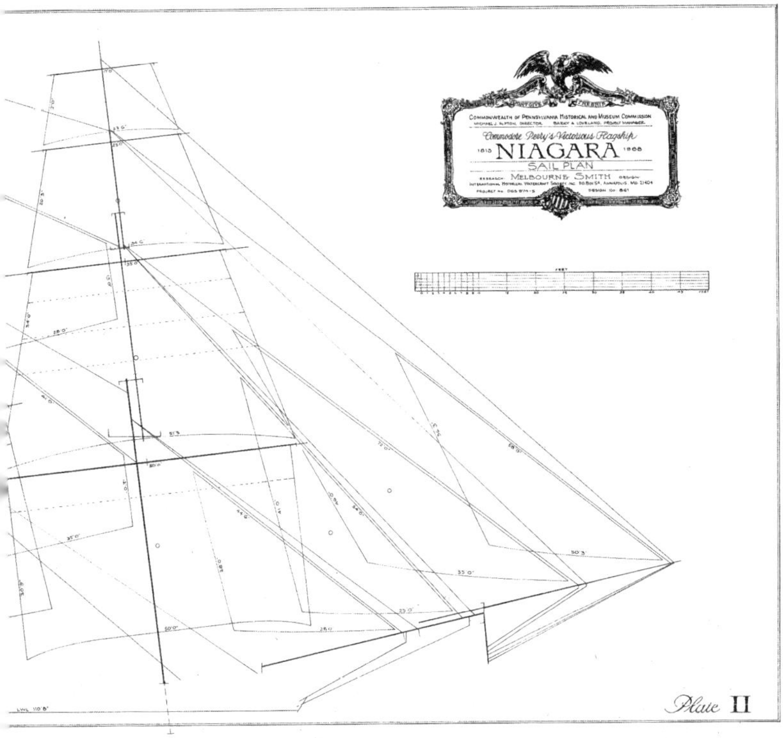

Plate II

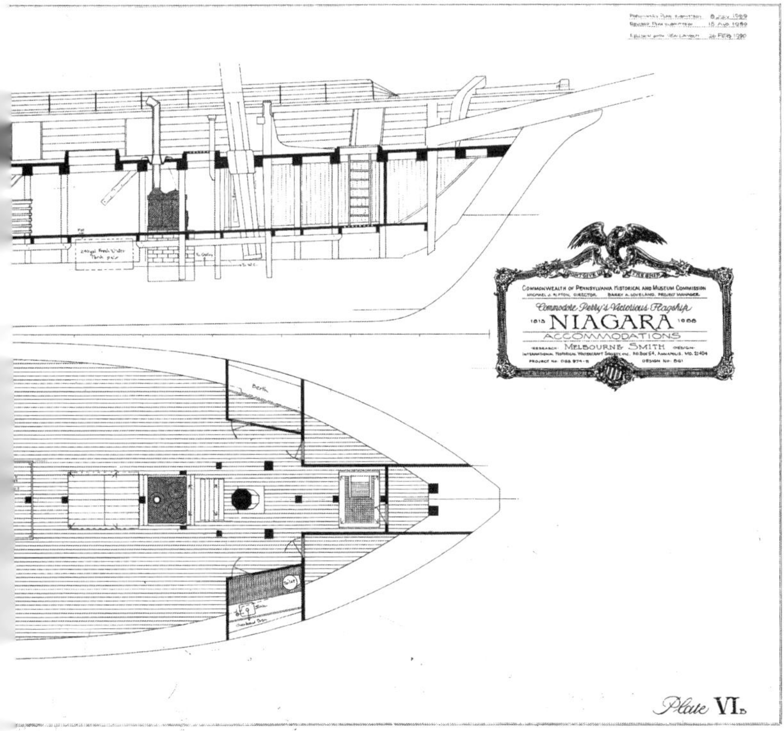

Plate VIb

Bill rented some thirty-inch chainsaws and hired a crew off the street. Although the State Commission had estimated four or five months for the careful dismantling of the precious relic, Bill had the thing obliterated in a week.

"I got a guy with a forty-ton crane to come in with a series of thirty-foot hoppers," remembered Bill. "We used cables to yank the old junk into the bins. The bin drivers were all demo guys who had a lot of experience. They moved it all very quickly."

He filled twenty-eight dumpsters, filled them so fast that the trucks couldn't get into the city dump and had to be parked on the side of the road till room could be made. When the last loaded dumpster rolled away, it carried the queen of the beehive with a mob of her apian subjects swirling overhead and over the bogus steering wheel strapped to the top of the load.

The citizens of Erie came running. "What have you done?" they shouted. "That's our ship!"

THE REINCARNATION of *Niagara* was a "really big job," said Melbourne. He meant even more than its budget, and even more than the logistics of managing a large crew in an untried location with the paralyzing cold of the Great Lakes' winter sure to come. Beyond all that, *Niagara* was historic—the warship that helped to give the United States a respected place among the community of nations. She would sail again. She would live and breathe and beautifully tell her story.

By the end of his time in California, Melbourne had already responded to a request for proposals from the Pennsylvania Historic and Museum Commission. The commission sought an accurate and fully functional re-creation, but its request was limited to design only. The commission wanted a naval architect—that is, Melbourne—to draw up the new *Niagara's* plans and specifications. That was all; someone else would build her. This division of labor is standard practice with civil projects. Part of the designer's job is to oversee the builder and make sure the work is done properly. The designer cannot *be* the builder. The fox cannot guard the henhouse.

Melbourne won the bid and went to work. The research in itself was a serious challenge. The vessel had been constructed in haste in the wilderness, and only a crude drawing remained. Factual evidence was limited to the mummy-esque timbers that Melbourne had found in storage. Like fossils, these fragments helped Melbourne re-conceive the dinosaur to some extent (the size and notching of the frames and floor timbers, the placement of iron drifts and keel bolts, for example). He also had some hazy photographs from 1913, when the remains of the original vessel had been hauled up from the muck and onto the ice of Misery Bay for the hundredth anniversary of the Battle of Lake Erie. In these photographs he could see the full length of the keel, the placement of the gun ports, and the size of the knees that absorbed the strain from the fore-rigging. Melbourne also studied the customary shipbuilding practices of that particular decade as well as the documented practices of the *Niagara's* esteemed shipwright, Noah Brown.

As he worked at the research and drawing challenges, Melbourne grew increasingly determined that he would build this ship. No one else had his skills. No one else could be trusted. This one could be his all the way, a fair run from port to port, so to speak.

So he created plans that were so detailed and fine that he knew no one else would ever bid on the job. "I designed the ship calling for laminated frames. And I set the price at roughly three million dollars. I built my own bid into the contract. They put it out for bid and couldn't get any builders. According to them, [potential bidders] said they would have to use traditional sistered frames. And they couldn't possibly do the work for three million.

"So the commission found a way to hire me. They hired another naval architect to supervise the project. He knew less about it than we did. After that everything went very smoothly."

HERE'S the paradox of the *Niagara* reconstruction project: Melbourne's task was to create a timeless and enduring exact copy of a ship that was originally built to be disposable. In a series of articles that Melbourne later published in *Seaways* magazine (1991–92) he wrote: "In reality the ship was a swift, but simple, gun platform [built] to perform briefly."

The original *Niagara* and her exact twin, the war-brig *Lawrence*, as well as four smaller companion war vessels, were all fashioned in 1812 in a furious hurry in a wilderness far from maritime supplies. For lack of oakum and pitch, the hulls were caulked with lead foil. The framing timbers didn't necessarily fay (fit tight) against the planking. And all the wood was cut from the surrounding forest—white pine, red cedar, black walnut, even tulip tree (poplar)—and used still green. It was said that many timbers were in the ship the same day they were cut.

One hundred and fifty shipwrights—carpenters, block-makers, sail-

Controlling the tiller with his leg, Captain Smith guides the Brig *Niagara* as she is towed out of the harbor for her first trial sail.

makers, and riggers—trekked from New York out to this obscure spot in the Pennsylvania wilderness. Manufacturers in Pittsburgh sent iron, canvas, cordage, anchors, and cannonballs via mule-drawn wagons over former Indian trails. Fourteen wagons with four men each hauled the cannon from Washington, D.C. These cannon were forged in the Georgetown foundry of George Foxall, who vowed to build a memorial church if Perry were to win. Today you can visit Foundry United Methodist Church on 16th Street, proof that Foxall was good for his word. These guns were primarily carronades—short, light-barreled cannon that could throw a heavy ball (thirty-two pounds) with smashing delivery, but only within a short range, no farther than half a mile. This caravan of sixty-five carronades took over a month to reach Erie.

That was a speedy trip under such wilderness conditions in the early nineteenth century. Construction was just as fast. Bear in mind that these were planned to be very fine ships, with the sharpest lines and best design ideas of their day. To build two such vessels from raw timber, plus four small fighting escorts, in eight months would be astonishing even in a well-supplied shipyard of our own time.

Haste was certainly called for. The man who best understood the urgency was Captain Dan Dobbins of Erie. In July 1812, he was delivering a shipload of salt to Fort Mackinac in the northwest part of Lake Huron when British forces captured the fort there, and Dobbins along with it. Somehow Dobbins got himself released. He sailed down to Detroit just in time for the British to capture him once again. When he finally got back to Erie in August, he raised a ruckus that alarmed all of northwest Pennsylvania.

Later that same month Dobbins went off to Washington. He gave a full report to President Madison and his cabinet and suggested a strategy for defending the northern border—namely, to float warships in Lake Erie and so take the fight to the enemy. He also knew the perfect spot for the shipyard, a place where they could work undetected even if the British ships came scouting along the shoreline. That place was Presque Isle Bay.

Presque Isle, situated just off the Erie shoreline, is not an island but a long narrow peninsula that arches into the lake then curves back to shore again, completely enclosing a large placid bay—almost six square miles in area with an average depth of twenty feet. This forested peninsula effectively masks the bay (and any shipbuilding activities there) from the view of ships traveling the lake. The trick would be to get the finished vessels out of the enclosed bay and into the open lake. For that they would have to work the ships over a submerged sandbar located at the easternmost end of the peninsula, right where the rim of forested land seems to reconnect with the shoreline.* Water level over the sandbar in those days was never more than six feet. But the draft of the two big war-brigs, which were each one-hundred-eighteen feet in length, was more like nine feet.

Captain Dobbins, though, had no doubt that the vessels could be sallied—coaxed and towed—across the barrier. He proposed the use of "camels" to

---

* These days Presque Isle is a state park, and the sandbar has been dredged open so that ships can pass freely.

lift the brigs just high enough to clear the barrier. These camels, specially built for this purpose, were oblong barges ninety feet long whose holds were about six feet in depth. The camels could be flooded with water, sunk, and lashed to both sides of the vessel. As they were slowly pumped free of water, they would lift a hull sufficiently to clear the sandbar.

On August 2, 1813, *Lawrence*, ready for battle, was kedged to the entrance channel. ("Kedge" means to warp or pull a vessel forward along a line fixed to a carefully placed anchor.) She was stripped of all guns, ballast, and heavy materials, lifted twice by the camels, then successfully floated into the lake and secured with anchors. That process took two days. Then it was *Niagara's* turn to be lightened and lifted.

Suddenly in the midst of this operation the British fleet hove to. The enemy warships stood about seven miles off and reconnoitered within clear view for an hour or so. Then they sailed off. The hazy sky, the southerly sun's glare, and the difficulty of perceiving masts against the shoreline forest had prevented the certain annihilation of Perry's fleet. Meanwhile, Perry sent armed forces around the lake to choke off the British supply lines, thereby forcing the enemy to take a stand in response to the Americans' hoped-for full-scale attack.

The battle came on the cloudless dawn of September 10. The American ships had anchored at Put-in Bay, near the eastern tip of Lake Erie. A lookout on the mast of *Lawrence* spotted the British ships across the glimmering water, shouted, "Sail, ho!" and Perry went to work. Using *Lawrence* as his flagship, he led a single-file direct attack against Commander Barclay's squadron.

For unknown reasons, *Niagara* fell behind—a mishap that could have proven disastrous. *Lawrence* sailed ahead with the four smaller vessels in train (*Porcupine*, *Tigress*, *Scorpion*, and a pilot ship named *Ariel*) joined by three other vessels that had been adapted for battle. The big American brigs had both been outfitted with eighteen short-range carronades each. But the British ships were mounted with a full complement of long-range cannon. The long guns brutalized *Lawrence* as Perry kept sailing towards them, striving to get her carronades within striking distance. The pounding killed or wounded eighty percent of *Lawrence's* crew. Once she was finally within range, though, she gave right back. Most importantly, she disabled the captains and first lieutenants of every British ship. After that she was dead in the water—sails, sailors, and guns all out of service.

This painting depicts Oliver Hazard Perry transferring the ensign from *Lawrence* to *Niagara* before rallying to victory in the 1813 Battle of Lake Erie.

When Perry realized that *Lawrence* was lost, he ordered the battle flag ("Don't Give Up the Ship!") lowered. With the flag in his arms, he boarded a small cutter, taking with him a few unscathed sailors including his own brother, and he retreated to *Niagara*. To reach her, they had to row for half a mile, dodging gunfire and cannonballs.

The decision to leave his ship won Perry the battle. When he reached *Niagara*, the stricken British ships silenced their guns. Their junior officers, suddenly thrust into command positions, assumed that the Americans were about to surrender. But Perry raised his blue-and-white battle flag on *Niagara* and sailed directly at the enemy ships, two of which had become entangled in their own rigging. Perry closed to within a hundred yards and raked the enemy ships with broadside after broadside. Within fifteen minutes the British struck their colors and surrendered. The Battle of Erie was over by three in the afternoon. Americans took control of the lake and soon reclaimed the strategic city of Detroit. The confidence of a young nation bloomed.

Afterward, U.S. Brig *Lawrence*, having accomplished her purpose, was converted to a hospital ship. *Niagara* stayed in service for a while, covering the army's advances up the Great Lakes region. The next year, she patrolled with a convoy that captured several other British warships, then for a while served as a receiving ship in Erie. But within a few years both brigs were respectfully sunk in the shallows of Misery Bay as a way to preserve them in case they were needed again. Submersion reduces oxygen and stifles the slow burn of decomposition.

Misery Bay is a small natural shelter near the mouth of the much larger Presque Isle Bay. Before the Battle of Lake Erie it was called Little Bay. But after the battle most of the surviving U.S. sailors were quarantined at that site because they suffered from smallpox. Many of them were buried on that shoreline. After that, Little Bay became known as Misery Bay.

Oliver Hazard Perry, of course, became a national hero. He quarreled publicly in the newspapers with the captain of *Niagara* about why that ship had fallen behind the others. (It is surprising how often ship captains in a line of battle used to disobey the battle plan, sometimes for revenge, sometimes for personal advancement as they gambled on the battle's outcome. This treachery occurred several times in the naval engagements of John Paul Jones, who had a knack for alienating his fellow officers.) Six years after the Battle of Lake Erie, while on a special diplomatic mission, Perry died near Trinidad from the effects of yellow fever.

In 1875 *Lawrence* was raised from her liquid slumber and moved to Philadelphia for the Centennial Exposition of 1876. The pavilion in which she was displayed caught fire, immolating itself and the now-ruined brig.

In 1912 the people of Erie pulled up U.S. Brig *Niagara* in time for the hundredth anniversary of her famous victory. They cut a huge hole in the ice, hauled up the wooden bones (so to speak), and slid them across the ice to shore. Once above water, the hulk rotted at a steady pace. Over the next seventy-six years numerous efforts, mostly unskilled, to preserve the wreck succeeded mostly in eliminating every authentic piece of her original structure and design.

The only hope in 1988 for meaningful restoration was to bring in the man who could think, design, and build in the manner of two centuries ago—and to do that with modifications necessary to keep the ship in service longer than a few years. Melbourne Smith.

And just like his predecessors, he had to work on site and fast. Erie, Pennsylvania, is the sixth-snowiest place in the U.S.A., and he had no interest in driving trunnels in blizzard conditions. "It went very quickly," he recalled. "From laying the keel to launch, just ninety-nine working days [within a four-month period]. At the launch we all wore T-shirts that said 'The Ninety-Nine-Day Brig Builders.'"

B ILL ELLIOTT served as construction manager. "It was pretty cold all right," he said. "Back at Spanish Landing we were building on the beach in gorgeous weather. The guys all had binoculars in their toolboxes so that during the breaks they could look at the bikinis. In Erie we lofted the ship on the ground floor of a building downtown in February and March of 1988."

In February and March in Erie, the temperature would have been right about freezing. "By April we moved outside to lay the keel, and we were bringing guys up from California. first thing, they all made a beeline to Kmart to load up on long johns." They constructed the hull outdoors on the waterfront but kept the shipsaw and piecework in an abandoned warehouse, a shabby building with no roof. "This was an industrial area between the waterfront and downtown. It had the air of a place on the downhill slide. Decaying rustbelt country."

Bill said this without a pejorative slant. He liked the place, not just because "they'd built machinery, foundries, industrial shops—if you needed something done, you could find anybody to do it." Mostly he found it to be "real America, the real guts. There's no glossy in Erie. It's a great town. The ship was very important to them, sort of like their Eiffel Tower. Families would come around telling their kids about great-great so-and-so who had sailed on the ship. The local radio stations put us on their news. The *Niagara* was certainly much bigger in that town than the *Californian* was in that state. I guess there are just too many lifestyle options in California."

In the Melbournean manner, the crew identified its home bar, the Docksider, where they would gather at the end of the workday to talk about the job and tell stories. Bill said, "Beer was cheap, and the bartender got to know us. Everybody there drinks Rolling Rock. We didn't care for it so much. So the bartender imported cases of Anchor Steam. Lots of them."

As it turned out, this building crew was not a reunion. Jay Hazell from Bequia, said Melbourne, "had cracked his head in a car accident and was under doctor's orders not to undertake such work." Gerry Trobridge, the blacksmith, by now quite white-bearded, chose to produce the hardware back where he lived near Baltimore and ship it up to Erie.

The best can't-make-it-up story involves Baron Thomas, the one-legged salt who had formerly traveled the globe doing research for Scripps Institute and whose specialty was carving deadeyes and bull's-eyes. Baron wouldn't

"Praised by the Experts" | During construction of *Niagara* staff reporter Bill McKinney provided the following comments to the *Erie Morning News* | Summer 1988:

Replica, Reproduction, or "The Real Thing?"

RECONSTRUCTION of Erie's treasured Brig *Niagara*—really a national treasure—promises to add fuel to an already raging debate among maritime scholars.

As far as Peter Stanford is concerned, the *Niagara* will enjoy the best of all possible worlds, regardless of the debate.

Stanford is president of the National Maritime Historical Society based in Croton-on-the-Hudson, N.Y. and chairman of the American Ship Trust which is this nation's chapter of the World Ship Trust.

"I'm thrilled and delighted at what's happening in Erie," Stanford said. "It's absolutely wonderful. I salute this event and all of the people who made it possible."

The *Niagara* is much more than a simple reproduction, he said. Because the *Niagara* also enjoys a certain historical continuity, it comes close to being "The Real Thing" in Stanford's eyes. That it is being rebuilt to sail the lakes makes it an even grander treasure.

"Because it is not the original, it can be put at risk," he said. "Meeting the requirements of sailing gives it a whole new dimension. It will teach things that can't be taught by 'The Real Thing,' such as what it really felt like to sail aboard her."

Adding tremendously to the *Niagara's* value, Stanford said, is the choice of Melbourne Smith to oversee the construction. Where the first reconstruction was not a particularly good one, Stanford said, Smith's version promises to be as nearly perfect as is humanly possible.

"It will be much closer to the original than what it's replacing," Stanford said.

"We think very highly of Melbourne Smith, as you can probably tell. He is much more than a boatbuilder. He has a 19th century can-do that you don't find much anymore. He gets things done, no excuses."

Stanford said Smith, beyond being a master of the woods he uses, is a sailing man and knows the sea of the sailing man. He knows the purposes to which each item aboard the old ships were put, something that Stanford said has allowed Smith to bring authenticity to all his past projects.

—BILL MCKINNEY
Erie Morning News

"You could not possibly have chosen a better person for this project," Stanford said.

Some three decades later, Stanford remembered the mood in Erie on the day Melbourne's reconstruction first touched the water:

"I was there for the Niagara launch. Melbourne had kindly asked me, and he got his sponsors to pay the fare.

"Melbourne had everything just so. The whole town had changed. There were 'Don't Give Up The Ship' flags everywhere. Canadians were all there. It was all Melbourne's doing. His creativity includes this spirit that begins to affect everything and everybody. It was one of the finest visits I had anywhere.

"Of course, the atmosphere was heightened by the fact that he'd lived in Canada. You don't get a trace of that kind of cheap pseudo-patriotism in Melbourne." ★

fly to Erie. He just wouldn't. "I'll float on anything," said Baron. "But I'm terrified of flying. I have to be drunk or wiped out to get on a plane."

His reluctance derived at least in part from experiences he'd had in Samoa. "There were about seven of us [researchers with the Scripps Institute] over in Apia, West Samoa, and we had to get back to our ship in Pago Pago. We boarded a DC-3. Then I realized the runway was a grass field, not tarmac, and the field was covered with water. And there was a big mountain right in front of us." As soon as the plane started its run across the field, it began fishtailing. "I jumped up and started yelling, 'I want out of this plane right now!'" The pilot revved up, fought for speed along the sloshy field, then braked sharply when he ran out of room and turned back to try again. That's when Baron lost his self-restraint. He began shouting, "'I don't care what you do, I'm getting off this plane before the next run!'" He stood by the door with his hand on the latch. "I'm going to open it if you won't do it." The pilot came out to explain why regulations forbade opening the door. "But he knew I was determined. 'Do you realize how far it is to the ground?' he said. 'It's a twelve-foot drop.' I said, 'No problem.' So they let me jump. I landed in six inches of water. Then I went to a bar and swigged a couple of beers." He watched that DC-3 try to take off three times. In the end, it barely cleared the mountaintop.

For a while after, his co-workers teased him without mercy. Then a year later that same plane in the same take-off failed to reach altitude and crashed into the mountain, killing all aboard including several of Baron's colleagues. The teasing stopped. So did Baron Thomas's history with air travel.

But he did cut *Niagara's* deadeyes and bull's-eyes. A brig such as *Niagara* requires a great many of these, and the largest, as much nine or ten inches in diameter, will weigh forty or fifty pounds.

Melbourne provided Baron with a "railcar of timbers from Belize." These had been hewn from a heavy tropical hardwood known as granadia (*Platymicium yucatamin*). Each timber was ten-by-ten inches square or else twelve-by-twelve, each one twelve feet long. To give an idea of density: a cube of this wood measuring one foot on a side weighs about eighty pounds. In other words, one of these sticks could have weighed almost half a ton.

Baron lived in Cardiff, a coastal town north of San Diego, and his property lay at the bottom of a steep grade. To receive the delivery, he built a flume that he greased with soap. Then he built an old-style sawpit in his back yard and set the sticks up on horses. From there it was fairly easy to drop blanks and haul them over to the lathe. It took Baron eleven months to fulfill the order.

Eleven months was quite a bit longer than the "Ninety-Nine Days" touted on the T-shirts, but no problem there. The push in 1988 was to get the hull in the water before winter began to refrigerate Erie and in time for the hundred and seventy-fifth anniversary of the battle on the tenth of September. Melbourne and his crew would have to come back in '89 for the spars and rigging.

They had to push to make their battle-anniversary deadline. "Bill was putting on six strakes [rows of planking] a day, each side," said Melbourne. "He got air hoses so we could work faster. A guy from Maine said, 'We only do one strake a day.' Bill said, 'We do six a day here.' He doesn't stand for standing around. He wants to go home. On one job site he threw away the coffee maker because people were standing around it. You go to Bill's own yard [Bay Ship & Yacht], he has bicycles all around so people can get between work areas as quickly as possible. And yet he is well loved by everyone in the yard. He's a straight arrow. He keeps no secrets."

Bill made several modifications to accelerate the work. The hull of a sailing ship is typically constructed on a single framing stage, but Bill set up three of them. He had four crews hanging planks, not just one. He also had Melbourne's organizational skills at his back. Timbers arrived on time in all the right sizes, also the tools, the plans, the money, the beer, and so on. By now Melbourne had mastered the art of the overview. Anyone who has worked on boatbuilding projects will tell you that glitch-free productions are quite rare.

The greatest test of Melbourne's ingenuity was finding the balance between authenticity and the compromises necessary to make a vessel that would actually last long enough to merit the public's investment. The historic commission insisted on authenticity. There would be no engine installed, for example. And the ship would be seaworthy and swift like the original. That fidelity, of course, pleased the builders no end. Nevertheless, Melbourne had cautioned the commission that they should consider adding propulsive power, watertight bulkheads, and extra keel ballast if they ever considered offering the vessel for public use. They refused even to talk about it.

But there were adaptations—adaptations beyond the required instal-

The reincarnated U.S. Brig *Niagara*, under full sail, once again sails Lake Erie.

lation of safety and navigational gear, also beyond the use of Melbourne's innovative laminated timbers.* For example, a ship with such heavy guns on deck would, if sitting idle, tend to hog—that is, to sag at each end. Heavy guns can make a ship dangerously unstable. So Melbourne designed the new cannon to be forged from aluminum. The results would have been half the weight of cast iron and look the same. But the idea was not accepted and no guns were provided. The rigging looked original even though hemp of original quality was not available at that time. Melbourne opted for a weave of polypropylene around a wire core, and the work of serving and tarring (in other words, wrapping the wire) was all done on site. For the sake of longevity, the sails were made of a synthetic cloth that looked quite like cotton duck.

---

*Lamination solved a problem with timber supplies. The big stuff was getting harder to obtain. Now when Melbourne went to Belize, if he wanted a tree, he had to fell an acre. That act of deforestation would free the land for farming. "The country was being flattened," said Melbourne, and he hated that. He could see that that the very landscape of the Earth had changed since the peak days of sail, when shipyards were producing wooden vessels at almost Model-T speed.

IN THE FALL of 1989 Melbourne and crew took the new *Niagara* out for a shakedown cruise with Captain Carl Bowman, USCG (ret.) in command. All the state officials were aboard. This was their chance to discover what it was they had actually commissioned.

"A tugboat pushed us out—because the design called for no engine. We took everybody for a sail for the day. It was an astounding success." Niagara's building crew had practiced at dockside for several evenings after work. Their first attempt at tacking (changing direction into the wind) went perfectly, to the delight of everyone. Melbourne had ordered no smoking aboard during the V.I.P. cruise, but some of the dedicated tobacco enthusiasts can be seen in pictures taken from the accompanying fleet of yachts, puffing away while crouched in the outboard rigging chains.

"At the end of the day I asked the visitors, 'Do you want to go sailing again tomorrow?'" No, they said. They all wanted to get back to Harrisburg.

Melbourne was surprised to learn that the state officials actually had no idea what they were going to do with the ship. They said they would start looking around for a captain. "I told them that they should have begun that search a year before. But they just left and went back to the capital. We said, 'At least let us take the sails and lines off.' We stowed them below and went home. A month later the State of Pennsylvania delivered the rest of the pay. Later, the director of the museum sent a beautiful commendation diploma."

Two years later Melbourne was dismayed to find that the *Niagara* was still sitting idle. "That's the worst thing for a sailing ship—to leave it unattended. It needs attention, daily upkeep. It needs to sail. Otherwise, it starts leaking. Freshwater on or in a hull causes real problems." So Melbourne started squawking. With phone calls, letters to the newspapers, and the rallying of more voices, he got the state commission to wake up to its own investment. They finally engaged a captain, Walter Rybka, to bring the project forward. He had a lot of clean-up to do. Then the commission decided that it wanted an engine installed after all, so the new skipper had to deal with that. Captain Rybka stayed with *Niagara* thereafter.

With work, though, the U.S. Brig *Niagara* was finally given the life she was ready to live. She is in beautiful shape today, maintained by the nonprofit flagship Niagara League and berthed when in port within yards of its sponsor, the Erie Maritime Museum. She is used for sail training and experiential learning. She towers over the Erie shoreline, a most formidable flagship for Pennsylvania and a vivid reminder of the nation's bold youth. Best of all, she's no toy.

Melbourne wrote about the challenge of old-style shipbuilding in *Seaways* magazine (November/December 1991): "It is often argued that all vessels, especially those of historic design, should be made safe and foolproof for the untrained or amateur to participate in their operation. Certainly if the public is to be entertained or the crew to be fledglings, all ships must be foolproof. The commission decided to replicate the original vessel and not to create a bastardized or Disneyland version, and in so doing they sired a racehorse (not a child's pony), a rare tiger (not a pussycat), or more precisely, a brig-of-war (and not a ferry boat). In doing so, they chose a highly dangerous but wonderful machine. And like a racehorse it is only useful and exciting for viewing in the paddock or in professional hands on the home stretch.

"She was designed to not only appear as the real thing but be capable of performing as the original 1813 sailing vessel, with many of the same unavoidable frailties, dangers, and excitement."

Fortunately *Niagara* has met with none of the excitement that took down the *Pride of Baltimore*. ★

The reborn *Lynx* rounds Upolo Point to finish her 2,500-mile run from Newport Beach, California, to Hawai'i Island.

Penobscot Bay | 1998

*"In these days of competition and hard utilitarianism,
[the intellectual arts are] not only a pure relief to the mind,
but a source of high enjoyment to the man who has kept an idea
constantly before him, and has followed it with a fearless
and faithful heart."*

— JOHN WILLIS GRIFFITHS, 1849
*Treatise on Marine and Naval
Architecture; Or, Theory and
Practice Blended in Ship Building*

"'OH, you're going to meet that son of a bitch.' That's what people would say to me when I told them that I was going down to check out the *Californian* project and try to introduce myself to Melbourne Smith."

Woodson Woods didn't understand why he heard such comments, and he still doesn't. But every society has its form of gossip. Even though Woodson was living in Phoenix, he kept a vintage yacht at a slip at San Diego Harbor—a 1930 yawl he'd bought cheap after the publishing heir Hastings Harcourt died up in Santa Barbara—so he was privy to the general drift of Southern California nautical off-gassing.

"They said he was a 'my way or the highway' kind of guy."

Nothing about their grumblings could dissuade Woodson, who was fundamentally enamored of beautiful wooden ships. But the thought of those comments did make him feel wary as he walked up to the rude shipyard at Spanish Landing, the bright sand, the ad hoc pavilion, the roar of traffic nearby passing the U.S. Coast Guard Station. When he asked, a burly bearded man, holding a mallet and chisel, said, "Melbourne? Oh yeah. Hang around. He'll be back sooner or later."

So Woodson hung around watching the crew dub the framing timbers and hang planks in the old style. He wasn't the kind of person who was particularly comfortable just hanging around.

SOME TIME later he noticed a fellow in a railroad cap moving quickly from place to place on the construction site. The man was slighter in build than most of the crew, shorter certainly than the lanky Caribbean man who walked with him and kept calling him "Cap." The fellow in the cap was white-haired but fully vigorous. Woodson put him at about his own age, mid-fifties. He moved with wind-up-toy energy from place to place at the worksite, dropping a joke at every stop. While the others laughed, Woodson noticed, this one went "heh - heh - heh," then his eyes would shift back into searching mode. This had to be Melbourne Smith, Woodson figured.

Woodson introduced himself. Melbourne listened in one ear. Woodson tried to express his love for sailing, using blunt but earnest sentences as though to strike up a conversation. He'd sailed his yawl twice to Hawai'i, the first time with his two sons, that sort of conversation. But almost instantly Woodson realized that his admired shipbuilder, though physically present, was not picking up the phone at this time.

If Melbourne had turned and paid some attention to his admirer, he would have seen a virile outdoorsman, his scissor-trimmed hair and beard now getting a first dusting of snow. He looked like a guy who might have a few poems in his pocket. Woodson might have suggested (he doesn't remember for certain) that the two of them do a project together someday. If he did, then Melbourne certainly said, "Sounds good," and quickly excused himself to deal with an urgent design detail.

Melbourne later admitted that he didn't remember that encounter at all. "I talked to so many people who told me, 'I've got the next job for you.' All of them were blue-sky things. You get kind of used to it. Then you discover that the man has a motive, something else he wants you to do. I guess that's why I distrusted Woody or anyone else until I got to know them. The amount of misinformation you get. You spend all your life sifting it. I remember my grandmother saying, 'Oh, these times in the world are so bad now.' I guess I wasn't that friendly to him. I don't remember that, though.

"I guess that worked out in our favor," he added. "You find out who are good people—if you're still friends over a long time."

Woodson remembered the encounter this way: "I could see he was definitely on his own track here, didn't want to be disturbed." And added, "I was intimidated by the guy."

Woodson Woods was a sailor, leader of back-country hunting treks, publisher, pilot, owner of a statewide Hawai'i charter flight service, and national competitor in racing unpowered sailplanes—in other words, not the kind of person who normally admits being intimidated.

AND YET this meeting was not a quirk. It was a seed that took a decade or so to sprout.

"It dawned on me," said Woodson. "This was in ninety-six. Or ninety-seven. I woke up one morning and had this wild feeling. I knew I was going to build a boat. It was an epiphany of some sort."

Woodson had enjoyed very good fortune in his life and he wanted to give something back. The best thing he had to give, he figured, was his love of sailing in wooden ships. He wanted to build a vessel that would be just as exciting to anyone who saw it or climbed aboard, a vessel that would fill children with enthusiasm for this faded history and technology.

"What happened then—I remembered Melbourne Smith. I decided to give him a call. I kind of ran it by him."

Woodson admitted later that he called Melbourne with a "counterpoint of doubt" based on the prior experience in San Diego. "We talked, and I liked him better on the phone. There was never one inkling of the stress I might have expected. As we got together planning to build that boat, things just continued to get better. I've never been happier.

"In fact, the two years we spent building that vessel were the happiest years of my life."

WHEN WOODSON made that first phone call to Melbourne, who had returned by then to Annapolis, he was earnest and clear about his purpose—educational, enthusiasm-igniting—but still blurry about the boat itself. He was drawn to the look and lines of the Baltimore clipper style, in part because the style was so purely American. Woodson was unapologetically patriotic about this project. It bothered him that his daughter's American history textbook contained only a single paragraph about the War of 1812, which he felt was the war that had completed the American revolution and confirmed the national character—brash, self-reliant, inventive, and rough-hewn.

Melbourne listened and made some suggestions for Woodson's research. Woodson kept calling, each time with more information, clearer ideas. Melbourne "began to actually like" this persistent guy from the West Coast. "He struck me as being reasonable—practical, not just romantic. He wanted things to work. He really wanted to take kids sailing. And he was a real student. He was willing to learn. So I figured, if he kept up his end and I kept up mine, we could solve this thing."

THE CLICK that turned an idea into a campaign happened when Woodson spotted the *Lynx*. He'd been studying Howard Chapelle's classic 1967 text *The Search for Speed under Sail*, and there he found the lines, carefully recorded, of a sharp-built topsail schooner by that name. She had just the look and pedigree he wanted. The very fact that her lines had been recorded was a fluke of history, but that fluke would certainly facilitate the task of designing some kind of replica.

There have been several U.S. built ships called *Lynx*. It's a very desirable name for a fighting ship. The name evokes a native predator of North America, swift, secretive, and sharp-eyed. For this reason, the ship depicted in Chapelle, the original *Lynx*, was well named. She had been commissioned less than a month after the beginning of the War of 1812. Thomas Kemp's shipyard at Fell's Point, Maryland, built her for the express purpose of eluding the British—slipping in and out of guarded ports in order to engage in North Atlantic trade.

Today Fell's Point is a Baltimore waterfront neighborhood renowned for its pubs. Two hundred years ago the area was despised by the British because, under the protection of Fort McHenry, its shipyards produced fast, armed sailing ships that could outrun any of King George's blockades. These new vessels were called privateers—privately owned ships that carried a commission from the U.S. government, a "letter-of-marque," a form of enlistment in the U.S. Navy. These privateers could confiscate an enemy's cargo and keep a portion of the spoils.

The notion seems weird today—the government recruiting the assistance of private boat owners in defending the country.* But in 1812 the U.S. Navy

---

* And yet something similar took place along the New Jersey coast in 1941.

consisted of only seventeen ships, compared to the thousand vessels of Great Britain, who clearly ruled the Atlantic. Even though the British had signed the Treaty of Paris ending the Revolutionary War, they still intercepted American ships at will, impressed (captured) American sailors as though they were homeland deserters, and seized merchant vessels who had traded with the enemy (France). England still occupied her forts on American soil, still engaged in the fur trade, and flagrantly behaved as though she had never lost the colonies. In order to preserve the integrity of the United States, President James Madison needed to push back. In order to push back, though, all Madison had (besides debts left over from the Revolutionary War) were those seventeen ships, which the British press had derided as a "handful of fir-built frigates... manned by bastards and outlaws."

Bastards or not, the Yankee shipbuilders were quite ready for the challenge. They were eager to outperform the British in home waters. These shipyards were defending their regional and business interests as much as they were defending a country. They hated seeing big British warships bruising their way into Chesapeake Bay, and they delighted in zipping past the brutes and pouncing on British merchant vessels, partly out of revenge and partly because the terms of warfare allowed that they could.

It was in this spirit that Kemp's shipyard produced *Lynx*. She was larger than most commissioned vessels of her time—ninety-four feet in length on deck, over twenty-four feet beam, with a displacement of two hundred twenty-five tons. She was not, strictly speaking, a privateer, meant for battle. Though she carried a letter-of-marque, *Lynx* was fitted out for illicit trade, not for capturing enemy vessels. As a result, she carried a relatively small crew of forty with a defensive complement of six twelve-pounder long guns. If she had been outfitted for the bagging of warships, thus operating as a privateer, she would have carried a hundred men—extras to replace the crews of the captured vessels—and a lot more firepower.

Imagine life on a privateer—a hundred men in a ninety-four-foot boat for a couple of months. Even for *Lynx's* crew of forty, the living conditions must have been scarcely tolerable. The speed of these schooners resulted in part from the clean emptiness of their decks. There was no gear or deckhouses above decks that might create "windage" or wind drag. As a result, below-decks space was tight. Everyone walked bent over. The only time a man could stretch full length was while working above, or else when he was lying in a hammock—which he swapped with other crewmembers depending on the order of their watches.

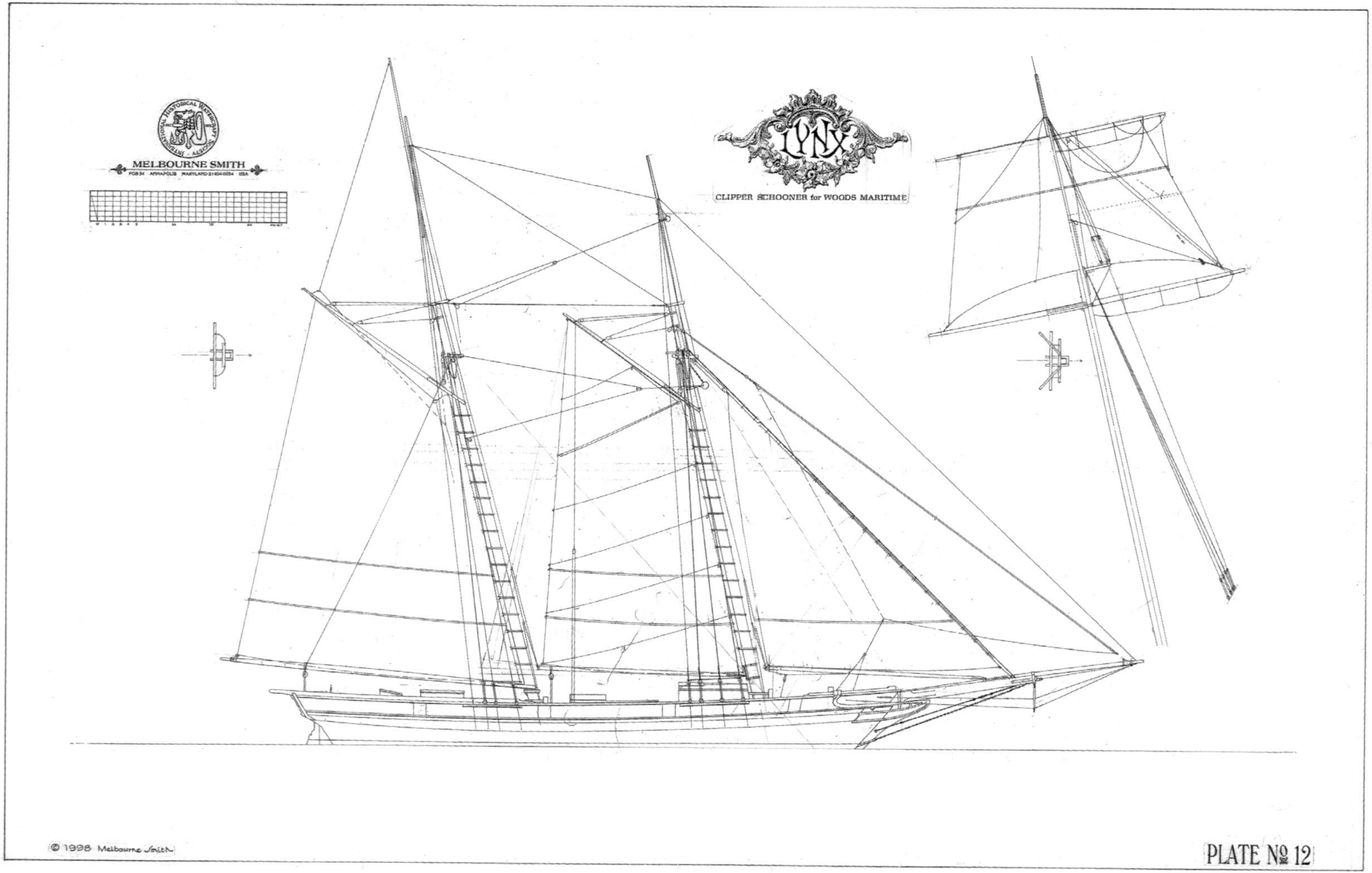
LYNX
CLIPPER SCHOONER for WOODS MARITIME
MELBOURNE SMITH
BOX 34 · ANNAPOLIS · MARYLAND 21404-0034 · USA
INTERNATIONAL HISTORICAL WATERCRAFT SOCIETY
© 1998 Melbourne Smith
PLATE No 12

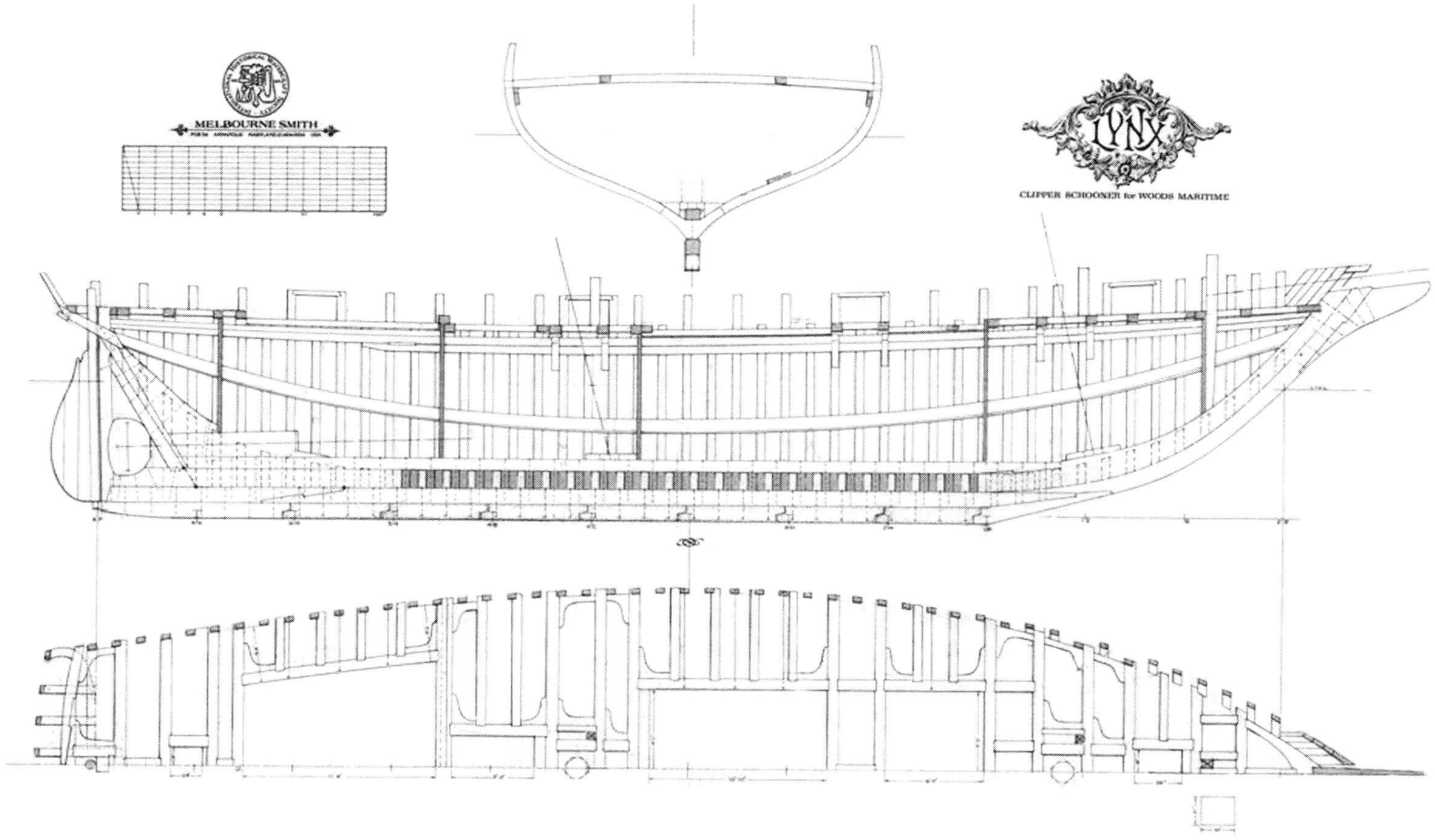

MELBOURNE SMITH
LYNX
CLIPPER SCHOONER for WOODS MARITIME

PLATE № 4

Despite its discomforts, this *Lynx* was a beautiful machine. It had a fierce profile that came from the rake of the two masts. The taller mainmast was raked proportionately more than the foremast. This look, plus her sharp lines and low-in-the-water profile, gave her a dangerous swagger. Basically fore-and-aft rigged, she had the additional ability to deploy square sails for off-the-wind courses and light breezes.

She was so beautiful, in fact, that the British took her into their service after her capture. There are no tales of battle heroics associated with this *Lynx*. Just a few months after her launch—she made one successful run to Bordeaux for a luxury cargo of perfume, wine, and stockings—*Lynx* was lying just up the Rappahannock River by Carter's Creek when the British trapped her.

This was spring of 1813. *Lynx* was huddled along the riverbank with three other American vessels. The captains were discussing how best to run the British blockade. Suddenly seventeen British boats thick with armed marines and oar-pulling sailors entered the river under the command of Lieutenant James Polkinghorne. There was no wind. Polkinghorne brought his force along to the farthest ship down the line, knocked her into submission, then came up to the next in line, the *Lynx*. She hauled down her colors. So did the next ship, the *Racer*. That left the *Dolphin*, who refused to surrender. So the British used the captured American warships to bombard her. *Dolphin* surrendered after a two-hour melee during which Lieutenant Polkinghorne died and a one-armed lieutenant named Brand had his other arm severed. It was a bad day on both sides of the fracas.

In the long run, though, a good thing resulted: The British Admiralty, as they were wont to do with well-designed captured vessels, "took off her lines"—recorded her dimensions and preserved evidence of her design. By contrast, Yankee shipyards almost never drew plans. They would carve a half-model of the hull and yell orders from there.

So, thanks to the British, Woodson was able to find her as a drawing in Chapelle's publication. With this drawing he was able to pursue his own search, using her as the model for his privateer.

Ironically, despite their careful measurements the British never quite caught on to American ship design. Melbourne explained: "When the British captured a Baltimore clipper type, they were always disappointed with the construction and how it was built. They said, 'This is very poor work.' Many privateers were taken back to England and rebuilt. The masts were

On the way to her launch site in Rockport, Maine, *Lynx* gets hauled over the Goose River.

straightened. Everything tightened up. Then of course when they were 'fixed' they wouldn't sail as well."

ONCE the decision was clear that Woodson's educational vessel would be a reincarnated *Lynx*, much larger questions arose. All of them were variations on the main puzzle: how could they adapt to late-twentieth-century circumstances without compromising the ship's historical essence?

Melbourne started with questions about the ship's size. The *Lynx* was oversized even in her own day. Her two-hundred-twenty-five-ton displacement was far too big for contemporary practices. He wanted to know, "Where are you going to keep the vessel, and how much water is there?" In those days Woodson was living in Newport Beach, California. And he was still thinking regionally, of a boat built and docked in the same harbor, just like Melbourne's previous creations. Newport Harbor was about ten feet deep.

"That limits the vessel right away to nine feet of water," said Melbourne. "The original *Lynx* drew twelve feet. Now I've got a number to work from."

In the next phone conversation Melbourne said, "A practical vessel of that size is going to be about seventy-two feet on the water line. That's quite a bit smaller than the original *Lynx*." Woodson was not taken by surprise. He had certainly been thinking on those lines. He said he was okay with the idea of a proportional reduction.

That wasn't all. Woodson was keen on even more radical compromises with historical fact. If this ship were to function as a living classroom, he couldn't have the students always walking bent-over below decks, rotating hammock-times, and defecating over the side. There had to be instructional space. Bunks. Electricity. A galley that could produce something more like pizza than salt pork and hard tack. And an engine!

"Woody wanted headroom and all the comforts, so in other words, he did not want to build a replica," said Melbourne. "There would be no comfort in the original vessel." As the two worked together, they became increasingly comfortable with calling this project an "interpretation."

Melbourne continued to enjoy the fact that his client did his homework, understood the practical parameters, wasn't a "blue sky" romantic. Even so, Woodson actually *was* a romantic. As much as he was engaged in the mechanics and methods of Melbourne's high-velocity mind, Woodson was even more captured by the charisma of everything Melbourne made. "What a thrill to start getting Melbourne's drawings in the mail," he said later. "Hand-drawn with pen and ink. Those wonderful drawings."

In fact, the entire collection of Melbourne's drawings and plans for the interpreted *Lynx*, which includes twenty-five plates and two books of detailed illustrations, deserves attention as a singular work of American art. Melbourne focused entirely on accuracy of detail. And yet the uncalculated side-effect of his focus was simple beauty. Beauty is very compelling, and it was beauty above all that Woodson wanted. "Melbourne's work has a mystique of the past. So does his mind. When I worked with him on design, I felt I was stepping into the past. That's the kind of stuff I love." And Woodson understood that to create a lasting educational experience, he would need this mystique more than anything else.

Melbourne: "We talked this over for weeks. We talked about use. Afterwards Woody said, 'I wish I'd built the original one.' That's like saying, I wish I'd bought the racehorse and not the trotting horse. But he could never have taken passengers in that." In the end, Woodson knew the difference between wishing and doing.

THEY BOTH agreed to break the pattern that Melbourne had begun in Belize over thirty years before—that is, the practice of building ships on the shoreline under wildly unpredictable conditions. With a miscellany of one-job workers. With vagaries of weather. With public staging. With bureaucratic meddling and funding hang-ups. With stone-age tools.

After all, even the original *Lynx* had been built in a shipyard, not on the sand. Maybe Melbourne felt his point about pre-industrial genius had been amply made by now. Maybe he realized that he was approaching seventy years old. Maybe Woodson felt the same way.

They put the job out for bid, and the contract went to Rockport Marine, situated on Penobscot Bay, Maine. This was a small shipyard. In fact, *Lynx* was much larger than anything they had yet built. To fulfill the contract, Rockport repurposed an adjoining building and expanded its shop.

By this time Woodson had become a regular visitor to Melbourne's house near Annapolis. "He had a wonderful home on five or so wooded acres, a big two-story house with a widow's walk, a cupola, and a barn. He loved that house. He would play the piano. Whenever I visited I kept marveling at this Renaissance man. He was a free-spirited artist just as much as a top-notch mechanic!"

They worked together on plans. For Woodson it was a humble collaboration. "I took over one part of the project with my love for arming the vessel. I had the cannon made in England, the Iron Brothers Foundry. They were cheaper than I could get in the U.S., even with the shipping." The interpreted *Lynx* ended up with four six-pounder carronades, four swivel guns, and a stand of muskets, cutlasses, and pikes.

Together Melbourne and Woodson developed plans for two aft staterooms, also a large main saloon amidships with entertainment center, fireplace, and dining for eight. The split-level galley, forward, included a berth for the cook

For Melbourne, this whole working arrangement was unprecedented. His client was not a state commission, a city council committee, a civically funded museum, not even the corrupt government of Guatemala. This was one man. The man had the means and the plan. In one way of thinking, here was a set-up for disaster. Any solo client could become cranky, autocratic, idiotic, psychopathic, could drift off, or could have darker motives, vanity being the most likely. But Woodson just wanted what he wanted. He wanted a ship that would startle the imagination of everyone who touched her or approached her. He planned to establish a foundation that would manage this ship as though she were a private school, which is in fact what she became. He would give that foundation, of course, to humanity. A true gift, nothing expected in return.

And he admired and trusted Melbourne.

You don't get many jobs like that in a lifetime.

Once Rockport Marine took on the work, Woodson and Melbourne began a monthly pattern of traveling to Maine. Woodson would fly to Maryland from the John Wayne Airport in Orange County, then he and Melbourne would fly north to Manchester, New Hampshire, then drive a rented car into remote Maine. They were a pair. The three-hour drive to Rockport was mostly straight-shot tedious. "Deadly boring for most of the trip," said Woodson, whose speaking style tends toward short clear noun-verb sentences.

"I don't like to get too familiar with people. But I really wanted to learn as much as I could about Melbourne. About him and what he did. So I'd be asking him questions. There were these pregnant pauses. Sort of embarrassing. I didn't know what to do."

Melbourne had his own conversational style. After a quiet couple of minutes he would thrust a forefinger into the air and proclaim something like, "Now here's something interesting!" And he would start talking about something that was more than a long pause away from the original question, usually something about the mechanics of sailing ships.

They learned to enjoy being together.

"He and Woody would come up. They would mostly hang around the yard while the work went on," said Eric Sewell, Rockford Marine's main man for the *Lynx* project, fifteen years later. "Anything Woody questioned, they would talk about it. Sometimes Woody won, sometimes Melbourne."

A born flannel-and-down-clad Downeaster, Eric grew up on a chicken farm, studied forestry in college, surveyed the Allagash Waterway for the State of Maine, then took a job in a boatyard because "it was a lot warmer than digging clams." It took him a few years to work his way out of the fiberglass boatyards into the wooden-ship specialty of Rockport Marine. He has the Mainer speech style—open R's and A's that sound as in "Maggie" (ma-velous, a-chitect), a laconic pace, plenty of sentences starting with the word, "Well...."

He said, "Well, this project was new for us, but Melbourne knew just how to do it. We talked almost daily on the phone. Any question I had, he'd draw it up and fax it over. He had ma-velous details."

Eric described Melbourne in the same terms that are used by nearly everyone who has worked with him: "easy-going and friendly, not at all tense. Sometimes the a-chitect wants everything exactly a certain way. But

To celebrate *Lynx*'s launch, the guests dressed in period costume. Woodson and Ali Woods outshone them all.

Melbourne was more the old way. He would draw up plans and trust you to do it." He added, as most do, "He loved to have a drink in the evening."

He also added, as all do: "He was very competent. He'd look at things. If it wasn't right he'd tell you." The example Eric gave had to do with the ship's rigging—that is, the arcane world of the sailing vessel's ropes, stays, sheets, halyards, grommets, and so on. The riggers hired to make the standing wire rigging for *Lynx* were independent contractors, obviously experts in rigging New England schooners, but with little patience for clipper schooners on the Baltimore model. Melbourne gave them very detailed plans and pretty much left them on their own. They misread the scale on the plans. When *Lynx*'s masts were hoisted in place just before the scheduled launching, every piece of the standing rigging was about a third too long. So, all the marline servings on the wire were in the wrong places.

The riggers were embarrassed, but they managed to re-cut all the wire to the proper lengths, re-serve the wire with new marline, and finish the job in time for the launching. Melbourne caught all this in time, and Woodson was compensated for the wasted materials. Impressed by Melbourne's attention to details, Eric Sewell hung a piece of that leftover seizing on the wall of his office, a lasting reminder.

Eric was also impressed by Melbourne's artfully calculated power of persuasion. At one point, visiting inspectors found that one of the companionway widths was slightly narrower than permitted by code. Melbourne countered that the sliding hatch cover open area was twice what was required, and he quickly calculated the total open square surface area. The inspectors capitulated to Melbourne's plain math. Eric phrased it this way in classic Mainer style: "He's a gifted talker. In a way. Sometimes. Basically he would say, 'This is the way it's going to be because everything else is there, and so this is the way it's going to be.'"

Meanwhile Woodson raised a motto in the shipbuilding shed: "Be excellent to each other and to your ship." Toward the end of the building project, Eric said, "Woody was practically staying here." He set the tone of the project.

Melbourne concurred. "Everything went so well because Woody always treated the crew so well. He showed up with a couple cases of beer, he did little things, he held parties and had them catered. Owners in shipyards are usually horse's asses. But Woody was a good customer. They just love him up there. Woody knows how to get the best out of people."

The launch involved a party that eclipsed anything Thomas Kemp's yard might have done in 1813. There were period costumes enough to bewilder any time traveler. It was Rockport's first launch of a square-rigged ship since 1885. Hauling her hull over the Goose River Bridge to the launch site was harrowing in itself. Spectators started filling the launch area twenty-four hours before the event, thirty-five hundred of them, with some three hundred fifty small boats dotting the harbor. The launch site was choked with bunting and flags and bonnets and brass-buttoned navy shortjackets. Woodson's wife Alison made a grand speech and smashed the champagne bottle. Woodson himself appeared in the form of a prosperous merchant of the day with tailcoat and ruffled shirt and a vertiginous top hat. There were pipers and a fife-and-drum corps. As *Lynx* slid down the launch ramp and splashed into the blue, cannon and muskets fired and air horns blasted from spectating ships that clogged the harbor. The crowd shouted "Huzzah!" again and again.

Melbourne had designed the commemorative posters, and he spent most of the event signing them. Woodson invited him to sail on the *Lynx*, but he turned down the offer. He had to get home, he said, where his wife Lulu was waiting for him.

MELBOURNE later explained why he needed to get home: "After building the U.S. Brig *Niagara*," he said, "I moved to a five-acre farm in Arnold, Maryland. I was living alone there in 1993 with my dog Spanker when I met a young lady. One thing led to another and we were married on the twenty-fourth of May, 1996, the day in Canada we called the Queen's Birthday.

"Lilith Arenas is a naval architect from the island of Cebu in the Philippines. Before making her own way to America, she worked with a boatyard in Cebu and with the Hans Christian Yachts in Nationalist Taiwan. While on that Chinese island, she picked up the nickname Lu Lu (璐璐), meaning "morning dew." With me, she has been evermore my Lulu and I have never had an eye for anyone else.

"Years before, I had read Daniele Varè's romantic *Novels of Yen-Chen,* and this lovely woman seemed to be a reincarnation. *The Maker of Heavenly Trousers* told the story of how a young Asian girl captured the heart of her Italian diplomat guardian in China. Lilith became my wife, and if you know that story, you know what I mean.

"With Lilith's attention, the homestead became a paradise. She planted a massive garden of flowers, bushes, and trees. Thanks to the contribution from horses we had on the property, her garden grew at a rapid rate. And her cuisine skills made every meal a banquet.

"Twenty years later," he said, "nothing has changed."

It wasn't until 2013 that the *Lynx*—by then a thriving school just as Woodson had envisioned, and a well-crewed schooner that had journeyed from Nova Scotia to Hawai'i—stopped in Florida to bring Melbourne aboard as a short-run pilot. Melbourne was eighty-three years old at the time. His philosophy of life was, "Never sail a ship that's shorter than your age." He broke that rule for one day. But the smile on his face in photographs of that occasion suggest a different motto—that rules are always to be broken, as long as you break them surpassingly.

There has been much praise of *Lynx*, much of that praise being historical and passionate and sometimes patriotic. But here's how Melbourne praised her in talking about adjusting the sails for balance. "By balancing, I mean having *almost* no pressure so that the vessel tracks straight with the rudder *almost* not needed. I say 'almost' because you want the vessel slightly out of balance so if you let the rudder go free, the ship turns very slowly up or into the wind.

"If the sails are not balanced properly, the correction must be made by the rudder. Dragging the rudder to one side corrects the balance, but it slows the vessel down considerably. It's amazing how many sail vessels

Lynx **passes under the Golden Gate Bridge, California.**

have to drag the rudder to one side to correct the balance. Such helm correcting is called a 'lee helm' or a 'weather helm.' A lee helm is the more dangerous.

"*Lynx* has been known to sail alone for hours on end with about one inch of weather helm."

From a true, Griffiths-minded "mechanic," what greater praise is possible?

I N LIEU of praise, here is Melbourne Smith's own description of the *Lynx* undertaking. These are the words of the Artist/Mechanic:

"The only restriction as to the size of the vessel was to keep her draft at eight and one-half feet. From this, I was able to give *Lynx* a seventy-two-foot waterline with a maximum beam of twenty-three feet to accomplish the required stability that would carry the traditional rig of a square fore topsail schooner having a jackyard topsail on the main topmast.

"Most clipper schooners had a pronounced drag to their keels, the draft being much greater at the stern end. To maintain balance with the required reduced draft, the keel was laid parallel with the waterline. Designing a near perpendicular rudder post—and making up the lateral area by filling in the space (except for a propeller aperture) between the stern post and a prick post—allowed the underwater center of the lateral plane to remain in the same vicinity as that of the original schooners. And it allowed her to carry a similar sail plan with less drag and draft.

"Preliminary lines were drawn, and a half-model was carved for approval. Final hull lines were completed with a hydrostatic characteristic study to assure that the vessel would be capable of her intended purpose. We found that a lofty rig could be set to show the authentic sail-to-hull relationship for schooners of 1812. To ease sail-handling, especially for novice training crews, the traditionally overlapping foresail was fitted with a boom, and the staysail was designed loose-footed on a boom as well. This change simplified tacking and sail-handling.

"To facilitate maintenance considerations, the keel, keelson, stem, and frames were all laminated in single pieces from treated yellow pine. This method, first tried on the frames of the topsail schooner *Californian*, has proved indestructible and impervious to deterioration. To increase further the life of the vessel, the sternpost, bitts, and planking were fashioned from durable tropical hardwoods. And she was bronze fastened." ✭

Melbourne, his ducks in a row, bends a batten.

West Palm Beach | 2012

"I've traveled a lot but never got very far."

— MELBOURNE SMITH

DESPITE his familiarity with maritime disasters, warm-latitude misadventures, and historic naval shoot-outs, Melbourne's greatest flights of seamanship occurred in his small studio. His design den. Since about the time he turned eighty years old, this den has been situated in West Palm Beach, Florida, where Melbourne kept developing a project to re-create the U.S. *Hornet* to serve as the State Ship of Florida. He worked in his home, a rented apartment on an upper floor overlooking the Intracoastal Waterway. Though he kept the blinds slanted against the afternoon sunlight, he could peak through to see the sparkling sea channel. The light on his matte-green work surface shone in a soft twilight illuminated by side incandescents. The small room was carefully stashed with paper storage—filing cabinets, drawers for flat artwork, a wooden bin with gridwork within for storing scrolled plans. A large vertical painting of *Niagara* under full spread of sail hung over his computer station. He used the computer for correspondence and for document storage. At his design table, however, there was nothing electronic. He had his eighteen ducks all in a row—each an identical flat-bottomed lead weight easily moved or nudged over the work surface. Each looked like a chubby narwhal with tusk bent into a downturned hook. With these he could pull and push a long batten—a thin, very limber strip of wood set on one edge. As he slid the ducks around, the batten naturally shaped itself into any curve Melbourne desired. The proper term for that style of curve-making is "fairing."

"You can always tell when a boat is computer-designed," he claimed. "When you designate a line, that's what you get. But when you put the duck down and bend a batten, it'll all balance on its own and form a natural line. With the computer you get a stuffed animal, but this way you get one that's alive."

His apt analogy: "A good singer is always behind the note, ahead of the note, all over the place. That takes real talent. If you're an amateur, you have to hit every note."

Then he produced a beautiful steel-and-brass instrument, completely mechanical, about a foot long, consisting of several rods jointed loosely, a pin at one end, a stylus at the other, and some gear-driven measuring devices in the middle. "This is my computer. It's called a planimeter." He pinned the device at one end then drew the outline of an irregular curved shape. Then he checked the tiny calibrated wheels. "With this planimeter I can find the areas of the sections and the displacement of a boat in an hour. I learned this from John Willis Griffiths. It gives you the area of an odd shape. You add up the sections and multiply by their distance apart." He worked out the calculations with pencil on paper.

"I wouldn't recommend anybody do this. I do it by hand then give it to a fellow at the Coast Guard, who does it again on the computer. It's amazing how identical they are. I don't know anyone who does this anymore."

In the living room he kept a dry compass that he once built for *Pride of Baltimore*, also a classic one-eye collapsible telescope whose fixed length was wrapped in a fancy whipping made of traditional marline. Nearby was the sea chest designed by Melbourne and fashioned in exactly the manner of *The Marlinspike Sailor*, a brilliant collection of line drawings by Hervey Garrett Smith, the foremost marine illustrator of the 1950s and '60s. (The older Smith used to introduce Melbourne as his nephew.)

From a perch as small as this he labored to resuscitate the human passion for sail—that is, for free travel on wind and water via rope, cloth, and curved wood.

In a very real sense he was simply doing what he'd learned as a kid. Painting signs. Defining accurate lines. Setting type. Working for himself entirely, but willing to make practical compromises. Avoiding authority politely. Being fascinated with pre-electric building technology such as he'd discovered at the Farmer & Son carriage factory. Respecting the honest enterprise of Mr. Collins and his small sheet-metal-products factory.

These childhood skills turned to mature purposes gradually through decades of immersion in the world of sail—its language, its mathematics, and its aesthetics. Its history, its vision, its disasters, and its abundance of particulars. From experience he learned the nature of wood, rope, canvas, steel, the wind against the sea and the sea's particular argument with land, the fixed and moving positions of celestial lights, the relationship between the center of buoyancy and the center of balance, the art of handling the ordinary madness of committees and clients, and the way to know that a whale is about to breech next to the ship (you can smell its bad breath). And where did all this brilliance come from? This ferocious appetite for research? This easy way with the most complex three-dimensional thinking? From a high-school flop whose primary interests were art and playing the drums and following the sheet-metal motto: "Never Say Fail. Say Never Fail."

Everything Melbourne Smith created caused countless people to talk about, invest in, even throw parades for the love of the history of sail. He never set out on a career path. Obviously he invented the story as he went along. You could say it was a string of accidents driven by high-speed enthusiasm—for example, building an eight-foot aluminum dinghy, wrecking a Brixham trawler off the coast of Normandy, romancing the tragic *Annyah*. But when he brought his innate brilliance with design and mechanics into the foreground, he changed minds. Most of all, he helped reverse the United States' amnesia about its own achievements in the technology of sail.

He never set out to do that. "It just happens that I was right, that's all," he said.

THE OCTOGENARIAN was sitting in an armchair in his rented apartment. It was a fine Asian-made armchair in a large and almost museum-quality apartment. His posture fit the chair as though the two of them had spent a fair amount of quality time together.

But Melbourne was never sedentary. That same day he had moved through the town like a very focused twenty-year-old, driving and stopping to talk with people, checking in, not much idle chat. He always had a small smile under his white moustache. Always fishing for ideas, thinking about people, looking attentively and patiently for the punch line.

Then sitting in his armchair he said, "Sometimes I run for half a mile and find out I'm still on the porch." That's a joke. He had rivers of energy, though most of it came from his mind.

"When I retire, I have all this unpublished artwork," he said with a gesture of one hand. "This may get me some rice and beans." He paused and looked straight ahead. "Then again, maybe it won't."

He kept tipping his attention outward as though reading cue cards from his own mind.

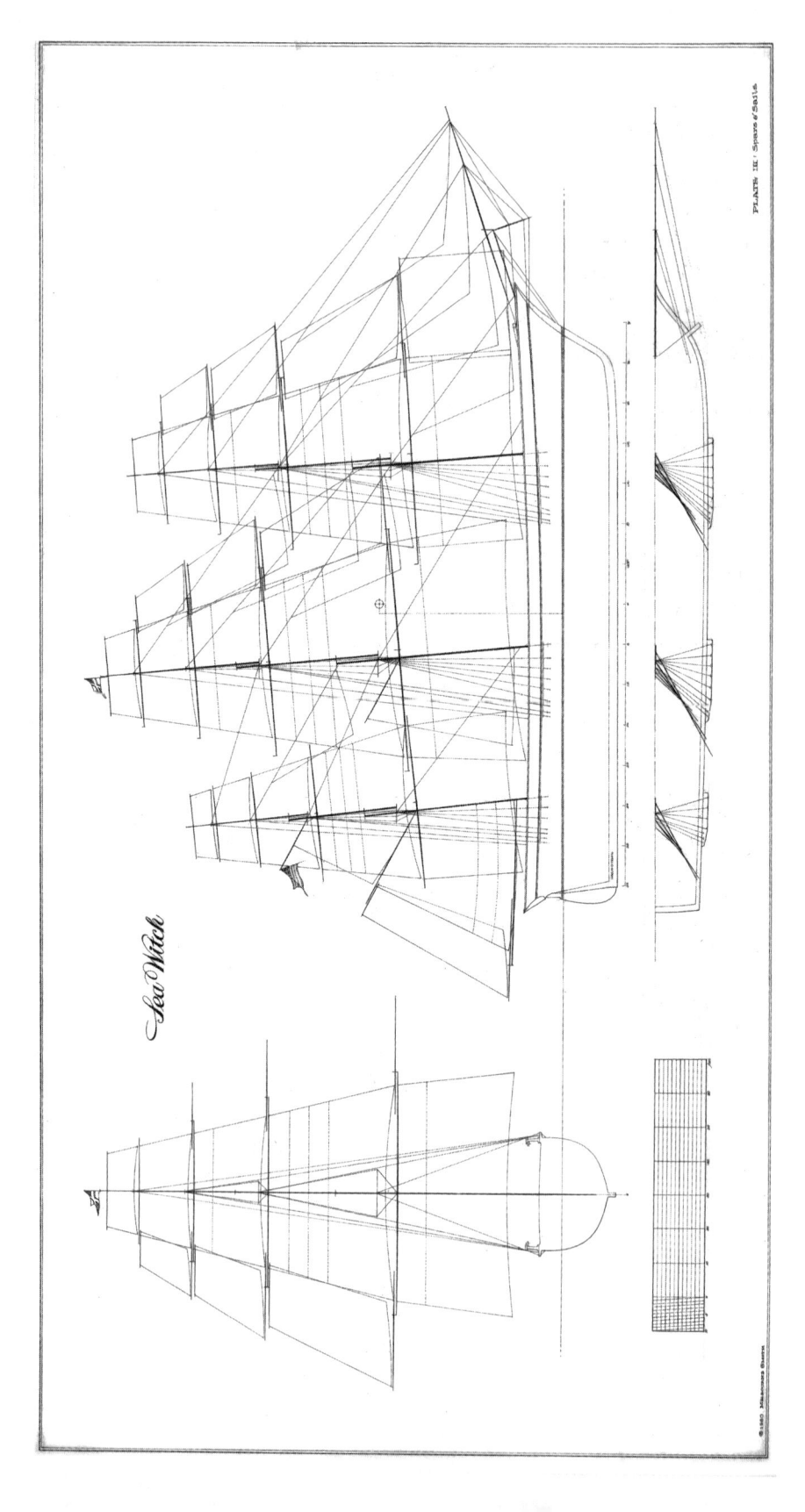

Sea Witch

PLATE III. Spars & Sails

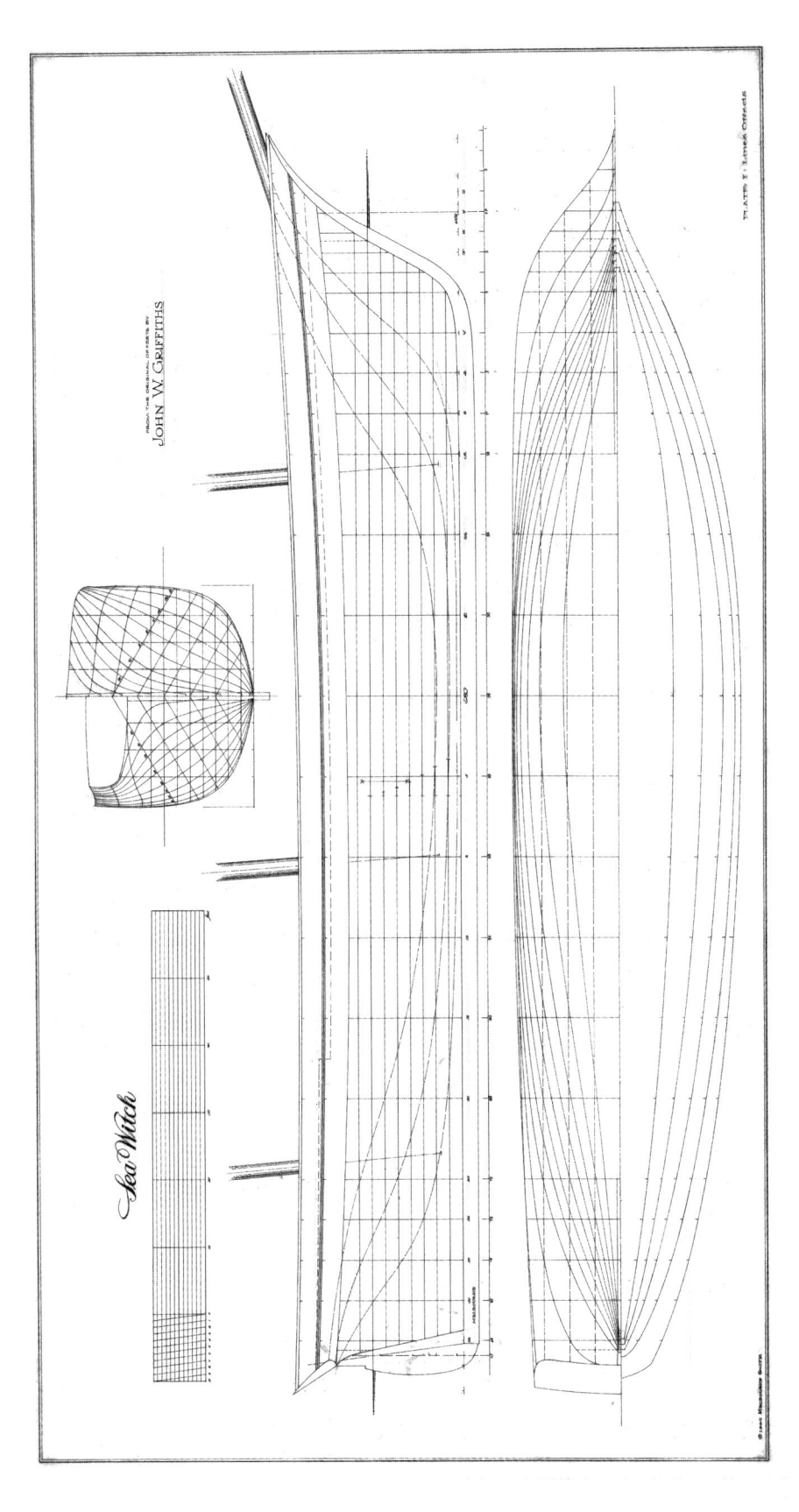

Sea Witch

FROM THE ORIGINAL DESIGN BY
JOHN W. GRIFFITHS

"I guess I'm enjoying success," he said, "but I wouldn't mind a little more money. A lot of the jobs, I'm so eager to do them that I don't make any money on them."

He shook his head then gazed far away. "Maybe it's like the old bread wagons," he wondered. "People just won't order any more of them. Nobody wants any more buggy whips."

He held that statement in the air for a moment, shook his head, then thrust his forefinger in the air and said, "You know, I have had some nice guys working with me who know the old skills. You have to admire the old skills. It's amazing how much work would get done in a day.

"Ever watch a cooper work? It's amazing how fast they can make a barrel and make it watertight. Nowadays a person can make one a week. They used to make five a day.

"Even the whalers. Some of the barrels they took out filled with water. But most they took out knocked down. Later they would put them together on the ship. To do that—and not have them leak—god, that's amazing.

"They built a whole clipper ship in three months. Unbelievable."

IN FACT, what verges on the unbelievable is the fact that Melbourne Smith had as yet been unable to build one particular clipper ship in a span of intention that began about four decades before. Melbourne was no Ahab, but he was just as persistent, and the great white whale of his career was certainly *Sea Witch*.

Beginning with his discovery of John Willis Griffiths during the latter seventies he dreamed of bringing this paragon of American shipcraft back onto the open seas. She should be America's flagship, he felt deeply. Living evidence of Yankee ingenuity. And he was the one to see her built. But this prize had eluded him.

"The clipper ship *Sea Witch* was launched in New York on December 8, 1846, and her ten-year career spanned the apex of American sail vessels. Ships of twice her tonnage were built specifically to beat her, but her passages home from China have not been equaled to this day. Regrettably, this champion of the ultimate class of sailing ship has been lost in romantic haze and distortion.... She was described as the most beautiful ship of her time, but what did she look like?"

Melbourne wrote these sentences in the opening paragraph of an article he published in *Nautical Research Journal* ("To See Which is Sea Witch," June 1980). In the article he painstakingly described the details of his research into the little

NEWPORT BEACH THE SITE FOR
Building an American Clipper Ship

As MELBOURNE Smith's plans to build *Sea Witch* evolved in 1997, several supporters were intrigued by the possibility to build the ship in a setting that would attract attention to the project and would help raise funds and awareness. With initial supporters Woodson K. Woods and Jakob Isbrandsen, Mr. Smith approached the City of Long Beach about a site on which to build the ship. "A fine location was enthusiastically suggested, with the requirement from the city that an immediate development plan be put in motion," said Mr. Woods. He continued, "Due to undeveloped funds, this was impossible."

The next site considered was McFadden's Landing in Newport Harbor, Newport Beach, California. Owned by the Irvine Company, the site was four acres at the waterway entrance from Newport Harbor to the Back Bay, bordering the Pacific Coast Highway. A master plan for the site was developed in 1999, pictured above, and submitted to the Irvine Company. It included a shipyard for the construction of *Sea Witch*, a wood boatbuilding school, and a new home for the Newport Harbor Nautical Museum. The site would also feature a park-like atmosphere that would welcome the public.

Efforts to raise necessary funds and to relocate the Newport Harbor Nautical Museum were slow and unproductive. In mid-August of 2000, the Irvine Company decided against the McFadden's Landing plan and withdrew its offer to gift the site.

It would be another ten years of effort to again try to make a reborn *Sea Witch* a reality. A proposal to build and utilize *Sea Witch* as the United States pavilion at the 2010 World's Fair in Shanghai, China was developed and submitted to the site selection committee. Once again, that effort went the way of the earlier ones and another proposal was selected as the Shanghai site for the U.S. pavilion.

—ED WOODYARD
Lynx Educational Foundation

evidence remaining. He studied two "rigged models of excellent workmanship." One model, made in 1936, resides at Mystic Seaport in the Stillman Building. A larger model is displayed at South Street Seaport Museum at the New York launch site. Both of these miniatures based their lines on assumptions derived from the books of John Willis Griffiths. Maritime historian Howard Chapelle made quite different assumptions in his 1984 book *The Search for Speed under Sail*. Discrepancies were sufficient to cause Melbourne to keep searching. He located a third model, housed at the Museum of the City of New York, purported to be a contemporary work by one of the shipwrights who made the original vessel. "Like most 'sailor's models' it is not in exact proportion and was probably built from memory."

He also studied the two paintings that exist of *Sea Witch*, both done by very observant Chinese artists. (One is at the Peabody Museum in Salem. The other can be seen at India House in lower Manhattan.) They differ slightly in details, and both "do not support" the models nor the drawings by Mr. Chapelle.

Then on a tip from farmer/guru Eric Steinlein, Melbourne traveled to the Smithsonian Institution to search the John W. Griffiths file in the Museum of History and Technology (Washington D.C.). There he uncovered an original lines drawing and sail plan that had been prepared for Griffiths after the ship had been built. With those, plus a scrupulous reconsideration of all Griffiths's published works, Melbourne created a new set of plans that he believed beyond doubt accurately represent the original.

The remainder of Melbourne's *Nautical Research Journal* essay was loaded with minutiae that dazzle the mind of lay readers. He touches on the stern framing, the waterline, the calculated meta-center, mast diameters, the presence or not of a topgallant rail, even the exact size and placement of the ship's dragon figurehead. By the end of the article the reader is convinced at least of one thing: Melbourne did his homework.

The plans to rebuild *Sea Witch*—plans developed over decades—were ambitious and practical. The rejections he received would have made a lesser man bitter. "I got good at writing letters—and not getting answers," Melbourne said. "It took me a long time to learn that the important person you are writing to probably never sees the letter. You can't go in cold yourself. Chances are thousand to one against you."

His last and most ambitious proposal was truly global in scope. Working well in advance, he attached the *Sea Witch* vision to the World Expo 2010, staged in Shanghai, China. For this event Shanghai, declaring itself to be the next great world city, built the largest and most expensive site in the history of world fairs and attracted an all-time record number of visitors, seventy-three million. Melbourne envisioned *Sea Witch*, reborn, once again making that record passage between New York and China, arriving in Shanghai in time to help open the World Expo. In fact, she would be the Expo "pavilion" for the United States. Her appearance would affirm the earliest interactions between the U.S. and China during a time of peaceful free commerce. After the new *Sea Witch* spent six months pleasing the crowds and taking excursions along the Huangpu River, and then of course being celebrated along all the waterways of the United States, she would find a permanent home in drydock —but not hidden among shipyards and wharves. Melbourne saw her immortalized under glass on a Manhattan waterfront or in Washington D.C. He imagined her enshrined in a glass-faced museum alongside a major financial tower, somewhere people rose to greatness in a glass elevator, so that as they rose they would get to look at *Sea Witch* from below and above. They would see how beautiful she is. When they looked they wouldn't think much about rigging and hulls and navigation. Instead they would feel happy to behold an honored symbol of American exceptionalism.

PETER STANFORD made the same point while talking about Melbourne and *Sea Witch*. Peter, at age eighty-seven, was retired as co-founder and president of National Maritime Historical Society. Prior to that he served as founder and first president of South Street Seaport in New York. Peter had supported Melbourne's research and tried to set up partnerships, and now regrets that he didn't do more for *Sea Witch*.

"I have often thought—if I could have only dropped all that and just gone to work for Melbourne on the great *Sea Witch* project. There were so many promising starts that seemed to attract the kind of people to get the project underway.

"America needs to recover this kind of thing from its past. It's an alien experience for most of the people, and that's what we need. Americans, we love to break records. We love to be exceptional. And we are. We love this kind of thing. And Melbourne is a leading actor in the quest for excellence.

"And *Sea Witch* just radiates this quality. She had ten years to do her wonders and by god they were wonderful.

"I'm convinced that there will be a *Sea Witch*. She stood for things the world cannot afford to lose." ★

Artist David Thimgan's painting imagines *Sea Witch* passing the California coast.

Sandy Hook | 1849

"It took a hundred years to build clippers.
It took a generation of undiluted hell to develop the men to sail them."

— CARL C. CUTLER
Greyhounds of the Sea

IN THE YEAR 1849 the horizon still hung like a curtain between the known world and the unknown beyond. No flying machines overtopped it. No electronic signals penetrated it. No fuel-driven engines of any kind yet challenged it. In the United States, where nearly every state fronted and relied on the Atlantic Ocean, the turbid wall of the horizon marked a real boundary. Anyone who stood on that seashore, who looked out across the three miles or so of visible gray sea, knew that the horizon was it. The limit.

Never mind the idea of going west, creeping across obstructions of land with horse expeditions or tragic wagon trains. When you stood on the eastern shore, the boundary was clear and god-like. There was only one way to penetrate it, only one way to escape the tedium and bondage of the land, and that was by sail.

In those days the telegraph operator at Sandy Hook watched the horizon daily for the sight of sails. He had his finger on the fastest way to get to New York—the dot-dash code that he ticked over a great ugly stretch of electric wires. But telegraph was the height of electric technology at the time. No such wiring could challenge yet the supremacy of the natural world, not for a man who came to work on a horse. No, the only technology that could meet the natural world on its own terms—harness it, rise to its challenge without engines, steam, petroleum, electricity, employing only carpentry, rope, cloth, muscle, and wits—was the do-or-die technology of sail.

Sandy Hook, a six-mile-long barrier spit of land, thrusts itself north from a New Jersey headland straight into the sea. It slightly blocks the wide entrance to Lower New York Bay. In 1849 Sandy Hook was the finish line, the "we have arrived" moment for ships wanting to measure their speed in competitive runs to Canton, China, and back. But this day, a Sunday afternoon in March, no ships of the American tea fleet were expected, not for another two weeks. They would not have left Canton until the close of the monsoon season.

And yet by god here was a set of sails.

At first the watcher on the shore could discern nothing but bulging whiteness, as though a distant cannon had shot forth a cloud. But at each glance the apparition came clearer. Cloud quickly became canvas, then became swollen bellies of canvas crowded against the wind and shimmering in the grip of ropes. Each time he glanced at the offing, the ship had surged closer than expected. Her speed slapped his experience, excited him, startled him.

The telegraph station operator at Sandy Hook had seen countless merchant sailing ships appear like this in the offing. Usually they dawdled, or tacked, or rumbled along like ice-delivery wagons. Ten years before this, the run from China to New York had required nearly half a year. But this unexpected vessel surged at him with all sails spread—"wing-and-wing"—exploiting a spanking breeze from the south-southeast.

Certainly she was one of the new breed, an extreme clipper ship.

Just the other day he had read a statement in the newspaper, a kind of Yankee brag. It said that to be called an "American clipper ship" was to earn the highest honor any vessel could claim. Then the writer went on to define what such a sailing ship might be:

> "Clean, long, smooth as a smelt. Sharp arching head. Thin, hollow bow; convex sides; light, round and graceful stern. A genuine East Indiaman or Californian. Aloft, large built, iron-banded lower masts; taut tapering smaller masts, long-proportioned spars from lower to skysail yards. Above board, she towers up with strong, fibrous arms spreading a cloud of canvas to the gale."

A MERICA'S SHIPYARDS were building and launching these speed-demon nautical experiments almost faster than the newspapers could report them. Many believed that these ships were over-sparred, in other words that they carried too much sail. Too much for hulls designed to slide across the sea surface like a skate on slick ice, the bow knife-narrow, the midship beamy, the ship's penetration of the water minimal.

Well before this arriving vessel had hoisted her colors, the telegraph operator guessed who it was. She had three towering masts each with five tiers of sail. Staysails flying before every mast. A long jib boom like an archangel's spear. A sleek black hull, and a gilded dragon figurehead with a coiled tail.

Sea Witch.

Launched three years earlier from the New York shipyard Smith & Dimon at the foot of Fourth Street, *Sea Witch* had been setting new speed records with each voyage. With each voyage her captain, Bob Waterman, a larger-than-life figure on land, had continued to learn how best to play this racy vessel, how to manage her in order to extract velocity from the winds. Her designer, John Willis Griffiths, had been jeered by other shipmakers for his radical ideas, which were supported by his brainy discourses on the mathematics of displacement, center of gravity, center of effort, and so on. Ignoring the jeers, Griffiths was now proving himself to be a true Yankee genius.

As the telegraph operator tap-tapped reports, he watched the pilot boat come out from the harbor. The harbor pilot and a steam tug would bring *Sea Witch* home from here. He watched for a glimpse of Captain Waterman. Sure enough, the notorious captain came off *Sea Witch* dressed in a new suit, stiff collar, and top hat, wielding a cane. No doubt he had purchased the suit before setting sail, ordering it to be delivered off shore upon his return. Waterman was a celebrity and always dressed the part, and he always went ahead of the cargo to the shipping office with manifest in hand. That way the goods would go on the market as fast and as pricey as possible—money changing hands even as the crew was still removing the baggy wrinkle[*] and stowing sails.

The telegraph operator had a hunch that this unexpected arrival might be one for the history books, and it was. The next day, newspaper headlines

---

[*] Baggy wrinkle is a hand-tied, brush-like matting around the standing rigging that prevents sails from chafing.

shouted the news that *Sea Witch*, sailing against the monsoon, had broken all records by a wide margin. She had sailed the fourteen thousand miles from China to New York in seventy-four days and fourteen hours. In other words, she had cut the voyage from half a year to fewer than two and a half months.

However, in 1849 the maritime world was beginning to change utterly, perhaps forever. The clipper ship era was declining in 1854 when Griffiths wrote: "It don't pay to go fast and carry nothing"—referring to the clippers' usual lightweight cargo of China tea. He added that "the almighty dollar presents more absolute resistance than the wind and water combined."

Nearly four hundred American clippers were launched in the early 1850s, but in 1857, one year after *Sea Witch* finally wrecked, only ten left the ways. At the time of the American Civil War, the country and the world were turning rapidly to metal hulls and steam engines, then to fuel-driven mechanization and the snap of the electric wire. As railroads proved their power, America's attention swiveled from east to west and to its own great exploitable interior. The "march of progress," as we used to say, tramped on.

In 1846, the year *Sea Witch* first touched the sea, the United States began annexing Texas and California and started a war with Mexico in order to facilitate the transition of power. Henry David Thoreau was jailed for tax resistance, his protest against that war. That same year, the first baseball game was played (Cartwright Rules), the New York Nines winning twenty-three to one against the Knickerbockers. The saxophone was patented, so was Elias Howe's sewing machine. Elizabeth Barrett and Robert Browning eloped, and astronomers discovered the planet Neptune. The Mormons moved west. The Donner party was trapped by blizzards.

Then in 1849 America's new Californians found gold. The clipper ships were readied to round the Horn at record speed for the hysterical transfer of shovels and miners, mules and store goods, returning occasionally with treasure. *Sea Witch* was put to that service.

Carl C. Cutler, scholar of the clipper era, wrote this: "The years just before 1850 were extraordinarily colorful years. They gave to the world... the most poignantly beautiful pageant the world has ever seen, when the clipper ships, visions of almost ethereal loveliness, moved on the face of the waters." No one will ever match that sailing record because no one would ever again dare to build such risky, lovely, handmade sailing machines.

In fact, though, Melbourne Smith would gladly build *Sea Witch* again. And he knows how. There is no way to understand the shipwrecks and successes and meaning of Melbourne Smith's life without having some feeling for the spell of the sailing life. To board a wooden ship that you have built yourself with hand tools, to hoist sails, and to force the wind to haul you far from the sight of land—and then to know how to navigate from there—this is a natural science that should remain at the very top of the stack of significant human achievements, next to farming and the concept of democratic government. The resonating glamour of the great sailing ships—such as *Sea Witch*—was enough to fire the imagination of an unusual lad named Bill Smith almost a century later, a boy from Hamilton, Ontario, a boy whose family was as un-nautical as can be imagined.

So, at age about seventy, Melbourne Smith bought a plane ticket to Cuba via the Bahamas. (The flight was not illegal, as Melbourne still possessed Canadian citizenship.) By then, after a couple decades of research and design drawing and project development, he felt that he knew *Sea Witch* as well as anybody—except of course for those New York shipwrights who had built her in the first place.

He had researched her as far as he could in the U.S. "After ferreting everything I could possibly learn about Griffiths," he said, "I chased down the first captain, Robert H. Waterman. After all, Griffiths made the horse, but every horse needs a rider!" Melbourne discovered that the flamboyant Waterman retired from sailing during the Gold Rush years. The former "driver" became the Surveyor of Wrecks on the California coast and then, financially secure, he sent for his wife in New England. Cordelia Waterman sailed without escort to the isthmus of Panama, crossed Central America overland, then went north to San Francisco by steamboat. She carried cuttings of rose bushes from their previous home in Fairfield, Connecticut. Reunited, the Watermans bought land west of San Francisco and founded the city of Fairfield, California. The captain built a fine house with cupola and marble fireplaces. When Melbourne visited the old house in California, those Connecticut roses were still blooming. He took some cuttings back to Maryland. Later, he placed them at the Watermans' gravesite in Mountain Grove Cemetery, Bridgeport, Connecticut—which also happens to be the final stop for showman P.T. Barnum and for that municipality's native son Charles Stratton, aka Gen. Tom Thumb.

In contrast, John W. Griffiths plot at United Methodist Cemetery in Queens draws few, if any, visitors.

Only one other final resting place remained subject to investigation—the wreck *of Sea Witch*. As far as Melbourne knew, no one had ever looked for her remains. He knew they were somewhere off the coast of Cuba where she had foundered in 1856. He had recently unearthed some newspaper clippings from that year, contemporary reports on the death of *Sea Witch*, and he felt the time had come for a pilgrimage.

All Melbourne knew from the records was that *Sea Witch* had sunk some miles west of Havana. On that run her crew, as usual, consisted of twenty or twenty-five sailors. Her cargo, locked in the hold, he learned, was five hundred human beings. These were Chinese laborers contracted to work in the sugar plantations—virtual slaves. They'd been packed in worse than hogs.

Searching the deep-buried records, Melbourne found two mentions from 1856 in *the New York Daily Times*. The first, dated April 7 (Vol. v, No.1416), bore the headline "LOSS OF SEA WITCH WITH CHINESE EMIGRANTS." The recovered news reads: "The clipper ship *Sea Witch* from China, loaded with Chinese apprentices, went ashore on the Island, 12 miles west from Havana, on the morning of the 28th, and will prove a total loss. Several Spanish steamers went to her assistance, and succeeded in taking off the passengers and crew. No lives lost."

Then Melbourne found a prior dispatch, "WRECK OF THE SEA WITCH," this one sent directly from Havana on March 31, the previous Monday: "The beautiful clipper ship *Sea Witch* lays [sic] a wreck upon our coast about fifteen miles to the westward. She was from Hong Kong, having 500 Asiatic colonists on board, for the labor hands of Cuban cane fields. Eighty of these ignorant forced emigrants died on the passage, —and if the rest have not perished, we shall have tidings this morning. (They were brought in by the Spanish steamers *Guadalquivir* and *Congress* last evening.)"

He found no further record of those "tidings." No telling how many of these "Asiatic colonists" survived.

NO ONE sent Melbourne on this mission. He simply went, employing the privilege of the maple-leaf side of his dual U.S.-Canada citizenship. He went with no clear idea how things might play out. He just wanted a few clues about the maritime past. He was a humble investigator who reported to no one except himself.

SEA WITCH, 1846

Melbourne's watercolor of the great American Clipper Ship *Sea Witch*

CHAPTER 19 | 231

For months he had been corresponding by letter with a helpful, English-fluent Havanan—Melbourne's queries typed on the letterhead of the International Historical Watercraft Society, the respondent's answers neatly handwritten on plain sheets. These exchanges led to a contact, a historian at the *Susonian Institute of Archealogy*, who had located a document in the Cuban National Archives. The document referred to a "frigate" being wrecked, and it was signed by a certain Vicente de la Guardia la Torriente. There was also some documentation from twenty years previous stating, "We believe the name of the ship, Seabichi or Seabitch is a variant and the same as *Sea Witch*." The documentation pointed toward a shipwreck spot some distance west of Havana. The vessel had wrecked on Punta Mirado, a quarter league from Playa Santa Ana, a beach on the north coast of Cuba. Evidence suggested that the vessel had been salvaged by rescuers from Havana "who removed ingots without having ownership of the cargo or the ballast." The remains of the vessel were towed to Muelle de Saba, the estate of landlord Don Francisco Garcia Gutierres. On March 6, 1857, "unknown persons" set the hull on fire. The hulk burned to the waterline and sank.

"This was more than enough encouragement to have me visit Cuba," said Melbourne.

AS THE RUSSIAN-BUILT airplane approached its landing, its cabin filling with alarming clouds of water vapor, Melbourne could see out the window rough shrubby hills and plastered stone buildings that were crackling from disrepair. He stepped out into the blast of a Havana evening, the sky solid black, the air hot. He felt a familiar and pleasant sense of adventure. He picked the first cab in the taxi rank.

"Marina Hemingway, okay," said the cabdriver.

Then the cabbie turned off his lights, including the interior lights, explaining that he didn't have a license to pick up fares at the airport. After about a mile he turned on the lights. "It's okay now."

"Oh, this is wonderful," thought Melbourne. "I'll get arrested as soon as I get to Cuba."

To the contrary, however, this taxi-driver proved to be the kind of godsend that all free-form travelers crave—resourceful, fluent in English (though he had never left the island), a mature family man hustling for a living in a depressed economy, in other words a savvy entrepreneur. He said, "Next time you come, I have two apartments to rent, with all the meals." Right away he picked up on Melbourne's mission—to locate some kind of old shipwreck—and he offered to take Melbourne wherever he needed to go, to the national archives, the national museum, along the coast to look at bays and coves.

"He did everything for me," said Melbourne. "In the end I paid him, maybe, twenty-five dollars a day. Later I was told that I'd given him too much."

THE NEXT morning the taxi-driver returned to Hemingway Marina and picked up Melbourne, then drove him into Havana to explore the historical archives. The day's research reached dead ends, but the drive through Havana exposed Melbourne to exciting, potholed streets with no sidewalks, rubble lots, cracked plaster walls formerly painted in great tracts of single colors—geranium green, burnt orange, weary red. Intense sunrays pounded against dense darkness of inner recesses with old men sitting solitary in the borderland between those extremes. Kids played stick-games in the street and did handstands against the old walls. Eventually the complete absence of commercial advertising anywhere in the streets struck him like a peculiar aroma.

There was little traffic but there certainly were cars. Melbourne was delighted to see so many that that were forty or fifty years old, buffed and running like new, with fins and chrome, with hydromatic transmissions and (somehow) whitewall tires, '57 Chevies and lavender Chryslers, gleaming Plymouths, Buicks, and Packards. These cars rolled past men wearing straw cowboy hats and tank tops, women in loose floral shifts, people leaning on each other or yelling at each other in the streets, every shade of skin mingled together, all one people.

"I love the people there," he said. "They're industrious and smart. For the most part it's quite an honest place." State-employed uniforms were everywhere, Melbourne noticed, but for the most part these police seemed to have little to do but direct traffic and say no. "I found that no one had the authority to grant permissions. The answer to every question was simply to refer me to a higher authority, one that would take forever to respond." Cuba was an odd but somehow happy and very human place for *Sea Witch* to have gone and died.

Melbourne was delighted to meet Sr. Dionisio Vives Rongel, the native Cuban historian who helped locate the resting place of *Sea Witch*'s bones.

THE TAXI-DRIVER, Señor Gómez, returned the next morning and drove Melbourne west along the shoreline. In the neighborhood called Barraco, closest to the sites named in previous correspondence, they were directed to the local historian, Dionisio Vives Rongel. A small, wiry man of about age sixty, Sr. Rongel listened intently to Melbourne's requests. He asked them to return the next morning.

Rongel was indeed prepared when they returned—not only with delicious coffee served kindly by Señora Rongel but also with three fat ledgers, including maps, in which much of the information was handwritten. The historian read aloud whatever could still be harvested from the records. He said that the enormous clipper ship, lightened of contents, had drifted on the high tide close in on the beach. Then she was towed to a small jetty owned by Don Francisco, who was a wealthy landlord from the Canary Islands to whom authorities in Spain had given a large tract of land here. Don Francisco's house still stood, as did the hulk of a large sugar mill he once owned. After he had tied the derelict clipper to his jetty, Don Francisco had his counsel inquire as to the value of his acquisition—which, according to the owners of *Sea Witch*, turned out to be nil.

The earnest historian spread out an ancient map, waved his hand over the large tract that had once belonged to Don Francisco, then pointed to the spur of land where *Sea Witch* had been tethered, and where she had burned and sunk. Then Rongel produced a more contemporary, Russian-made map to show that the spit of land, and certainly Don Francisco's wooden jetty, had long since disappeared. In fact, Melbourne and Señor Rongel surmised, the coastline had changed over time precisely *because* of *Sea Witch*.

"When you put something like that in the water," said Melbourne later, "the water surges behind it and washes out the jetty, and washes out the land. The little point of land that supported the pier is now gone. I could see that the wreck is about a hundred yards off shore now, under maybe three fathoms of seawater."

Later that day, Melbourne stood on a nearby cliff and stared at the place where *Sea Witch* slumbers in the muck. It was a dry-rimmed cove outlined in chapped boulders and stunted shrubbery. The deep-cobalt water lay like glass over its dark secrets.

"I wanted to take pictures of the land and the site." But of course there was a policeman watching him. So he asked the policeman for permission to take pictures. The policemen said no pictures. To take pictures you have to go to back to Havana for permission. Señor Gómez, the taxi-driver, pointed out that to get permission would take at least a year, if he could get permission at all. "In Cuba nobody has authority to give permission, nor do they want to get in trouble for granting permission." Technically Señor Gómez shouldn't have taken him out to the site in the first place. So the whole expedition resolved in a teeter-totter of would-be could-be.

If Melbourne could have dived at the site, he would have verified the wreck's identity in a glance. "Basically, there's just the bare bones of the keel timbers down there. The keel, keelson, frames, a lot of fastenings." But the J.W. Griffiths arrangement of frames was distinctive. *Sea Witch* was built with double frames—two twelve-inch frames paired and set at thirty-six-inch centers.

Melbourne yearned to take a piece of her hull back to his studio. The idea was absurd, of course. How could he explain to the customs official that a long, sodden, rotting, antique sliver was actually a souvenir? Rather, was actually the Grail of Sail?

And yet he knew she was down there. At least he could have touched her. But for one impediment:

Melbourne never did learn how to swim. ✶

Bibliography

Anderson, Captain Lindsay. *A Cruise in an Opium Clipper*. London: Chapman and Hall, 1891.

Chapelle, Howard Irving. *The Search for Speed Under Sail, 1700-1855*. New York: Norton, 1967.

Cutler, Carl C. *Greyhounds of the Sea*. Annapolis, Maryland: Naval Institute Press, 1984. Third edition designed by Melbourne Smith with the addition of *Five Hundred Sailing Records of American Built Ships*.

Griffiths, John Willis. *The Ship-Builder's Manual and Nautical Referee*. Memphis USA: General Books, 2012.

Griffiths, John Willis. *The Progressive Ship Builder, Volume 2*. United States: Nabu Press, 2013.

Griffiths, John Willis. *Treatise on Marine and Naval Architecture; Or, Theory and Practice Blended in Ship Building*. New York: D. Appleton and Company, 1849.

McEwen, W.A. and A.H. Lewis. *Encyclopedia of Nautical Knowledge*. Cambridge, Maryland: Cornell Maritime Press, 1953.

Meloney, William Brown. *The Heritage of Tyre*. New York: The Macmillan Company, 1916.

Robinson, J. Dennis. *America's Privateer: Lynx and the War of 1812*. Newport Beach, California: Lynx Educational Foundation, 2011.

Smith, Hervey Garrett. *The Marlinspike Sailor*. Camden, Maine: International Marine/McGraw-Hill, 1993.

Spears, John R. Captain Nathaniel Brown Palmer: *An Old-Time Sailor of the Sea*. New York: The Macmillan Company, 1922.

Spectre, Peter H. *Different Waterfronts: Stories from the Wooden Boat Revival*. Gardiner, Maine: The Harpswell Press, 1989.

Wilson, Evan. *Epitaph for a Beautiful Ship*. Austin, Texas: Evan Wilson, 2010.

ILLUSTRATION & PHOTO CREDITS

All photographs, illustrations, and architectural drawings by
MELBOURNE SMITH,
unless otherwise noted.

1: *Sailing Trawlers* by Edgar J. March, M.S.R.R., 5: Edgar J. March, M.S.R.R.,
53: John Horn, 60: Jane Roberts Henry, 69: Jane Roberts Henry,
73: John F. Kennedy Library and Museum,
77: Oil painting by A. Redford, Montreal, 102: Richard Kibbe,
105: Fred Hecklinger, 111: US Coast Guard, 118: Tracy Fiege,
125: Bob Dollard, 130: Fred Hecklinger, 136: Potomac Riverboat Company,
141: Smithsonian Institution, 154: Eliot Hudson
170: Bob Covarrubias, 176: Lynda Lee, 184: Lynda Lee, 187: Pennsylvania
Historical & Museum Commission, 193: Commonwealth of Pennsylvania,
196: Woodson K. Woods, 205: Kip Brundage, 209: Kip Brundage,
214: John Bildahl, 212: Chris Woods